Sanjeev Kumar

Sanjeev Kumar

The Actor We All Loved

Reeta Ramamurthy Gupta
and Uday Jariwala

HarperCollins *Publishers* India

First published in India by HarperCollins *Publishers* 2022
4th Floor, Tower A, Building No. 10, Phase II, DLF Cyber City,
Gurugram, Haryana – 122002
www.harpercollins.co.in

2 4 6 8 10 9 7 5 3

Photos courtesy: Sanjeev Kumar's family's archives

P-ISBN: 978-93-5629-141-6
E-ISBN: 978-93-5629-167-6

Typeset in 12/16.2 Dante MT Std at
Manipal Technologies Limited, Manipal

Printed and bound at
Gopsons Papers Pvt. Ltd., Noida.

Every man's life ends the same way.
It is only the details of how he lived and how he died that distinguish one man from another.

—Ernest Hemingway

For

Jyoti, Uday, Neelam, Aryan, Saachi, Prithvi, Rishika, Krishiv,
Ekta, Fiahan, Ashish, Artee

and the late Jethalal, Shantaben, Kishore, Nikul, Gayatri,
Ashok and Jamnadasji

Jyoti, Colin, Neena, [illegible], Sandra, [illegible], Kunika, Krishiv,

Ekta, Hudson, [illegible]

and the late [illegible], [illegible], [illegible], [illegible]

[illegible] and [illegible]

Contents

SECTION V: WAXING, WAVERING, WANDERING

SECTION VI: TALES OF FRIENDSHIP

SECTION VII: HURRICANE HARI

SECTION VIII: THE LAST LAP

ना ले के जाओ

ना ले के जाओ मेरे दोस्त का जनाज़ा है
अभी तो गर्म है मिट्टी ये जिस्म ताज़ा है
ना ले के जाओ ...

उलझ गई है कहीं साँस खोल दो इस की
लबों पे आई है जो बात पूरी करने दो
अभी उम्मीद भी जिन्दा है ग़म भी ताज़ा है
ना ले के जाओ ...

जगाओ इस को गले मिल के अलविदा तो कहूँ
ये कैसी रुख़सती है ये क्या सलीका है
अभी तो जीने का हर एक ज़ख्म ताज़ा है
ना ले के जाओ ...

An Ode to My Friend

Don't take my friend away, just yet,
his body is still warm
feels alive.
Don't take him away, just yet.

He's perhaps at unease
Let him say his piece
His hopes are alive
His sorrows still hurt!
Don't take him away, just yet.

Shake him up, will you;
I haven't bid him a proper goodbye.
How can he be so still!
when the wounds of life still hurt ...
Don't take him away, just yet.

—Gulzar

Sanjeev Kumar with a young Uday Jariwala.

Foreword

When the Almighty decided to bless Hindi cinema with largesse, he sent Haribhai Jariwala to earth. A 'parasmani' who could deliver a stellar performance even in a simple role or convert an ordinary dialogue into an auditory odyssey, Haribhai Jariwala was a performer nonpareil. I am always humbled when spoken of in the same breath as Haribhai, courtesy our work and our home state of Gujarat. Our journey from theatre to cinema is also a common thread that connects our career paths.

My experiments with theatre started in the early 1970s. Haribhai, a superstar at the time, came to see my play *Kabro* (based on the English play *Equus*) at Bhaidas Hall in Mumbai. This must have been around 1979. On another occasion, he came to see one of my plays at Prithvi Theatre. He had mentioned then that he was staying in the same complex at a friend's home. I remember this distinctly because shortly afterwards he suffered a heart attack and I went to see him at Nanavati Hospital. This was in 1983.

However, the last time I saw him was at a shoot in Mumbai's Film City in 1985. He was doing Nitin Manmohan's film *Baat Ban Jaaye*. He had just returned from his cardiac surgery in the United States. I went over from my set to his to pay my respects. What I saw was a blanched apparition of the happy man I had seen before! In all fairness, I had only known him as a big star—so he wasn't particularly accessible to or communicative with me. But thanks to a few common friends, like actors Amrit Patel and Chandrakant Thakkar and producer Jayant Malkan (who had produced his film *Namkeen*), he was always polite and courteous to me. I will never forget what I saw on the set that day. But when the camera turned on, Haribhai resurrected himself into the character he was playing.

Theatre is an excellent training ground, and Haribhai was already a thespian when he sought roles in cinema. Theatre requires exceptional memory. There are no 'short takes' that can be patched together. It is an actor's medium, and the performance is organic and live. Once the curtains open, the actors have to hold the audience and assay the plot. Theatre gives you confidence and instils discipline and alertness. The subjects theatre deals in are also intense; the literature is fine and the writing is exceptional. You mature as an artiste around sensitive subjects. But here's the key: theatre prepares you for a marathon, whereas cinema is a 50-metre run. Haribhai understood this intuitively.

In cinema, theatricality is not considered good, so you have to adjust your sense of proportion and become more subtle, temper your loudness and your tonality. Moreover, cinema is a director's medium. An actor is just doing his or her part and may not even know what else is being shot where for the film. The movie comes together only in the director's mind and, hence, overconfidence can kill you. Haribhai knew exactly 'how much' to act. That is not easy!

In the initial days of his career, he was extremely good looking—as charming as Cary Grant and as timeless as Dilip sahab. Directors noticed him because you couldn't take your eyes off him. He used his voice exceptionally well. He didn't have the baritone of Amitabh Bachchan, but he was extremely intelligent and knew what to do with his voice. He was a powerful actor; he owned the screen when he was on it. His performances in *Aandhi, Koshish* and *Anubhav* are a course in acting itself. And what a terrific exponent of comedy he was in films like *Angoor* and *Pati Patni Aur Woh!*

For all great character artistes, the bulk of earnings and recall come from the big multi-starrers they feature in. For Haribhai, these were films like *Trishul, Sholay*, etc. Jamnadasji, Haribhai's manager, used to tell me, '*Paresh, agar Amitabh Bachchan ka baap banna hai to Sanjeev Kumar hi ban sakta hai! Aur kaun banega?*' (Who but Sanjeev Kumar can match Amitabh Bachchan on the screen?)

Haribhai was pensive and observant in nature. While he never craved glamour, he was a gifted exponent of the art of make-up. The film *Naya Din Nayi Raat* is a case in point. During an early chance encounter, I had seen him reading a book by Richard Emerson Smith—the American special make-up-effects artiste, nicknamed 'Godfather of make-up'. His own make-up artiste, Sarosh Mody, was trained abroad and was an absolute genius. Haribhai had the ideal actor's face—there was a lot of space for expression and it had an excellent sense of proportion. His face was also very versatile—he could pull off expressions for any emotion, any character without looking awkward. He also knew how to keep it real. I can say with certainty that Haribhai's loose kurta pyjama and ruffled hair were not the result of carelessness. That's how people dress when they're at home, and he was playing a part!

I remember that the late Satyen Kappu used to reminisce about Haribhai a lot. '*Uske jaisa kaun risk leta hai?*', he would constantly say. The audience used to sigh with relief when Haribhai entered the frame, 'Nothing can go wrong now!' He was every director's fail-safe artiste, an avatar all in his own league to perform and enthral. His performances will be studied by generations and in perpetuity.

I would love to reprise *Koshish* some day! Maybe in my own way and maybe as a tribute to Haribhai. His performance in that film was not just about playing a character with disability; his touching portrayal elicited a response from everyone in the audience. What greater paean can I write for Haribhai?

Paresh Rawal

Introduction

There are two distinct elements to being a great actor—one is the ability to play a variety of roles and the other is the audience's willingness to accept the actor in those roles. Audiences often reject their favourite stars when they digress too far from their 'star' avatar. Haribhai stands tall—in a category all his own—because his audience was convinced that he could play anything. His work is a testimony to that.

As a director, I can vouch for the fact that in the history of world cinema, there are very few who can transcend this dreaded 'slotting'! Haribhai never played the character—he became the character. To be fair to actors, this rigorous typecasting is often a function of the industry itself making a commercial judgement of them. It is not uncommon for producers to slot an actor in terms of 'Can he romance the heroine?', 'Can he dance?', 'Can he fight?', 'Can he do comedy?' … Haribhai was beyond these boundaries. In fact, he had created a space for himself where the audience expected him to be different and enjoyed the infinite talent he displayed. He was comfortable with the thought of interpreting a character in his own unique way and did not want to play it according to someone else's idea of it. I am sure if he was ever asked the question, 'Can you perform the role?'—Haribhai would have replied with a twinkle in his eyes and a smile, 'Let's give it a shot!'

If I'm a student of cinema, then Haribhai is an exposition of it. Besides all the shades he had, I always found him extremely romantic—right from one of his earliest films *Nishan* in 1965 and all the way to *Qatl*, which was released two months after his death in 1986. Midway in his career he played a role in *Aandhi*, which he made distinctive by his portrayal of a husband's silent appreciation for his ambitious wife in the film. It will forever remain a classic. Haribhai interpreted love according to the age of the character and not his own age. Was there any mystique to him? The thing with mystique is that if you look for it, you will find it!

This book fills a gap in the history of Hindi cinema—how can an industry not chronicle its greatest performer?

Rakeysh Omprakash Mehra

Prologue

Aficionados of world cinema will appreciate why Hari is often compared to Hollywood actor Philip Seymour Hoffman, who also died at the age of forty-seven, almost three decades after Hari. Both had film careers spanning twenty years and were highly respected as performers, and neither had the conventional 'looks' of a movie star.

Filmmakers trusted Hoffmann and Hari to assay the most challenging lead roles as well as character roles with equal gumption. Hoffman won the Academy Award for best actor in a leading role for *Capote* and was nominated on three more occasions as actor in a supporting role. Hari wasn't to be left behind. He won the Filmfare Award for best actor twice, for *Aandhi* and *Arjun Pandit* (he was nominated eleven times for best actor in his career). He also won the Filmfare Award for best supporting actor for *Shikar* (Hari was nominated thrice in the best supporting actor category). His greatest paeans, though, were the two National Awards he won for *Dastak* and *Koshish*.

Millennials and Gen Z may not know much about any of these award-winning performances of Hari. Perhaps, at some level, this book is an attempt to bridge that gap. At best, they know him as the Thakur in *Sholay*. A handful might associate him with other multi-starrers like *Trishul* and *Silsila,* which are still alive in the public discourse. However, the mere mention of Hari to the generation born in the 1950s, '60s and '70s and to a certain extent even the '80s, may herald a lively discussion on who the best actor in Indian cinema really is! A debate as to the best ten (of the 164 films) that comprise his filmography, might not reach any consensus!

As an actor, Hari has many firsts and crazy risks to his credit. He was the first actor to introduce prosthetic make-up in Hindi cinema in 1981 with *Chehre Pe Chehra*. He was also the first actor to play nine different roles in one Hindi film, *Naya Din Nai Raat*. It may also be said that Hari's *Aandhi* was one of the first films to be banned in independent India. In *Encyclopaedia of Hindi Cinema,* Gulzar writes:

> During the Emergency in 1975, the film *Aandhi* was banned. I was at the Moscow Film Festival, where the film was to be shown. I received orders that the film had been banned and must not be shown at the festival. We were also told that all posters and publicity material for the film must be removed. The front page of *New York Times* carried the news that the film had been banned because it was said to be based on Mrs. Indira Gandhi's biography.[1]

1 Gulzar, Govind Nihalani, Saibal Chatterjee, eds., *Encyclopaedia of Hindi Cinema* (Encyclopaedia Britannica India Pvt. Ltd. And Popular Prakashan Pvt. Ltd., 2003).

For the uninitiated, *Aandhi* is a film that many consider to be one of Hari's finest works. Its female protagonist is the character of Aarti—an ambitious politician, whose hair had a streak of silver and who wore saris in a manner that reminded people of Indira Gandhi, the Prime Minister of India at the time of the release.

Thanks to Hari's vast repertoire of performances, the cohort for whom he will be perennially relevant are students of cinema all over the world. His performance in Satyajit Ray's 1977 film *Shatranj Ke Khilari* is considered 'riveting', as described by Ray's wife Bijoya in her book *Manik And I.*[2] It is also significant that Satyajit Ray made Hari a part of the only full-length Hindi film he ever made. *Shatranj Ke Khilari* received extensive coverage across the world. It was India's entry for the best foreign language film at the fifty-first Academy Awards. The film's theme was that the self-centredness, detachment and cowardice of India's ruling classes were the reasons a kingdom like Awadh could be annexed by a handful of British officials. Gary Arnold, in his review of the film for *The Washington Post* on 6 April 1978, wrote, 'Kumar and Jaffrey create a marvellous tragicomic impression of a ruling class in complacent, irreversible decline.'[3]

Hari had a favourite chair in his drawing room and a picture of K. Asif (the maker of *Mughal-E-Azam,* who was the first to visualize Hari in the role of the lead in his magnum opus *Love and God*), hung above it. Hari would seek Asif's blessings on his way to work every day. In 2013, *Forbes India* magazine published

---

2 Bijoya Ray, *Manik and I: My Life with Satyajit Ray*, trans. Indrani Majumdar (Penguin India, 2012).

3 https://www.washingtonpost.com/archive/lifestyle/1978/04/06/the-chess-players/f6cddf62-1567-4a21-8ff0-6ecd9f923aa2/

an article titled '25 Greatest Acting Performances of Indian Cinema'. One of them was Hari's performance in his 1982 release *Angoor*. The citation goes thus:

> Normally great acting performances are associated with tragedy, or the character exhibiting a panoply of emotions. It is not often that a comic role gets this status. The one exception is Sanjeev Kumar's double role in *Angoor* (based on Shakespeare's *The Comedy of Errors*) where he makes you joyful with effortless acting and amazing comic timing.

Those who google Sanjeev Kumar will discover to their delight gems like the progressive *Anubhav* by Basu Bhattacharya, where a couple's estrangement, as well as the reality of the ubiquitous, customary sex between them, is embraced in a matter-of-fact manner. Others will discover his celebrated films directed by Gulzar. Their partnership was eternal, and the songs written by Gulzar, composed by R.D. Burman and rendered by Hari on screen, are absolutely timeless.

Gen Z may connect better with the mischievous tipsy song '*Rang barse*' from *Silsila*. If there's one song to celebrate Holi with, it may well be this! Just the disgust with which Hari 'looks' at his wife, played by Rekha, flirting shamelessly with her lover, played by Amitabh Bachchan, in the song, by itself calls for a PhD in acting.

But this book aims to unearth what's not commonly known about Hari. Born on 9 July 1938, Hari began his film journey with black and white cinema. He was a mainstream hero doing action, romance and stunt films convincingly before a premature paunch asserted itself. The trams he travelled in were discontinued in 1964, around the time when he started earning enough money to buy a car. Hari's career is a virtuoso slice of Indian cinematic history.

Whether you're ranking Hindi cinema's best lead roles, comic performances, character performances or negative roles, at least one movie of Hari's is sure to make it to each list. Hari's life epitomizes the saying: 'A flame that burns twice as bright, lasts half as long!'

1

The Family Tree

Young Hari was born into plenty.

Grandfather Shivlal had a haveli in Surat, Gujarat, with a ghoda-gaadi and all the trappings of wealth. Father Jethalal Shivlal Jariwala became a zari trader, keeping up the family tradition. Those were the times when a ceremonial gun mounted on the wall of the palatial family house was symbolic of grandeur. It was the era of British rule when one needed a license to even own a radio. And Jethalal had one!

Let's go back to the early 1920s. Jethalal's first wife bore him two daughters, Laxmi and Jasu, before she died of illness. His second wife bore him a daughter, Bhagwati, but died in childbirth. Hari's mother, Shantaben (hereafter referred to as Baa), was Jethalal's third wife.

Baa was from Bardoli and hailed from a family of rich zamindars. Her father was the sarpanch of his village, and it was only because he was powerful that he could even think of getting his daughter married into a wealthy family in Surat city. Baa bore Jethalal five children: first a daughter who passed away in her infancy, followed by Hari, Kishore, Gayatri and Nikul.

Baa was sixteen years younger than Jethalal. Young girls being married off to older men was very common in those days. So, Jethalal's daughters from his earlier marriages—Laxmi, Jasu and Bhagwati—were almost Baa's age. The first two were already married when Baa came into the family, circa 1933, and Baa was a part of the third one's wedding rituals.

As Jethalal had no sons, it was Baa's wish to bear him a son. There was a Maata ka Mandir in Charoti on the Maharashtra–Gujarat border, a couple of hours' journey from Surat. Baa used to travel all the way there to pray for a son. The word for these prayers is 'mannat'—Baa pledged to God that if he gave her a son, she would make him wear only 'donated clothes' for the first ten years and bring him back to the same temple for his mundan ceremony. After five long years of marriage (it was common then for a child to be born to a couple within the first year of marriage itself), a providential son, Harihar Jariwala, was born on 9 July 1938. Three more children followed—Kishore in 1944, Gayatri in 1946 and Nikul in 1947.

Hari went on to become Sanjeev Kumar, an actor who was loved by millions of Indians. He chose to remain single. Baa's second son Kishore Jariwala grew up to be an actor and musician. He was estranged from the family for several years. Later in life, he married Prafulla. They lived separately and had no children.

Hari's sister Gayatri got married to Ashok Patel and settled in America. Ashok passed away on 18 April 2017 and Gayatri on 17 February 2021. They have two children, Alex (Ashish) Patel and Artee Patel.

2

Reliving 6 November 1985

Hari Jariwala lived on the second floor of a rented flat in Perrin Villa, a residential building in Bandra, Mumbai, as part of a large joint family. Mother Shantaben, younger brothers Nikul and Kishore, Nikul's wife Jyoti and their children—all lived together. The house was blessed with the laughter of children and the sanctity of faith, which the ladies kept alive through their prayers and rituals. It was a regular, traditional, vegetarian Gujarati household.

Kishore Jariwala shifted out of Perrin Villa after his marriage to Prafulla in 1981. Baa and Nikul had succumbed to heart disease in 1979 and 1984 respectively. During Hari's last days, only his sister-in-law Jyoti, her three children—Uday, Prithvi and Ekta—and an entourage of domestic staff lived with Hari at Perrin Villa.

When the sun rose on 6 November 1985, Jyoti Nikul Jariwala was at the holy site of Jagannath Puri. She and the kids were visiting her parental home in Kolkata for the Diwali holidays. Jyoti had left Uday behind in Mumbai with Hari for company and had taken along only Ekta and Prithvi. But Hari was to go to Fiji for a show, so on 5 November, Uday, too, joined his mother in Kolkata. That was when Pushpa Patel, Jyoti's mother, made an impromptu plan to visit Puri with the family.

For Jyoti, it was a time of hope. Hari's successful surgery at the Texas Heart Institute had given the family a much-needed breather and a positive outlook. Hari had been operated upon by one of the world's top surgeons and had lost a great deal of weight. It seemed that he would recover his health. The staff back at Perrin Villa was very reliable. Hari's long-time personal attendant, Pandit, was trained to manage the medicines. Driver Sharmaji, cook Ramji, maid Rukmini and Jamnadasji, Hari's trusted manager, were looking after his affairs.

After Hari's surgery, a bell had been installed next to his bed, just in case he needed something urgently. It was normal for the helps to do their chores and not enter Hari's room until they were summoned by the bell. On the morning of 6 November, Hari had returned home at 4 a.m. from his friends Shabnam Sippy Pillai and Prem Pillai's house. So, it wasn't unusual that the bell didn't ring till about 10.30 a.m.

That's when Jamnadasji arrived every day; it was his usual time. He had a free pass to enter Hari's room, without being summoned by the bell. When he entered the room that day, he discovered that not only had Hari woken up but was also vomiting severely. Hari asked Jamnadasji to cancel his shoot for that day. He was very remorseful because it had slipped his mind that it was Baa's death anniversary that day! Hari wanted to observe solitude and silence.

Looking at Hari's condition, Jamnadasji first did as he was bid and then went to call Dr Gandhi. Meanwhile, Hari gathered his wits and called close friend Shabnam Sippy Pillai.

The Last Supper by Shabnam Sippy Pillai

Shabnam, the daughter of producer Nari Sippy, whom Hari had worked with in Paras *(1971) and* Devata *(1978), gets a lump in her throat every time she recalls what had happened on Haribhai's last night:*

> On 5 November 1985, Haribhai came home for paya, a mutton dish. My husband Prem and I always maintained an open house for Bhai. I had known him for so many years—I was seventeen when my father was making *Paras*. Haribhai used to call me Babli and I would call him Bhai.
>
> Bhai had a shoot during the day. [Actress Ranjeeta Kaur confirms that Haribhai's last day of shooting was with her for R.K. Nayyar's *Qatl,* in which he was playing a blind man's role. They had shot in Juhu and had wound up by about 5 p.m.]. That was followed by some dubbing and a party that he had to attend. He reached my house at about midnight, and we were together till 4 a.m. In his trademark style, Bhai asked me to show him the empty kadhai in which the paya was cooked so that he could be convinced that the dish was indeed over. He took a last playful lick from the kadhai too! In the wee hours of the morning, he left for his home, which was just a minute away from ours.

On the morning of 6 November, at around noon, the phone in my house rang. It was Bhai. He told me, 'Babli, I am a very big idiot. Today is Baa's barsi and I never go anywhere. By oversight, a shoot has been fixed but I've cancelled it. You come home.' I told him, 'We were together till 4 a.m.! And you want me to come now?'

'If you don't come today, you won't see me again,' he replied. I told him I'd get some work done at my boutique and then come over.

The End ... by Sachin Pilgaonkar

In a couple of hours, back at Perrin Villa, another friend, Sachin Pilgaonkar, was by Hari's side.

On the evening of 5 November 1985, I met Haribhai while he was dubbing at Sumit Studio. We spoke for a while and, instinctively, I promised to meet him the next day at his home. Here's how that conversation went:

Haribhai: I have to go to my optician's tomorrow. Come after 12.30.

Me: I have some work too. Would it be fine if I came by 2.30?

Haribhai nodded.

On cue, I reached the second floor of Perrin Villa between 2 and 2.30 p.m. on the afternoon of 6 November and rang the bell. 'Is Haribhai home?' I asked the housekeeper who opened the door for me.

Housekeeper: He's bathing.

Me: Where is Jamnadasji?

Housekeeper: He has gone to fetch Dr Gandhi.

Jamnadasji was Haribhai's manager, soul provider and dependable lieutenant—all rolled into one. I waited for a bit, as the housekeeper looked very scared to open the door to Haribhai's room.

I was wondering why Jamnadasji had gone to fetch the doctor. So I asked again, 'What time did Haribhai get home last night?' He answered, '4 a.m. He was at a friend's house.'

I could imagine what had happened! After his dubbing, he would've indulged in his usual late-night binge. I felt a rage seethe within me. Haribhai had just had an open-heart surgery—why was he abusing his own health again? He seemed to be living his life unchecked and unfettered! I was preparing to give him a piece of my mind. I loved Haribhai beyond measure. It was not just about respect for him as a performer; our relationship was deeply personal. I couldn't bear to see him in this state of atrophy!

As the seconds ticked by, my anxiety was rising. There was no sign of Haribhai having finished his bath yet! I confronted the housekeeper again.

Me: How long ago did he enter the bathroom?

Housekeeper: About thirty minutes before you came.

Me: How can anyone have a bath for over an hour?

As the housekeeper stood meekly before me, I felt great relief as Jamnadasji entered with Dr Gandhi.

Me: 'What happened, Jamnadasji?'

Jamnadasji: He vomited black phlegm in the morning. He was supposed to go to the optician's in the morning, but didn't!

Me: So, he's been inside all day! Let's open the door and see how he is!

Jamnadasji hesitated. Concerned, I opened the sliding door to Haribhai's room. I imagined that if he were changing or getting ready, I would politely apologize and shut the door. But none of us were prepared for the sight that met our eyes!

On the carpet, I saw Haribhai fallen down! He was lying on his stomach with his head down and his hand pointing towards the door, as if reaching for it. A bottle of sorbitrate tablets (emergency medication) was lying next to him.

Dr Gandhi rushed towards Haribhai and turned him! As he tried to pump and revive Haribhai's heart, his face fell.

'He has passed away some time back,' Dr Gandhi declared.

An avalanche of emotions came over me! As tears welled up in my eyes, I felt like a fool for not having opened the door sooner. Would it have made a difference if the housekeeper had had more courage? Who knows?

One of the finest, most iconic, naturally gifted performers in Indian cinema had breathed his last. My dear friend who lovingly called me 'Chachin' was no more!

The Phone Calls

The doctor had declared the time of death must have been around 2.30 p.m. It was about 2.45 p.m. when Sachin Pilgaonkar discovered the body.

Jamnadasji tried to reach Jyoti. But she and the children were in Jagannath Puri. In the pre-mobile phone era, there was no way to track them down. So, Jamnadasji left a message with Jyoti's brother Sunil Patel.

Jamnadasji also called Kishorebhai, who rushed home immediately, and then called Babu, Moushumi Chatterjee's husband, who in turn called Shabnam Sippy Pillai at around 3 p.m. Sachin Pilgaonkar informed Shammi Kapoor and Shatrughan Sinha. The news spread like wildfire.

Meanwhile, Sunil Patel left his home in Kolkata by road and reached Jagannath Puri. He checked hotel after hotel to see where Jyoti and the family were staying. When he found them, all he said was, 'Haribhai is serious. Jamnadasji had called. You need to rush back.'

There was an urgency in Sunil's voice, which made all of them drive straight to Kolkata airport the next morning, 7 November 1985, to take the first flight out. On the flight was that day's edition of *Times of India* with the headline: 'Actor Sanjeev Kumar no more'.

'We were all in complete shock. It seemed so recent that we were all celebrating his successful surgery and recovery; and then this!' remembers Jyoti.

At the Bombay airport, Viresh Patel, another brother of Jyoti's, received them. The drive home seemed longer than usual, and emotions were welling up. At Perrin Villa, there were crowds of people overcome with grief. It took a while for Jyoti and her family to navigate their way through them and reach their own house. When they entered the house at Perrin Villa, Hari's body was on ice in his favourite place in the house called 'jhupti', which had glass walls. This was the room in which Haribhai used to meet his directors and producers, have script readings, etc. It could seat around twelve people. Jamnadasji and Kishore Jariwala had overseen all the arrangements. The hall was cleared, and the impossibly long line of fans was being allowed to enter the home; they saw the body through the glass, paid their last respects and left.

For Jyoti, 6 November 1985 is a blur.

On the one side, bhajans were being sung by both Hindus and Sikhs. On the other, swarms of people were expressing their condolences. Sunil Dutt, Dilip Kumar, Sachin Pilgaonkar, Shatrughan Sinha, etc., were sitting in the jhupti next to the body. Jyoti's whole life collapsed in front of her eyes. She was grateful that Kishorebhai and Jamnadasji were around to manage Hari's passage to the other world.

The body had to be kept on ice for a couple of days until Gayatri Patel, Hari's sister, could come from Texas, with her husband Ashok and children Ashish and Artee. Gayatri reached at around midnight on 7 November. The last rites were set for 8 November.

It was the end of the story of Harihar Jethalal Jariwala, more of a sasur (father-in-law) than jeth (brother-in-law) to Jyoti. He had joined his mother on the anniversary of her demise.

But Sanjeev Kumar, one of the finest actors on the Indian cinematic firmament, remains alive through his performances.

SECTION I

Early Days

1

Hari's Acting Bug

There are scores of media reports that say Hari spent his childhood in Bardoli, near Surat. This is completely untrue. Hari's family had always lived in Santa Cruz in Mumbai, and that is where he was born. Gayatri says, 'My brothers and I were born in Shanta Bhavan, in Chapel Lane in Santa Cruz West. Shanta Bhavan was named after my mother and was a bungalow; we had tenants on the ground floor and first floor, and our family lived on the second floor.'

Jethalal died at the young age of forty-seven in the year 1950. Baa was thirty-two years old at that time, and Hari twelve. The formidable task of raising four children single-handedly fell on Baa's shoulders. Hari, and to some extent Kishore, were the only children of Baa's who had had any interaction with their father Jethalal (called Babuji by all his children).

According to Gayatri, 'Baa did try to take care of the zari business for a while, but she was a really simple woman from a small village with no education. Besides, Babuji's partners had usurped everything. Neither Babuji's brothers nor Baa's family came forward to help in any way. Baa took on the role of both mother and father for us! When the resources ran out, we shifted to the small Bhuleshwar flat that Babuji used as his office, and she put Shanta Bhavan on rent. We survived on the Rs 600 rent that the tenants paid us every month as rent. I was just four years old at this time.'

Initially, the family used to visit their ancestral home in Surat only to spend their vacations there. To the outside world, Baa remained fearless as she put up a brave face. She borrowed some money and built two more flats in Shanta Bhavan, upping the rent to Rs 800 a month.

'Baa had a major setback while raising us. There was some law that a woman cannot have two properties to her name, so Shanta Bhavan was taken away by the government. We had to put the Surat property on rent for sustenance. She did whatever it took, selling her jewellery and trading utensils for other goods, and pressed on. In those days, we had to pay the school fees before the tenth of the month. If we did not, we would be asked to stand outside the class; it was very humiliating because I was late to pay the fees many times. We definitely had a lot of money problems as children. But what my mother lacked in education she made up for with grit and determination. Baa was working as hard as she could to make ends meet,' Gayatri remembers.

Young Hari saved coins to watch films. He finished his schooling from Sacred Heart Boys School in Santa Cruz (he is not a Gujarati school dropout, as widely reported) and joined Nanavati High School in Bhuleshwar to complete his eleventh and twelfth grades. In one of his stage performances in eleventh grade, he did a re-enactment of Raj Kapoor's song *'Awaara hoon'* and won a prize. That's when he realized he enjoyed performing.

He did not pursue further studies after the twelfth grade but joined the Indian People's Theatre Association (IPTA) instead and decided to learn the craft of acting. IPTA had been founded in 1942 by stalwarts like K.A. Abbas, Anil De Silva, Ali Sardar Jafri and Dada Sharmalkar and was very active at the time.

Actor Satyen Kappu remembers Hari Jariwala coming to see one of his plays at K.C. College in 1957. Fresh out of twelfth grade and introduced to IPTA by a common friend, Hari was asked to visit the IPTA office the next day. Senior actor A.K. Hangal met him, and Hari was enrolled as a member. In the book *Life and Times of A.K. Hangal*, the thespian recalls meeting Hari: 'Hari first came to IPTA when we had started conducting our rehearsals at the Bhulabhai Desai Institute. He was dressed in kurta-pyjama and was very shy and unassuming. None of us took him seriously during the initial days.'[4]

Let's revisit Hari's theatre days with a first-person narration by Amit Divatia, a veteran actor of the Gujarati stage, who met Hari at IPTA and witnessed his meeting with theatre doyen Chandravadan Bhatt, the man who gave Hari his first salary in theatre.

---

4 A.K. Hangal, *Life and Times of A.K. Hangal* (Sterling Publishers, 1999).

2

The Voice of Amit Divatia

Hari and I met at IPTA. We were roommates, co-actors and buddies since the late 1950s or early '60s. We had common friends too, such as the late Arvind Joshi (actor Sharman Joshi's father), Kishore Bhatt, Jayant Vyas and Kanti Madiya. Hari was a very friendly person.

I hailed from a family steeped in theatre. My sister Namita Divatia was married to actor Prashant Desai and my other sister Niharika was married to Chandravadan Bhatt, a theatre stalwart. Hari used to hang around where we rehearsed. As luck would have it, Prashant got a job in Goodyear Tyres and quit a play midway. One of the crew members suggested Hari as a replacement to director Chandravadan Bhatt, 'Look at that boy with curly hair. He is from Surat and knows Gujarati. He is a struggler. Let's try him.'

Chandravadan Bhatt looked up and 'noticed' Hari for the first time. This casual suggestion from the crew member and Bhatt's setting eyes upon Hari would eventually make history.

'Aye, come here,' said Bhatt. 'What's your name?'

'Harihar,' came the reply.

Bhatt: 'Where are you from?'

Harihar: 'Surat. I know that you are Chandravadan Bhatt.'

Bhatt: 'Yes. Will you do a play in Gujarati?'

Harihar's response was shocking but honest: '*Gujarati drama mein toh paisa milta hai!*' (Gujarati drama pays well!)

Bhatt: 'Yes, will you try out for the role? I will give you Rs 35 per show.'

Hari was ecstatic, '*Arre Baapre*! Rs 35! I will act exactly the way you want me to!'

Bhatt promptly conducted a rehearsal, after which Hari was selected for a small part in a play called *Choota Cheda* (divorce). I was the junior-most in the unit, followed by Hari. My job was to hold the dialogue and prompt him. We used to hang out together—perhaps he didn't feel intimidated by me and felt comfortable asking me the doubts that constantly cropped up in his busy head!

Even in those days, when he had nothing, he would always talk about his celluloid dreams. The rest of the crew used to tease him, '*Dekho, film ka hero aaya hai!*' (Look, the great film hero is here!) Hari was always honest about his desire to become an actor. In the words of American humourist Erma Bombeck, 'It takes a lot of courage to show your dreams to someone else.' It was almost as if he believed that the more he spoke about it, the more likely it was that his desires would come true. Our shows would be held on Fridays and Saturdays at the Tejpal theatre, Tardeo, Mumbai. It was difficult to get a free weekend there because the theatre was always in demand by musicians and Qawwali exponents like Shakeela Bano. I also knew that the very reason Hari had joined IPTA was to meet folks like Dev Anand, Khwaja Ahmed and Balraj Sahni. He was hoping that someone would notice him in a play and give him a break in films.

As Hari continued to work in theatre, our troupe was invited to tour Ahmedabad. We had a booking for almost twenty shows all over Gujarat. When I look back, a superstar like Sanjeev Kumar was living with me in ordinary motels like Pathik Ashram in Bhavnagar. But to Hari, these things didn't matter. He was just happy to be acting.

We did many tours. One of them involved a play that was truly memorable. It was called *Nyay na Panthe*. Sohrab Modi was the lead. Hari, Dinesh Hingoo and I had small parts; we played three gunmen. Given Sohrab Modi's stature, the Maharaja of Bhavnagar had come to see the show. Now, Modi was more than seventy years old. But when he saw Maharaja Krishnakumar Shreeji, he performed an elaborate Darbari Mujra, an artistic welcome befitting a royal family. All of us watched open-mouthed. We were stunned by Modi's litheness and his energy. Only a person who wanted to 'give joy' and surrender completely to his art would go this far!

The Maharaja was overwhelmed by the show of respect and said, 'We are grateful that a talent like you has come to the city.'

Modi replied, 'You are our Raja. *Raja ke saamne raiyyat sir jhukaayegi hi*!' (The subjects will always bow before the king). The Maharaja stayed for the play and met Sohrab Modi again before he left. For us newcomers, this incident was a game-changer. Mesmerized, Hari spoke to me about the power that Sohrab Modi commanded, while also noting his humility and complete submission to his art.

Hari and I went on to do Gujarati plays like *Manu ni Maasi*, *Lagn ni Bedi* and *Gunehgaar.* Hari also did Hindi plays like *Damru*, directed by A.K. Hangal, and *Ward No.6* by Anton Chekhov. I had seen him in the prime of his youth and together we had been in situations where the true character of the man emerges. What amazed me was how dignified he always was with women. He was brought up with exceptional values by his mother and was a very cultured young man. I never heard even the slightest murmur of any dalliances or indiscretions on his part. His ambition to become a great actor was the topmost mission of his life.

But he did have one weakness! During our many tours, even in the state of Gujarat with its Prohibition Act, he would always tell me, '*Amit, desi daaru ka bandobast kar*!' He was addicted to country liquor.

A friend would get us a potli (a plastic bag containing alcohol) for the princely sum of Rs 5. Hari also loved non-vegetarian food. After the drinks I would take him to Pathiyaar Gully, where he would enjoy his chicken. It was because of him that I started loving chicken too, despite having been a vegetarian until then! 'Amit, I can't control myself when I see chicken,' he always used to say. Having eaten to his heart's content and then some more, he would show up the next morning at 11 for rehearsal and deliver a very fine performance.

In his early twenties, Hari joined Filmalaya Acting School. It was through Filmalaya that he got selected for a small role in *Aao Pyaar Karen*. When the film released, Hari was so excited! He insisted that I take all my friends to see it. When I obligingly took my friends for the show, they openly asked me, 'That crazy friend of yours ... he had such a small role! What is he jumping about?' But Hari had the gift of positivity when it came to talking about his roles. His energy level was always high! He continued to work very hard. When *Khilona* released, Hari, my simple friend, became a big star. I was happy for him.

Hari was a very dependable friend. No matter what pinnacle of prestige he attained, he continued to come for our plays whenever possible. He would just come, sit and spend time with us. Our friendship was very much alive, but I knew that our backslapping days were gone. Hari had become a superstar. I still remember him coming to watch our play *Preet, Piyu ne Paanetar*. On another occasion, Chandravadan Bhatt was directing the Gujarati adaptation of Shakespeare's *Taming of the Shrew* and we were all rehearsing for it at Bhaidas Hall, Juhu. This was in 1979. Hari came in. He had by then acquired the eclat, urgency and mannerism suited to his stature, but at heart he was still the same simple man I knew from eighteen years before. 'Where is Bhatt sahab?' he asked me with a smile. People there recognized Hari and started crowding around us, but Hari waited for almost half an hour just to meet the man who had given him a break in Gujarati theatre. He met Bhatt sahab with humility and enquired after us with genuine concern.

Before he became a bonafide film actor, he joined the Indian National Theatre (INT) and became friends with the prolific Pravin Joshi. It was there that he also met Jamnadas Javeri, the man who would serve Hari all his life.

3

Jamnadas Javeri

The Indian National Theatre was backed by stalwarts such as Damu Jhaveri and Bachu Sampat. They had the vision and the capital to invest in theatre, and INT was known for its very fine plays.

Padmashri Sarita Joshi, one of Hari's oldest friends, has fond memories from those days. 'The Indian National Theatre was a highly revered establishment. You could say that it brought in the golden era of Gujarati theatre. From Dhirubhai Ambani to Arvind Mafatlal, Yash Chopra to Vyjayanthimala, people used to come to see plays written by greats like Kanhaiyalal Munshi, Gujarat's most-read author. Munshi was also the founder of the Bharatiya Vidya Bhavan educational trust. He coined the phrase '*Gujarat ni asmita*', a slogan which encapsulates the collective pride of Gujarati culture. Hari, my husband Pravin Joshi (theatre actor and director) and I were part of a generation of theatre actors who were building our future in this venerable ecosystem. Pravin eventually directed Hari in his adaptation of Arthur Miller's play *All My Sons*, for which both of them got a state award from the Government of Maharashtra.'

Bachu Sampat's daughter, actor and educationist Swaroop Sampat, also remembers Hari fondly. 'My father founded INT at the behest of the then Prime Minister Jawaharlal Nehru. Haribhai was close to my father and called him "boss".'

Theatre was very important to Hari, and it taught him a lot. He met many of his life's greatest friends and well-wishers during his theatre days. Jamnadas Javeri used to work in Bhuleshwar, at a cloth store near Haribhai's house. He would quietly observe young Hari coming and going for his theatre rehearsals. As he got to know him better, he realized that Hari wanted to become a film actor. So he approached Hari one day. Remembering that conversation as narrated by Jamnadas, Uday Jariwala reconstructs it:

> Jamnadas: I want to become your manager.
>
> Hari: But I am a nobody.
>
> Jamnadas: Just keep me ... *tumhari aankhon mein roshni hai.*

Somehow, in the bright eyes of this young man, Jamnadas had recognized a would-be star.

Over time, Jamnadas became more like a friend, philosopher and guide to Hari.

While accolades for his theatre performances started coming Hari's way, he also kept trying his luck in cinema. Jamnadas used to pitch him to various production houses and not tell Hari about all the rejections. He would just say, 'I'm trying.'

Jamnadas Javeri belonged to the Gujarati Soni community. A God-fearing man, he devoutly worshipped Lord Ganesha. His wife Chandaben was very friendly with Gayatri and Jyoti, and son Deepak was a regular at Perrin Villa, especially on Sundays when he, Prithvi and Uday would watch movies like *For a Few Dollars More* and *The Good, the Bad and the Ugly*.

Other than Jamnadas, people like Siraj Burmawala and Gulzar were also Hari's friends from his theatre days. The first validation of Hari's good looks, too, came from theatre. Gulzar, with whom Hari would eventually develop one of the most rewarding creative partnerships, says: 'They were rehearsing a play at Bhulabhai and I ran into Hari standing outside, looking very happy. Some Gujarati woman had remarked, "*Joy sarika dikhta hai*!", remarking on his resemblance to actor Joy Mukherjee. Hari was delighted and told me this, adding, "*Apna bhi chance hai*", with a winning smile! To him, the lady's remark translated into a sure-shot break in films.'

And soon enough, he got one too.

4

Hungry for Roles

Hari's willingness to work hard and regularly approach producers and directors to give him a break eventually seemed to bear fruit. In 1961, he was selected for the film *Aarti* that had Meena Kumari in the titular role. Hari was twenty-three years old at the time. He was over the moon.

Hari had actually debuted in films with a small role in the Sunil Dutt starrer *Hum Hindustani* (1960), but he hadn't received any credit for his role in it. So a film opposite Meena Kumari was a big deal!

'My dreams have come true,' Hari had said excitedly to Pravin Joshi.

But a couple of days later, Hari learned of a very upsetting development. Pradeep Kumar was finalized instead of Hari in *Aarti*. Hari felt that it wasn't right. 'પ્રદીપ કુમારે મારી જગ્યા લીધી છે. તે બરાબર નથી' (Pradeep Kumar has replaced me! This is not fair.)

Hari had complained woefully in Gujarati to Pravin Joshi. He had been shaking, trembling and crying.

Pravin Joshi, one of the biggest names in Gujarati theatre and one of Hari's close confidants in the 1960s, heard him out and let Hari vent.

'Can you get me a job in INT?' Hari had pleaded. 'I am not meant to be an [film] actor.'

Pravin had responded, 'Have some faith, Hari. Why do you want only big banners? If you really want to be an actor, you should not be afraid to start small! A job at INT will not give you any satisfaction.'

'But I'm being offered only mythological or stunt films! They will spoil my career,' Hari had insisted.

Pravin Joshi had said, 'You focus on doing your best and have patience.'

With wet eyes, Hari had continued, petulantly, 'I am such a good actor. I have got awards for theatre! Doesn't it count? How can they just replace me?'

It was a sad day for Hari. Pravin Joshi encouraged him to keep the faith, but Hari couldn't get his abrupt replacement out of his mind! He succumbed to depression and signed a very detrimental contract with Rajshri Productions in sheer desperation! Those were for bit roles for a monthly salary.

Hari was under tremendous financial pressure. He knew that despite being widowed and laden with debt, Baa had supported his passion for acting and allowed him to pursue his dreams, never pressuring him to earn any money for the family. There were people who would come home to recover debts and threaten Baa, but she never allowed this to come in the way of young Hari's dreams. His heart sank, and he wondered whether his talent would amount to anything at all! How would he start earning and taking care of his family?

When the full force of what he had done hit him, Hari was admitted to the Harkishandas Narottamdas Hospital for a month. As word of Hari's illness spread in Surat, family members were quick to declare, 'Hari has gone mad!' Depression wasn't understood well back then. It was Jamnadasji, Baa, her sister Rukmini and husband Jeevan Patel who stood with Hari day and night, bringing him back from the brink.

Luckily, somehow Jamnadas got him out of the contract that would've effectively ended his career! He and the others nursed Hari back to good spirits and gave him courage again. And he never looked back after that.

5

The Voice of Padmashri Sarita Joshi

Sarita Joshi (then Sarita Khatau) was Hari's first co-star in a lead role.

Both Hari and I have done good work in theatre and cinema from the 1960s. Our first meeting was in Baroda. We were cast together in our debut as lead actors in Gujarati cinema in the film *Ramat Ramade Ram*. This was around 1961. We shot the film in Baroda, and our financier, Manubhai, was a friend of the legendary Guru Dutt. The shoot was set up at the Sarabhai bungalow owned by the folks who owned MDL, the stained-glass factory. Directed by Dinesh Rawal, *Ramat Ramade Ram* also featured Tarla Mehta, Arvind Pandya and Mahesh Desai.

When I first saw him, Hari was very quiet. He had heard about me because I had worked with eminent playwright and director

Satyadev Dubey in theatre before and I used to command a reasonable price in those days. Actors like Hari were yet to get established, and they used to charge much less. One day our director Dineshbhai said, 'The hero of our film Hari—there is absolutely no sound in his laughter.'

In contrast, I was a live-wire, jovial and interactive with the cast and crew, keeping the environment positive and happy. I used to tease Hari, 'Don't worry, I can hear your voice.'

It took him a long time to open up. When the songs were being shot, we used to pull each other's leg—'I will run around the tree. You will run behind me.'

Our performance in *Ramat Ramade Ram*, which released in 1964, was received exceedingly well. Hari and I got an award from the Gujarat government. Manubhai wanted to introduce us to Guru Dutt. Hari was excited because he was very keen on a break in Hindi cinema. But Guru Dutt died in October 1964, and that was not to be.

Very few people know that it is thanks to Hari that I met my husband, Pravin. One day, Hari had asked me casually, 'Sarita, have you seen Pravin's shows?'

'Who Pravin?' I had asked.

'Pravin Joshi. I'm doing a play with him. Come and see it,' Hari had said.

He gave me two tickets of Rs 5 each. He was always generous—both in the small things and the big things. Hari took me behind the scenes to meet Pravin, and the rest is history.

Hari's struggle to become an established name in Hindi cinema continued, while I continued to work in drama and Gujarati cinema. His eventual debut as lead actor in Hindi cinema was in *Nishan* (1965), after which he got a couple of more stunt films like *Husn aur Ishq* (1966) and *Ali Baba aur Chalis Chor* (1966). He started getting appreciated, and, as we all know, there was no looking back for Hari after that. In those days, Pravin and I used to live on Nepean Sea Road. About ten minutes away was Lamington Road, the buzzing place where all the film studios were located. Often, Hari would come home after his shoot; he and Pravin would just sit in the balcony and talk.

Jamnadasji used to call in advance—'*Bhai aavana chhe*', which was a signal to my domestic help Dhakla to make some good food. To his credit, Hari used to talk to everyone. He had no 'attitude', as they say, and was happy to be in his chappals and kurta pyjama. He was a very simple person; just give him good food and he would be very happy. When I was pregnant, Hari would tease me—'*Bahut choti lag rahi hai.*'

I still remember how after *Zanjeer* released, Amitabh Bachchan, Jaya Bachchan (she was Jaya Bhaduri before marriage) and Asrani had come to Birla auditorium to watch one of Pravin's plays. Hari was also there. He had introduced me to Amitji then.

Hari was always keen to introduce people he cared about to others who could help them. He introduced me to Jennifer Kendal, the fine lady who ran Prithvi Theatre. On one occasion, Hari had gone to Prithvi Theatre with Shafi Inamdar. There he saw my daughter Ketaki and commented, '*Ekdum tere jaisi dikhti hai.*'

On another occasion, when I was learning to drive, I had met with an accident and my hand was swollen. 'Why did you hurt yourself, Sarita? We are artistes. Every part of ours is important,' Hari had said. I had got very upset when Pravin and he had ganged up and made me stop my driving lessons.

Pravin reciprocated Hari's friendship heartily. He would get coloured glasses for him, sometimes champagne glasses with bits of crystal; Hari was very fond of expensive glassware. We would visit Hari at his home sometimes, and Baa used to make turiya patra (a Gujarati delicacy of ridge gourd and gram flour patty) which I liked a lot. I would take pulao for Hari, made by Pravin's mother.

In 1975, when *Sholay* released in Minerva, Hari bought tickets for Pravin and I. We loved his role, and what happened after about three days of the release of *Sholay* is the kind of adulation that every actor dreams of. Hari had scaled dizzying heights of stardom. All the accolades Hari received for his roles were always about the courage and strength of his performance.

Pravin's reputation in theatre was also growing in eminence, year after year. His play *Santu Rangili* (based on Bernard Shaw's *Pygmalion*), which released in 1977, remains one of the most celebrated plays in Gujarati theatre to date. Hari wanted to plan a surprise for Pravin. So he hosted a party for him, which Raj Kapoor also attended. There, Hari declared that he would produce a film with Pravin as the director and that he would also act in it. Hari also attended the mahurat of another film which Pravin was to direct, featuring Jeetendra, Shashi Kapoor and Sharmila Tagore. However, destiny had other plans. Pravin died in an accident in January 1979. Hari cancelled his shoot and came home. The entire theatre fraternity got to know by word of mouth about what had happened, and it didn't take very long for our friends to come and share their condolences. Dilip Kumar and Saira Bano, who were very close to Pravin and I, also came. So did Shashi Kapoor.

'Kitna chalte rahte hain cigarette peene wale,' Dilip sahab had said to Hari, expressing shock at Pravin's early demise—Pravin was a non-smoker.

Hari had asked me that day, 'Do you need anything, Sarita?'

His question was genuine, and I knew it. Hari has a special place in my memories, not just as my first co-star but also as a very close friend of my late husband.

'On the stage, you perform with the voice. As Stanislavski said, "Three things are very important for an actor. First, the voice. Secondly the voice and last the voice." But in films, you've got your eyes, you've got your face. You've got your entire body to perform with. Eyes are very important in cinema. Sometimes, you can tell the whole story with your eyes.'

Sanjeev Kumar
Filmfare, January 1978

SECTION II

Becoming Sanjeev Kumar

1

From Hari Jariwala to Sanjeev Kumar

BY SAAWAN KUMAR TAK

In the early 1960s, I had gone to watch an IPTA play at Tejpal theatre. If memory serves me right, it was written by the great writer Sagar Sarhadi. His one-act plays used to be extremely popular. But I remember being spellbound by the actor on the stage—Hari Jariwala. I had remarked to Sagar, *'Yeh toh Dilip Kumar style ka actor hai.'* Later, when I asked Hari to meet me, I discovered that he was painfully shy.

'Chai piyoge?' I asked, and he nodded.

As the tea arrived, I started narrating the story of my film *Naunihal* to him. He listened keenly, but asked midway, 'Why are you narrating the story to me?'

It was my turn to be surprised. 'To cast you,' I said simply.

Disbelief was writ large all over his face. He took a moment to gather himself, asked for a beedi and continued to listen. I offered him *Naunihal,* but I made it clear that the offer was not for the actor named Hari Jariwala. A majority of the successful actors of the day had Kumar as their surname—Raj Kumar, Pradeep Kumar, Rajendra Kumar, Manoj Kumar, Dilip Kumar, etc. So I suggested that Hari should also take on Kumar as his surname. And since my own name began with an 'S', I gave him the name 'Sanjay Kumar'. But that wasn't the end of it, because at that time another young actor named Sanjay Khan was making his presence felt with films like *Dillagi* and *Dus Lakh*. So we decided to go with 'Sanjeev Kumar'.

We remained close over the years, and I saw his heartbreaks up close. *'Ishq mein dhokha'* (betrayal in love) can be a difficult thing to survive. Love is a very powerful emotion and can make or break a man. Hari had also seen a lot of monetary struggles in his childhood. So, when he finally made some money, he took to showing it off by drinking excessively—perhaps to show that he could finally afford to! He also developed very princely ways—his generosity with food and alcohol extended to others too!

Hari was born to act. What was interesting to me was that several of the playback singers suited his on-screen lip-syncing—Mohammed Rafi, Bhupendra, Kishore Kumar, Mahendra Kapoor, Mukesh ... they could all sing for him. My favourite song has to be *'Tumhari zulf ke saaye men shaam kar loonga'* from *Naunihal*. I must also credit the singers, who always made it a point to ask before recording, 'Whom is the song picturized on?' They would then make suitable adjustments.

An image that will stay with me is Hari taking a long drag on his cigarette—as if his life depended on the pleasure of that one puff!

2

The Infamous Grind

Once Hari set foot in the world of cinema, he never went back to theatre. His persistence stemmed from the fact that he had a family to feed. He couldn't afford to sit idle. There were days when he would meet many people in a single day, only to ask them if they would give him a good role in a film.

After losing out *Aarti* to Pradeep Kumar in 1961, Hari was to work in *Balidan* in 1963, but that didn't happen either. It is worthwhile to pause here and register that Hari, at this point, had been struggling since 1956, when he was only eighteen. When a conscientious man is ambitious and even at the age of twenty-five sees his mother keeping the hearth alive, it can bring him immense discomfort. A few magazine clippings suggest that Hari went hungry on the days when there was no work. Gujarati theatre, as Amit Divatia said, was Hari's first source of reliable income. And after a lengthy stint here, it had, at last, led to some meaty lead roles in Gujarati movies for Hari to start with.

There's a story behind how Hari made it from Gujarati cinema to lead roles in Hindi films—a transition easier talked about than done! Around the release of *Ramat Ramade Ram* in 1964, director Homi Wadia of Basant Pictures was running some screen tests for *Nishan* (1965). Hari appeared at the venue in white kurta pyjama. The scene given to him was to sit next to the heroine. She had to ask, 'Who are you?' and Hari had to respond, 'I'm Hussain.'

Although it was only a simple one-line response that was demanded of him, Hari was in the mood for some magic! He infused all his learnings into this line, bringing a unique, subtle, expressive nuance to this banal scene! Homi Wadia was taken aback by the newcomer's ease and natural grace and remarked on this to his director Aspi Irani, who offered him the film. Those who have watched *Nishan* will know that Aspi Irani offered Hari a wholesome opportunity to display his histrionics. In this debut double role as lead, Hari got to play the inebriated spoilt prince Kiran and the righteous hardworking Badal—twins separated at birth. Kiran's love interest was Helen, and Badal's was Nazima. The film also starred actress Shammi and Prem Chopra. In a magazine article of unknown provenance from that time, Hari himself says, 'There was a lot of scope for acting in that movie. I still consider it to be one of my best-acted films.'

Hari was twenty-seven when the film released. To offer some context, other great actors in Hindi cinema had their lead debuts earlier in their lives—Dilip Kumar was twenty-two when his debut film *Jwar Bhata* released; Rajesh Khanna was twenty-four when he debuted with *Aakhri Khat*; and Rishi Kapoor was twenty-one when *Bobby* released.

Hari came across as a young, vital performer. He was excessively lean, slim and eager. A few of his early films feature a prominent, well-fitted waistband. A healthy mop of hair crowns a tight, expressive face, and his smile could fire up a million watts! He had a completely new, unabashed, full-throated way of 'singing' on screen. Despite *Nishan* being his first film in a lead role, there was nothing raw or new about the way he performed in it; he was composed, consummate and clearly gifted.

Hari's youthful exuberance shone through in the song *'Humkadam humsafar humnashi humzubaan/ Mast apne hal mein zinda diilo ka karwan'* sung by Mahendra Kapoor, well-known for his rendering of patriotic numbers. A teenage boy in the opening lines of the song, Hari transforms into a young man in the first stanza of the song. Then there's the romantic *'Haye, Tabassum tera'*, sung by Mohammed Rafi, in which Hari belts out heartfelt praise for his lady love. The customary hero-bashing-up-the-goons scenes in the film ticked all the right boxes for the perfect debut lead performance for Hari. But *Nishan* was released in the thick of the Indo-Pak war of 1965. Whether the film would be seen at all and what would it do for its lead actor were all big question marks. Luckily, Hari was favoured by fate. Despite the film managing just one show a day, and for just three weeks, a few important people managed to see the film, and there was some buzz in the air.

An interesting anecdote from those days came from Subhash Indori, arguably Hari's closest friend, in his interview to journalist Anil Chitre in the July 1980 issue of *Cine Blitz*.

Sanjeev was still travelling by bus, even though he had a release to his credit, *Nishan*, his first film. During one such bus ride, a producer travelling in the same bus recognised Sanjeev as *Nishan*'s hero. When Sanjeev alighted at Grant Road, the producer hurried after him and told him that he was launching a film and he wanted to discuss things with Sanjeev. The producer took his residence address and promised to drop in the next day. The following day, the producer arrived at Sanjeev's one-room chawl at Bhuleshwar and saw Sanjeev sleeping in the kitchen. Sanjeev immediately woke up and prepared tea for his guest and carried the cup to him. During the discussion that followed, the producer enquired the amount he had received for his film *Nishan*. 'Rs 25,000,' Sanjeev told him.

'The producer was surprised and told Sanjeev, 'But I can offer you only Rs 10,000.'

'I know,' Sanjeev answered. 'When you saw me travelling in a bus, you deducted Rs 5,000, and when I prepared the tea myself and offered it to you, you deducted another 5,000. Now you're offering me the balance amount. But my price is still Rs 25,000.'

The deal was clinched, and Sanjeev was signed at his price.

Nishan may not have been the ideal launchpad, but it gave Hari his next few films, which released in 1967 and '68. These movies featured costumes, sword fights and stunts and Hari's immense talent.

3

1966: Implementing Plan B

As word of Hari's competence spread, *Nishan* caught the eye of none other than actor Mahmood. He had a wonderful instinct for talent and offered Hari a lead role in *Pati Patni* (1966), a feature film that demanded both comic timing and talent. *Pati Patni* featured Mahmood himself in a significant role as a music teacher and also starred prominent actor Nanda Karnataki opposite Hari, as well as Mumtaz, Om Prakash, Sujit Kumar and Shashikala.

In the same Subhash Indori interview in *Cine Blitz* that was quoted earlier, there is also an anecdote about Hari's equation with Nanda:

> During his struggling days, Mahmood had signed him for his brother Usman Ali's film *Pati Patni*, with Nanda, who was then at the top. Sanjeev used to travel by bus from his Bhuleshwar residence to the studios, and he had the habit of

tucking his bus ticket under his wrist watch. One day while shooting a scene, Nanda noticed the bus ticket and enquired, 'You travel by bus to the studios?' Sanjeev replied calmly, 'When I'm late I come by bus but otherwise I walk it to the studios.'

Nanda was aghast—her hero travelling by bus and having the cheek to snub her! A few days later, Nanda went to a theatre to see a movie. To her horror, from her balcony seat, she saw Sanjeev sitting in the front seats of the lower stalls. Next day, she confronted Mahmood instead of Sanjeev—'What kind of a man have you signed opposite me as a hero? I saw him viewing a movie sitting in a seat of the lower stalls.'

[When] Mahmood demanded, 'Why did you purchase a one-rupee ticket?' Sanjeev's prompt reply was, 'Because there wasn't any ticket of a lower denomination!'

It left both Mahmood and Nanda gaping.

Hari was a man of very simple tastes and had a likeable disposition. Thanks to that, Homi Wadia cast him again in *Alibaba Aur Chaalis Chor*, opposite L. Vijayalakshmi, in a fantasy adventure—this time as producer and director. Homi Wadia's genre was stunt and action, and that's what he made Hari do! There is a particular scene in which Hari rides on horseback, chasing the villain who has captured his lady love. Hari rides atop a hill and ambushes the villain with a clean jump! He displays acrobatic agility as he lands clean punches on his villain and rescues the lady. While it is difficult to venture to guess what percentage of the scenes were performed by a stuntman—the message was clear—a new romantic action hero had arrived! Viewers who know Hari only from his later multi-starrers will be surprised to see him walking around shirtless—with just an open waistcoat and a loose dhoti held up with a decorated waistband in the opening scenes of *Alibaba ...*!

It was Aspi Irani's turn to cast Hari again Hari in another directorial venture, *Smuggler*. Hari's character was portrayed in a completely new light here; the film had a very modern look, with Hari in suits and a tie. The role also saw Hari performing a sort of clap-dance in the song '*Kaise kaise kaam kiye*' with his leading lady Kumkum.

The blog 'MemsaabStory' remarks on Hari's looks in *Smuggler*. The review says: 'It stars a young and very handsome Sanjeev Kumar opposite the lovely Kumkum, and alongside Sheikh Mukhtar.'[5]

Greta Kaemmer, who writes this blog, is an American. A self-confessed fan of Shammi Kapoor, she makes an interesting observation about *Smuggler* and similar small-budget movies:

> Not only do these movies often have lovely songs by lesser-known composers (e.g., Ganesh, G.S. Kohli), but they very often have straightforward and fun stories too, and they give one an opportunity to see well-known actors as they were starting out (e.g., Feroz Khan, Sanjeev Kumar). B-movie directors often had the good sense to give ladies like Helen lots to do, as well. One of my favourites of these guys is Aspi Irani (usually credited as Aspi). He made the delicious *Daku* with Shammi, and the equally delightful Shabnam ...

Hari was committing to whatever came his way so that he could earn some money. There was *Husn aur Ishq* (1966), a fantasy film

---

5 https://memsaabstory.com/2009/08/19/smuggler-1966/#more-10008

by Naresh Kumar. This is where you will probably encounter Hari dancing the most he ever has. As he performs to '*Jinki tasveer nigaahon mein liye firta hoon*', to Mohammed Rafi's voice, he delights us with an impromptu jig—with his unique way of moving his shoulders and his walk! What's interesting is that it's not heavily choreographed and looks quite natural and credible. The title song '*Husn aur ishq*' also involves a very elaborate romantic sequence against the backdrop of rain. With his curls falling gently on his forehead, wide grin and honest expressions, Hari is the consummate chocolate boy! And yes, the waistband was intact!

In the book *Hero Volume I: The Silent Era to Dilip Kumar*,[6] Ashok Raj labels these early films as B-grade and observes that Hari's 'abundant talent was visible only to the discerning eye'. Naresh Kumar would later again cast Hari in 1971 in *Ek Paheli*.

Badal (1966) was also directed by Aspi Irani. This film has Hari playing the eponymous role of a village simpleton who witnesses the king's murder by his own minister. He takes an unusual path to rouse the villagers against the minister by writing verses targeting him. Hari sports a few disguises in the film and also woos the minister's sister, played by L. Vijayalakshmi. He looks the part of her wooer in a fitted angarkha, turban and cummerbund. The classic song '*Apne liye, jiye to kya jiye!*' performed earnestly by Hari is still remembered. A blog by Madhulika Liddle[7] credits Badal with 'taking the route of one of those classic novels that I've always wished Hindi cinema had adapted for the screen: Dumas's *The Three Musketeers*'. She further writes, 'I will admit

6 Ashok Raj, *Hero Volume I: The Silent Era to Dilip Kumar* (Hay House UK, 2010).

7 https://madhulikaliddle.com/2017/06/12/baadal-1966/

I watched this film mainly for two reasons: for Sanjeev Kumar, who is deliciously handsome in his early roles; and for the song *"Nain bedaardi chhalia ke sang lad gaye"*, which is total eye candy. [I am shallow, that way].'

Madhulika Liddle is a prolific writer of short fiction; she also writes on history, travel and classic cinema. She explains why she liked the film: 'Sanjeev Kumar as Badal. He is such a delight: handsome, very physical as he springs about, and—of course—a fine actor. This film, while pretty akin to one of those many Dara Singh starrers of the 1960s, is several notches above those simply because of Sanjeev Kumar. Dara Singh I find cute in a blustering, macho Punjabi way, but Sanjeev Kumar makes for a far more attractive hero.'

Hari had six releases in 1966 and was like a sponge, soaking in all the influences around him and discussing every small move with his trusted manager Jamnadas.

He also seemed to have imbibed an important lesson from fellow actor Nanda. When Hari was working on *Pati Patni*, Nanda Karnataki was already a big star. But Hari realized that she had had her own share of struggles, rising from being a child artiste to playing the second lead—to Mala Sinha in *Dhol Ka Phool* (1959) and Waheeda Rehman in *Kala Bazaar* (1960)—before she bagged lead roles herself in *Kanoon* (1960) and *Hum Dono* (1961), opposite stars like Rajendra Kumar and Dev Anand.

Hari realized that if he had to make the switch away from stunt films to mainstream cinema and hobnob with the big filmmakers, he would also have to play second lead in films that had sellable star casts and warranted large distribution. So he signed *Shikar* with the very saleable Dharmendra as soon as *Pati Patni* was released. It was a film that changed his career graph.

4

1967: The Breadwinner's Conundrum

Even though Hari signed *Shikar* with director Atma Ram, brother of the legendary Guru Dutt, he did not have the luxury of sitting around for the film's release. It was too big a risk. Hari wanted to continue to make a serious claim to being seen as a lead hero—and this opportunity was available for him only in smaller films. If this was ever in doubt, then the shaky print available on YouTube of Kewal Mishra's film *Aayega Aanewala* (1967) should suffice to convince the reader. In this suspense drama, Hari plays Inspector Raj. Dressed in well-tailored suits, the scene in which Hari reacts confusedly to the ghost that haunts him, leaving wet footprints and humming with nobody visible, suggests immense promise. Unfortunately for today's internet generation, the film has been simply out-googled by its namesake, the timeless haunting song *'Aayega aanewala'* rendered by Lata Mangeshkar for the film *Mahal* in 1949. The film's own title song, *'Aag se aag bujhane, koi aayega'* simply could not match the popularity of the 1949 chartbuster.

Naunihal came next, produced by Saawan Kumar Tak and directed by Raj Marbros, who, surprisingly, does not have any other movie to his credit. This was Hari's first cinematic outing that also featured Balraj Sahni, another accomplished actor, and Shaukat Azmi (mother of actor Shabana Azmi), with whom he had done theatre. The plot is about an orphan 'Raju' who is told that he is not alone because he will always have 'Chacha Nehru' (India's first prime minister, Jawaharlal Nehru, was fondly called Chacha Nehru, and his birthday on 14 November is celebrated as Children's Day in India) by his side. The film's music was composed by Madan Mohan, and the lyrics were by Kaifi Azmi. The romantic song *'Tumhare zulf ke saaye mein shyaam'* sung soulfully by Mohammed Rafi, gives viewers a glimpse of Hari's sensitivity as a romantic actor, a departure from his earlier film roles of frolicking romance. What was unique about this film were its last ten minutes dedicated to the funeral procession of Jawaharlal Nehru, who passed away on 27 May 1964. Featuring Mohammed Rafi's melodious *'Meri aawaz suno pyar ka raaz suno'*, the film was clearly a tribute to the leader.

The film *Gunehgar* followed in 1967, with Hari playing a police inspector in a crime thriller. Among the films produced by P. Daswani, a financier, *Gunehgar* was also the fourth of the five films Hari did with Sheikh Mukhtar. At 6'2", Sheikh Mukhtar was an imposing figure and often enjoyed the lion's share in film posters, *Gunehgar* being a case in point. The plot features Kumkum, who goes from her village to the city in search of her father and her brother. She is rescued from difficult circumstances and falls in love with Hari. Unknown to her, her father (Sheikh

Mukhtar) is a fugitive being tracked by Hari. When father and daughter reunite and she learns the truth, she is torn between her love for her father and Hari. *Gunehgar* is arguably director R. Thakur's finest work, who has a total of six largely unsung titles to his credit.

Hari also made a special appearance starring Vyjanthimala and Uttam Kumar, where he was unceremoniously left out of title credits again. Another film featuring Hari and shot around this time, *Mitti Ka Dev,* was unfinished and, of course, never released. This was made by Samir Chowdhury, the brother of gifted songwriter and music director Salil Chowdhury. The film and the soundtrack were completely destroyed before their release in a major fire that gutted the studio where they had been stored.

But Hari was destiny's child. He was not meant to grovel in the quagmire of movies that were not viewed widely by discerning audiences.

It was in 1968 that things began to pick up for him.

5

1968: The Needle Shifts

If there's one film in Hari's struggling days that opened his kismet, it would have to be *Sunghursh*, also starring Dilip Kumar. This was also Hari's first colour film if you ignore his blink-long appearance in *Chhoti Si Mulaqat*. Ashok Raj's *Hero Volume I: The Silent Era to Dilip Kumar* credits Dilip Kumar as Hari's 'discoverer'. According to Raj:

> During the preparations for the multi-starrer *Sunghursh*, the thespian (a reference to Dilip Kumar) and director H.S. Rawail were in search of a suitable actor to do the role of Dwarka, one of the powerful characters in the script. One night, they went to see *Nishan* at a theatre in Bombay and were greatly impressed by the hero's performance and readily signed him for *Sunghursh*. *Sunghursh* opened for Hari, the gateway to success.

In the film, Hari's character is supposed to serve poison to Dilip Kumar but drinks it himself by mistake. This was, at best, an extended cameo, but Hari's rendering of it made it a dynamic role. Dilip Kumar's praise for his acting prowess travelled far and wide. The screenplay for *Sunghursh* was written by Gulzar, another master craftsman with whom Hari would go on to create history.

Hari's other gamble—to work alongside Dharmendra in *Shikar*—his third role as a police inspector, paid off! Hari's strategy to be discovered by the big directors, who could compare his performance with that of the leading actors, was a propitious one as directors like B.R. Chopra recognized and acknowledged him. Hari also won the Filmfare Best Supporting Actor award for *Shikar*.

While there's no way to verify the order in which Hari signed his films, he was next seen in *Saathi* (1968), in a special appearance. It was a film that had Vyjanthimala and Rajendra Kumar. Hari seems to have done it by the same logic—becoming visible to the big filmmakers.

In the same year, L.V. Prasad's *Raja aur Runk*, an adaptation of *The Prince and the Pauper*, became Hari's first solo lead success story, despite a visible struggle on his part to hide an emerging paunch with a wide belt in some scenes. It also gave him something priceless—the instantly popular chartbuster '*Phirkiwali, tu kal phir aana*', a song sung by Mohammed Rafi. The film had many other hit songs like '*Mera naam hai Chameli*' and '*Tu kitni achchi hai*', which are still hummed today. Hari is also seen dressed to the nines as Lord Krishna in the song '*O Kanhaiya*'.

Kumkum was the leading lady with whom Hari had the most number of lead roles in his early days—*Smuggler*, *Gunehgar*, *Aayega Aanewala*, *Raja aur Runk* and even her last film *Bombay by Nite*. Kumkum was an important co-star and a dependable performer, with hit songs in other films like *'Ae dil hai mushkil jeena yahan'* from *CID* (1956), *'Reshmi salwar kurta jali ka'* from *Naya Daur* (1957), *'Daga data vai vai vai'* from *Kali Topi Lal Rumaal* (1959) and *'Madhuban mein Radhika nache re'* from *Kohinoor* (1960). She was the lead in smaller films, but when it came to the bigger projects, there was always another leading actress who helmed the film. *CID* had Waheeda Rahman, *Naya Daur* had Vyjanthimala Bali, *Kali Topi Lal Rumaal* had Shakila and *Kohinoor* had Meena Kumari. *Raja aur Runk* was Hari's first solo hit, and Kumkum played the lead. The point here is that it took a lot of momentum for a dependable, skilled performer to catapult from low-budget to high-budget directors, and Hari was one of the few who had the tenacity to do this.

As Hari's films started releasing, Baa was thrilled that her Haria's (Baa always fondly called him Haria) dreams were coming true. As is the custom in Indian families, Baa started scouting for potential brides for him. After all, Hari was already thirty, and that's late by Indian standards. Baa matched horoscopes and showed Hari pictures of prospective brides from 'good' Gujarati families. However, in the words of the great Henry Wadsworth Longfellow, 'Most people would succeed in small things, if they were not troubled with great ambitions.' Hari declined these matches built on a simple matching of horoscopes because he was consumed with being a successful actor. He wanted to work with all the senior actors and directors, learn the minutiae and improve his performance bit by bit. It seemed that Hari had his hands full.

The tear-jerker drama *Gauri,* starring Nutan, Sunil Dutt and Mumtaz, presented yet another performance-oriented role for Hari with its big star cast. It was also a successful film. Then there was *Aashirwad* by the celebrated director Hrishikesh Mukherjee, a film primarily featuring Ashok Kumar—a great actor and to whom Hari has often been compared. It won Ashok Kumar the National Award for Best Actor. Sporting a slightly fuller face and now much more stoic on camera, Hari rendered the role of a doctor in the film.

One of the hidden gems in Hari's filmography that discerning movie buffs will continue to discover for posterity is the brilliant *Anokhi Raat*. This is the first time that Hari works with the gifted director Asit Sen, and the film also marks Parikshit Sahni's debut. One of the big reasons for the movie's eternal appeal is that its music has survived the ages. One song, '*Oh re taal mile nadi ke jal mein*', is picturized on Hari, and the other, '*Meri beri ke ber mat todo*', is picturized on Aruna Irani, another important co-star who features in many of Hari's early films, including his Gujarati films.

Anokhi Raat had three parallel plots. The leading lady (Zaheeda) stays with her grandfather in a massive home. Zaheeda's late father had borrowed money, which she is bound to repay. Hence, she has no choice but to auction away all the expensive decorative vintage items in her home. The twist in the tale is that her creditor (Tarun Bose) is willing to forego the loan in exchange for Zaheeda's hand in marriage. In such a situation, a rainy night brings several visitors to Zaheeda's home—an old lawyer and his young wife, an artist seeking shelter (Parikshit

Sahni) and a dangerous dacoit (Hari). The environment is rife with conflict. As the night advances, they discover that the ransom on Hari's head is more than the debt owed by Zaheeda's father to Bose. Hari surrenders himself so that she can be freed from having to marry Bose. Hari does this because Zaheeda's face reminds him of his own sweetheart, Gopa.

6

1969: Hari Cements His Place in Cinema

If 1968 was the year Hari came into his own, then 1969 was the year in which a majority of his films were made with bigger budgets, featured mainstream stars and enjoyed massive distribution.

Hari made a special appearance in *Bandhan*, featuring the heartthrob Rajesh Khanna as the hero opposite Mumtaz. Produced by G.P. Sippy and directed by Narinder Bedi, this movie has Hari playing an eccentric lawyer. In a reel mirroring real casting, Hari plays Anju Mahendru's brother. This is probably the first film in which Hari has touches of grey in his hair, next to the ears and at the temples. Hari's famed voice modulation is in full display—and perhaps this was what got directors started with visualizing Hari in powerful roles.

Then there was *Oos Raat Ke Baad*, Hari's first film with Tanuja; an important pairing that would soon become unforgettable. A tale of two brothers—played by Hari and Madan Puri—where the latter wants to wrest their ancestral property for himself. This film has Tanuja playing Hari's daughter! In a foreboding role, Hari, with greying hair and pain writ all over his face, has three heart attacks and dies full of unreconciled regret. Tanuja's consort is played by Sailesh Kumar, a promising six-foot-tall actor in the 1960s. Sailesh Kumar is yet another important name in Hindi cinema who never made it big (he died in 2017, in Mumbai), despite having acted in more than thirty films and looking every inch the hero. The X factor required to succeed in cinema can be both puzzling and elusive.[8] It is to Hari's credit that he was bold enough to risk playing any part as long as he felt he would make an impact. He was only thirty-one when this film released.

Satyakam was Hari's second outing with Ashok Kumar, Dharmendra, and Hrishikesh Mukherjee, and his first with Sharmila Tagore. Hari also turned narrator for the film, which explores the importance of ideals and portrays the compromises and the struggles of a man, played by Dharmendra, who wants to keep his integrity alive. Among the highlights of the film are the scenes between Dharmendra and Hari, written by the gifted Rajinder Singh Bedi and with whom Hari was soon to earn his stripes! *Satyakam* won the National Film Award for Best Feature Film in Hindi.

In sharp contrast to his expedient morals in *Satyakam*, *Sachaai* featured Hari starting off as a man of unshakeable integrity. He

---

8 https://timesofindia.indiatimes.com/blogs/Addictions/secret-agent-077-sailesh-kumar-tasted-success-but-real-stardom-eluded-him/

argues with his pragmatic friend Shammi Kapoor for upholding the merit of truth at all times. The plot takes a U-turn, with Hari falling into bad company himself and Shammi Kapoor reforming completely to become an honest police inspector. This was a remake of the Telugu film *Manchi Mitrulu* by K. Shankar. It featured Sadhana as Hari's sister and Shammi Kapoor's romantic interest.

Then there was the film *Jyoti*, which was to initially feature Dharmendra and Meena Kumari. Later, Hari stepped in as the lead in this black-and-white film. Even up to 1969, a clear trend can be seen: A-league actresses were still not willing to work with Hari unless Dharmendra, Sunil Dutt or Rajendra Kumar was in the film. Libi Rana was roped in to play Hari's wife in *Jyoti*, and Hari plays a mechanic. The couple's relationship is strained because they are childless. Libi Rana's tireless devotion to Lord Krishna blesses the couple with a baby boy, who is named Nandan. However, there is a misunderstanding that creates friction between the couple. The film explores religious beliefs—a very sensitive topic in India.

Hari also made a special appearance in the Jeetendra starrer *Jeene Ki Raah*—a film that starred Tanuja in the lead. This was L.V. Prasad's second film with Hari, with story, production and direction by Prasad. This, too, was a major success at the box office. Laxmikant–Pyarelal's hit music had a major part to play in its success, with evergreen numbers like '*Aane se uske aaye bahaar*' and '*Ek banjara gaaye*'.

In B.R. Ishara's *Insaf Ka Mandir*, Hari plays an advocate again. At the start of the film, his character discovers that the man he lived with was not his father. As he goes in search of his real parents, he gets embroiled in a double murder involving a father and daughter. He appears in the case in court on behalf of the deceased. The courtroom drama sees some thrilling dialogue delivery by Hari, with Prithviraj Kapoor playing the judge; the thrilling climax is credible, except for the fact that the investigation process that led to the verdict is not clear to the audience. In the end, the woman whom Hari proves guilty of murder turns out to be the mother he had been searching for! 'There's a great future for you,' Prithviraj Kapoor tells Hari in a significant moment in the film, which the viewer can interpret conveniently in innumerable ways. The viewer also cannot miss Hari's massive weight fluctuations in the film, which probably suggests a lengthy shoot as well. Hari's trademark loose kurta pyjama makes its appearance in this film for the first time, alongside his loose half-sleeved shirts and the lawyer's garb. In the scenes where he is slimmer, he wears full-sleeved shirts and trousers.

Hari finally got his own mainstream heroine when Tanuja starred opposite him in *Gustakhi Maaf.* A modern comedy featuring twins, mistaken identities and all kinds of confusion, the film highlights Hari's comic timing like never before. The blog 'Atul's Song A Day' carries a wonderful narration of the plot:

> At first, it is established that Tanuja is romantically involved with Sujit Kumar, who plays Hari's elder brother. The appearance of the twin sister (Tanuja again) of course creates numerous hilarious problems. She falls for Hari and the scenes that follow are some of the best in the film – Tanuja is trying to woo Sanjeev Kumar out of genuine interest, and Sanjeev is horrified and appalled that his future sister-in-law, and the bride to be of his elder brother, is playing romantic

> hooky with him. With nobody the wiser, the situation creates confusions galore, as all well wishers get together and carry off the sister to a mental asylum in a straight jacket, believing whole heartedly that the young lady is struck with the split personality syndrome.[9]

The scenes in which Tanuja teases Hari and woos him as she sings coquettishly *'Sajana mera jiyara jale'* are priceless. Hari's dialogue *'Aap to dus mardon ki mard hain!'* to Tanuja, when she tries to project herself jokingly as innocent and vulnerable, is well-timed and a major departure from movies of the time that project women as meek.

Dharti Kahe Pukar Ke was Hari's second project with Jeetendra and Nanda. It featured the superhit song *'Je hum tum chori se'* and saw Hari once again paired with the gorgeous Libi Rana (who often appears in the film credits as Nivedita). The film shows the contrast between village life and city life through the story of three brothers. A sentiment that runs through the film is the immense value that every Indian farmer ascribes to his land.

Sachin Pilgaonkar remembers co-starring with Hari in *Chanda Aur Bijli*: 'When we got together to work in *Chanda Aur Bijli* (1969), directed by Atma Ram, I was twelve years old. I was playing Chanda and we needed a fine actress to play Bijli. However, Asha Parekh refused to play the part alongside Haribhai because he was not an established hero, and finally Padminiji filled in. Haribhai always joked that he was the "Aur" in the title of the film.'

---

9 https://atulsongaday.me/tag/gustakhi-maaf/

Professionally, Hari was on a roll. Not all his films were lead roles, and not all of them set the box office on fire, but he had achieved a tipping point of some kind where his performances were being talked about. Fortunately for him, films like *Bombay by Nite* that were delayed beyond measure could not tarnish the upswing that he was on at the time. The years between 1964 and 1969 also saw Hari star in three Gujarati films—*Ramat Ramade Ram* with Sarita Joshi in 1964, *Kalapi* in 1966 alongside Padmarani and Aruna Irani and *Mare Javun Pele Paar* with Aruna Irani in 1968.

It was the Hindi remake of *Mare Javun Pele Paar*, titled *Khilona*, in which Hari starred alongside Mumtaz in 1970 that brought him to the centre of the limelight.

7

The Southern Connection

In the late 1960s, a very important relationship in Hari's life started taking shape. It was one of mutual respect with the legendary actor of Tamil cinema, Sivaji Ganesan. Hari was given a character role in Ganesan's home production *Gauri* (1968), which was a remake of Ganesan's own *Shanti* (1965).

An article of unknown provenance titled '*Naan Sivajiyin Maanavan*' (I am a student of Sivaji's), which presumably was translated into Tamil, obtained from Hari's family archives, quotes him as follows:

> I first met him when I was but an extra on the sets of *Gauri*. One look at me and he said, 'In the future, you will be a very accomplished actor.' His words were like God's own words and he blessed my career. Whenever a Sivaji Ganesan movie had to be remade in Hindi, all of us actors would worry plenty. His prowess inspired fear. We would see the Tamil

> print again and again to observe his performance and learn! At a personal level, whenever I visited Chennai, I would seek his blessings. I am grateful for all the love he has given me. If he sees me as one of the finest actors in Hindi cinema, it is my honour.

The mutual admiration between Sivaji Ganesan and Hari and the latter's own quiet, easygoing nature eventually played a major role in Hari's success. When South Indian producers and directors wanted to remake their Tamil or Telugu films in Hindi, they often chose Hari. These remakes typically had long dialogues and demanded good histrionics, and this further augmented Hari's 'actor' tag. For example, Sivaji Ganesan's *Avan Thaan Manithan* was remade as *Shaandaar,* and *Gnana Oli* was remade as *Devata*—both featuring Hari. Among the Telugu films, *Takkar* was a remake of N.T. Rama Rao's *Devudu Chesina Manushulu* with Hari in the lead role. The winds blew the other way too. Hari's *Mausam* was remade in Tamil as *Vasanthathil Oru Naal*, featuring Sivaji Ganesan.

The other important southern connection was L.V. Prasad. Hari scored a hat-trick of hits with him—*Raja aur Runk* (1968), *Jeene Ki Raah* (1969) and *Khilona* (1970).

Hari's third connection to the south—actor Hema Malini, whom he would meet soon—was an intensely personal one.

8

The Fourteen-Year Itch

In the Ramayana, the principled Lord Rama had to perform a fourteen-year penance before he could rightfully take his place on the throne as the king of Ayodhya. He was kicked hard by fate, but this banishment from the kingdom had to be endured. It can be said that Hari, too, endured a fourteen-year ordeal—his struggle to become an actor started in 1956 and culminated in the year 1970.

On 8 April 1970, L.V. Prasad's *Khilona* released. In the film, Hari plays a sentimental poet who is beset by tragedy and loses his mental balance. Mumtaz, a poor courtesan, is hired to help him recover. The story is about how she helps Hari out of his trauma. *Khilona* also featured Jeetendra and Shatrughan Sinha. It was a milestone performance in Hari's life! He drew heavily upon his own experience of depression and was nominated for the Best Actor category at the Filmfare Awards.

Providence definitely had a hand in Hari's ascent to mainstay status in Hindi cinema, as some of his unusual choices ended up being big money spinners. For example, in 1970, Rajesh Khanna's *Aan Milo Sajna,* Dev Anand's *Johny Mera Naam* and Jeetendra's *Humjoli* were blockbusters. Yet Hari's small black-and-white film *Dastak* somehow managed to cut through the clutter and receive warm praise.

Made by Rajinder Singh Bedi and based on one of his own plays, *Naql-e-Makani*, *Dastak* was a risk from the word go. Hari and his co-star Rehana Sultan play newly-weds in the film. They move into a rental flat close to the local red-light district. Shamshad, the former occupant of their flat, had been a nautch girl, so men continue to knock at the couple's door ('Dastak' means to knock) in the hope of seeing her. The couple struggles with this ignominy. Hari exhibits both restraint and anger, raping his own wife in a moment of weakness in the film. The role of the paanwala, whose business suffers when Shamshad moves out and the couple moves in, is a particularly interesting social commentary on morality as viewed by Indian men.

Other than the merits of the film and Hrishikesh Mukherjee's deft editing, there was an element of luck in the success of *Dastak*. Hari's co-star in the film, the risqué Rehana Sultan, had just become an overnight sensation thanks to the bold posters of B.R. Ishara's *Chetna*. Audiences wanted to watch more of her. Even though her role in *Dastak* was demure and understated, she was de rigueur at the time. Rehana, Hari and music director Madan Mohan were nominated for several popular awards for the film. Despite being a strong nominee, Madan Mohan did not win any awards, and that made him very upset. So, when all three bagged the National Awards for Best Actress, Best Actor and Best

Music Director, respectively, a bitter Madan Mohan did not want to accept that either. His son Sanjeev Kohli remembers Hari's graceful intervention. 'Haribhai', as Sanjeev called him, came home one evening to persuade his father to accompany Rehana and him to Delhi. 'We have to show solidarity,' he remembers Hari telling his father. He even persuaded Madan Mohan to get a tuxedo stitched identical to his own for the occasion.[10]

This kindness and concern were just an extension of Hari's gratitude. He never grudged others their credit.

The last Gujarati film he did, *Jigar Ane Ami*, with Kanan Kaushal, was also in 1970, as was Hari's Sindhi film, *Ho Jamalo.*

10 Roshmila Bhattacharya, 'Salt-and-pepper memories with Sanjeev Kumar…', *Hindustan Times*, 4 November 2012; https://www.hindustantimes.com/india/salt-and-pepper-memories-with-sanjeev-kumar/story-MXYjycs53f0fxpXDQqQ6MO.html

9

Making It Big

After 1970, Hari's name in Hindi cinema was well and truly established. It is important to mention that Hari was an extremely good-looking man in the days before food and alcohol took over his belly and his countenance. An article in *The Guardian* on his film *Anubhav* (1971) says, 'He looks like an Indian Gregory Peck, exuding a similar warmth and intelligence ... '[11] High praise!

Lead roles in Hindi cinema were now very much open for Hari. Remarkably different in appeal from the brawny Dharmendra and the charming Rajesh Khanna, Hari had staked his claim on being a 'sensitive' performer, whom the audience could relate to. *Anubhav*, by Basu Bhattacharya, was one such film, and the box

11 Nirpal Dhaliwal, 'Anubhav shows the suprising truth about Indian marriage', *The Guardian*, 30 July 2008; https://www.theguardian.com/film/2008/jul/29/anubhav.bollywood

office gave a huge thumbs-up to Hari and Tanuja's exceptional performance in the film, which is something of a love triangle.

In the words of the veteran scribe and columnist Vithal C Nadkarni:

> When I joined The Times Group's trainee journalist scheme in early 1970s, the fourth floor with its warren of iconic magazines like *The Illustrated Weekly of India*, *Dharmayug*, *Filmfare*, *Femina*, *Sarika* and *Science Today*, etc. were considered to be the 'heaven of journalism'. After my training, I joined Sardar Khushwant Singh's *The Illustrated Weekly*. At that time Sanjeev Kumar was one of the topmost Bollywood stars and although films wasn't my beat, there was a buzz about the good-looking thespian which colleagues from the film magazines used to share with us during our 'extended' (scribes-sorority-wise) lunch breaks during which scribes hung out sorority-wise.
>
> I had watched quite a few of Sanjeev Kumar's movies. I particularly resonated with his performance in *Anubhav* (1971), which I had seen in Pune while working for an engineering firm as an intern. In the movie, Sanjeev Kumar plays the role of a newspaper editor, who is often so engrossed with his work that he tends to neglect his pretty wife. Things change when the wife's college friend joins the paper. Somehow, I was drawn and mesmerized by the settings (the movie was shot in *The Times of India* offices and presses and also at a posh building near Malabar Hill). In retrospect, it seems serendipitous how all these scenic locales became, in a space of couple of years, integral and intimate parts of my own personal and professional itinerary that has lasted for over four decades.

Sanjeev Kumar's glowing reel-life presence (as also his name 'Haribhai') resonated in my mind with a real-life historic Gujarat-born character, Haripaldeo aka Sri Chakradharswami; the founder of the Mahanubhav sect in thirteenth century Maharashtra renowned for his unsurpassable good looks. One of the earliest biographies in Marathi, *Lilacharitra*, waxes eloquent about the Master being as fair as the 'champa' (magnolia) flower, with long ears and mesmerizingly wide beautiful eyes (*'champe gour sri murthi; lamb karna, vishal netra'*). In fact such was the magnetic allure of Sri Chakradhar's physical attributes that the *Lilacharitra* describes him as 'the paragon of beauty for Kali Yuga just as Sita was the epitome of beauty for Dvapara Yuga'. I felt in films such as *Anubhav*, Sanjeev Kumar also seemed to radiate with a similar sort of dazzling intensity and melting sensitivity. What is more, upon being complimented for his beautiful eyes, the hero of *Lilacharitra*, Sri Chakradharaswami, himself goes on to describe the land of his birth, Gujarat, as 'an island full of beautiful eyes' (*Gujarat mhanije netra chi dweepa chi ga*)!

I confess when I read that line, I could immediately relate it in my mind's eye to Sanjeev Kumar, who had that perceptive gaze, endearing presence and delivered scintillating performances.

Naturally, Hari built a humungous female fan following. The year 1972 saw Hari teaming up with Jaya Bhaduri for *Parichay* and *Koshish*. In the latter, as a deaf-mute person, Hari acted with his whole being rather than just with his face or dialogues. In a scene in the film where his own son refuses to marry a girl because she too is deaf-mute, his expressions are priceless. *Koshish* gave him his second National Award.

Hari's stars were on the ascent. Uday Jariwala recalls that there was a time when a populous suburb of Mumbai named Andheri had three theatres in proximity, all running different movies featuring his uncle. It was a personal high for the actor who happened to drive past the place at that time. The lead roles and significant parallel leads continued. Hari explored situational humour and created room for himself in female-centric movies like Ramesh Sippy's blockbuster *Seeta Aur Geeta*. He glided effortlessly through his roles, thanks to his unique timing and acute sense of what he could contribute to the plot.

In 1973, Raja Nawathe's *Manchali* and Tahir Hussain's *Anamika* were released. Hari had done many lead roles by then, but his roles were different in these two. They were 'regular' lead roles and did not involve extraordinary histrionics. Hari was cast in them as a regular saleable lead hero. Hari, of course, pulled them off with elan. But those who were watching Hari closely were concerned.

Far from the Hari with a full mop of hair seen in *Anubhav*, later films like *Seeta Aur Geeta*, *Manchali* and *Anamika* featured a Hari with a sharply receding hairline to the left, his hair combed with a view to hide it. There was also the matter of Hari's girth, which had widened considerably, and face, which seemed to have expanded. One might ask that for all his ambition, how could Hari let his appearance change like this while at the helm of his career?

There is a popular German proverb, 'Ambition and the belly are the two worst counsellors!' In Hari's case, the penury of his arduous struggle had been replaced by the glut of success! Had he succumbed to the addiction of the 'good life' and allowed his weight gain to become a concern for producers who would now think twice before casting him in a lead role? Had he surrounded himself with sycophants who were inflating him with some idea of invincibility?

In an intensely competitive milieu that saw Rajesh Khanna, Amitabh Bachchan, Jeetendra, Vinod Khanna, Dharmendra, Vinod Mehra and Shatrughan Sinha compete for lead roles, Hari was intelligent enough to know the consequences of being overweight!

This brings us to the paradoxical reason for Hari's success as a character artiste. All the leading men of the day used to prefer to work with Hari for three reasons: he was happy to be overweight and was not competing with them when it came to looks; he elevated their level of performance in the film, and he never got the girl in the end. The only downside for them was that after the film's release, Hari would receive the lion's share of accolades. But since this praise was largely for Hari's performance and not for his glamour, the lead stars could live with that!

Hari might've had his own logic too. The fee offered to him to play a character artiste in a blockbuster headlined by Amitabh or Dharmendra was far more than what he was offered to play lead roles in smaller budget films. He had a lifelong ambition to buy a big house for his mother. He had even selected a bungalow in Juhu in the early 1970s for which a token amount was paid around this time! In this phase of his life, Hari was also hopeful that he would get married.

As of 1973, Hari was a successful actor, thirty-five years old and single. To put this in context, 1973 was the year both

Rajesh Khanna and Amitabh Bachchan got married, both aged thirty-one.

Despite being successful and eligible in every way, why did Hari remain single? What was happening in Hari's personal life? Let's hand the reins over to the two women who have known Hari best—his late sister Gayatri Patel and his sister-in-law Jyoti Nikul Jariwala.

SECTION III

Hari's Family Life

1

My Brother, My Hero

Gayatri Patel recalls life with Hari, whom she lovingly called 'Bhai'.

When Babuji passed away, I was just four years old. Baa told me that I kept crying even though I didn't know what was happening. Babuji's last words to me, as told to me by Baa, were, 'I'm sorry I didn't leave anything for you.'

Bhai had listened to that, and it had impacted him deeply. At that moment he resolved to take on the role of a father for all of us siblings. In a way, all of us looked up to him, and there was no question of disobeying his orders—in fact, Nikul and I were quite scared of him. Kishorebhai was something of a rebel and had his own opinions. This is natural among siblings, I guess.

Kishore, Nikul and I were enrolled in Nanavati High School, which was near our home in Bhuleshwar. As Baa worked hard to keep things going, Bhai had set his mind to pursue films and stopped studying at the age of seventeen.

Bhai was very focused on his talent, but there was a hitch. Bhai was not even twelve years old when Pappa had arranged his engagement! It was a common practice back then. The girl's name was Anusuya, and she was from Surat. Whenever we went to Surat on vacation, Anusuya would also stay with us the whole day. I still remember her face. She was very pretty. But Bhai never showed any interest.

It was Bhai who told Baa one morning that he was never going to marry Anusuya. 'I am not going to marry her. But you know that as her age increases, nobody else will marry her either. Please release her and me from this expectation,' he said. Baa understood. She spoke to Anusuya's family and separated them. Bhai was free to pursue his dreams.

During his struggling days, Bhai used to keep a diary. He would write about which producer or director he had met and about the plays he was doing. This habit waned over time. In our early years, Bhai's favourite food was baingan (eggplant) and bhindi (okra). Baa would make it as often as possible. Another thing he liked was patra (a preparation of colocasia leaves and gram flour). There were no birthday celebrations or cakes when we were growing up. The big day to look forward to was Diwali. Baa would give Bhai Rs 10, and all of us would get Rs 5 each to do what we wanted with it.

Our age gap being huge—eight years—his personal life was totally out of bounds for discussion. We only knew what we saw. He would share a lot with Baa, but us younger siblings had no clue. I was just happy being Bhai's favourite. I would take great pride in setting Bhai's thali. He always liked a pinch of salt and two chillies on the side in his thali.

Bhai used to call me 'Baby'.

Bhai Starts Earning

I don't know about Bhai's struggle in much detail. All I know is that it took him five to six years of intense struggle to get a break in films and many more years before he became as successful as he wanted to. There was a period of deep depression that he had to overcome to get there. But once he started earning, we lacked nothing! He worked long hours, took care of all of us all the time, and eventually we didn't need to rent the Surat house anymore.

We stayed in Bhuleshwar till 1966, after which Bhai took up the Perrin Villa house on rent. I was in my first year in Jai Hind College and stayed back with Kishorebhai in Bhuleshwar because of the proximity of the house to the college. But Bhai insisted that I shift to Bandra. So, in my second year of graduation, I transferred to K.C. College and moved to Perrin Villa. Whenever I wanted to go out with my friends, I would have to make up excuses saying I had to attend typing class or sitar class to avoid Bhai's questioning.

Bhai's work in cinema created a new set of glamorous friends—all of us were awestruck! The first actress that we became familiar with was Tanuja. She had even come to our small home in Bhuleshwar. She would sit, eat on the floor and was a very free and frank person. In one of Bhai's interviews, he was asked, 'You like Tanuja so much. Why don't you get married to her?' Bhai had replied, 'She is a Western-type of girl.' Then he quickly added, 'More than that, she's just a very good friend.'

I have read articles that said Bhai fell in love with a Muslim girl at the age of twenty-six. There were many Muslim actresses back then. Was it Saira Bano? They did a film together around the time when Bhai was twenty-six. Was it Nazima or Kumkum [her real name was Zaibunnisa], both of whom Bhai had worked with when he was around that age? The only person who could've answered this question correctly is Jamnadasji. I have no idea who she was, and maybe none of the above guesses are correct.

Another celebrity to come home was Nutan Samarth. This was in the late 1960s. She was very close to Baa and I. When she used to come to Perrin Villa, she used to share her problems with Baa. Bhai was soft-hearted towards her, and we all really liked Nutan a lot. But her husband found out, and things went wrong. She was a very kind soul and a very cultured and fine woman.

There was no dearth of marriage proposals for Bhai from our community. But Bhai had told Baa, 'I'm not interested. I won't be able to adjust easily. Why don't you get Nikul married so that someone can take care of you?' Kishorebhai was also not interested in marriage at that time.

2

The Family Grows

Jyoti got married into the family in December 1971.

'When Baa came to see me in Kolkata as a prospective bride for Nikul, my family was told, "these people are from the Jethalal family". Jethalalji was a well-known man. One can also imagine that only a wealthy man could marry thrice. [In] those days, traditional families wouldn't consider alliances with families of film stars,' said Jyoti.

Gayatri chipped in, 'Bhai was simply not interested in marriage. Kishorebhai was also not willing to get married. Baa, therefore, arranged for Nikul, the youngest of the brothers, to be engaged to Jyoti. Nikul and Jyoti got married on 10th December, and Ashok and I were wedded on 11th December. The year was 1971. As a gift, Bhai gave my husband Ashok money to invest in a motel and build a business in the USA. Bhai was like an eternal Santa Claus, always giving and ensuring that we were well.'

The weddings were well-attended affairs. 'We have lost the pictures, but I remember that Ashok Kumar, Biswajit, Dharmendra, Amitabh, Mahmood and his brother Anwar Ali had come for our wedding,' says Jyoti.

Due to the Indo-Pak war that year, the wedding reception for both couples was postponed to January 1972. There is a picture of Nargis Dutt attending the reception at Juhu Hotel, with a young Sanjay and Namrata in tow. Hari asked the newly-weds to take the blessings of three people who couldn't attend the wedding. So, when the couples headed to Ooty for their honeymoon, their first stop was at Sivaji Ganesan's house in Chennai. Jyoti recalls, 'Kamala and Sivaji sir met us with so much warmth and love. Bhai also asked us to meet Prithviraj Kapoor and Sakina apa, Dilip Kumar's elder sister.'

'After my marriage, Kishorebhai continued in Bhuleshwar for some more time. So it was just Baa, Nikul and Bhai and I at Perrin Villa. I was not much aware of films, but when *Khilona* released, I realized what a big star Bhai really was,' Jyoti recalls.

Jyoti fondly recalls the daily routine of the household.

'Baa and I would get up early and prepare for the day ahead. Bhai's daily routine was simple. He would get up in the morning at around 11 a.m. and have a cup of chai. This was Gujarati chai, with mint and lemongrass leaves, ginger and home-made chai masala. Jamnadasji would arrive by 10.30 a.m. As soon as Bhai woke up, Jamnadasji would update him on his day's schedule. Bhai's success brought in a stream of visitors; they would start trickling in by about 10.30 a.m. Some of them were what you would call friends who had time to spare, such as publicist K. Razdan, Satpal, Arun Verma, Johnny Whisky and lyricist Subhash Indori. Jamnadasji would entertain them till Bhai was ready to meet them. They would all have tea and snacks. Several others would drop in, too, as Bhai would offer help to anyone who asked. Restaurant owners, producers and directors used to come to him with their sob stories. Ravi Walia, who had a car business, was also a regular at home. Bhai used to treat him as a younger brother. The owner of Kachins—we used to call him Shahpurwala—used to come home to show him new clothing styles.

'Bhai was not one for breakfast, but if he saw his friends having something interesting, he would ask Baa to pack it for his shoot. In the afternoon, Bhai would leave for work and Jamnadasji would leave on his errands.

'If the shoot got cancelled, the friends would get to know from Jamnadasji and promptly come home for lunch. Bhai loved the food cooked by Baa. He was of the opinion that the house help could do all the preparation, make the rotis, etc., but that only the lady of the house should do the cooking. He was traditional-minded that way.

'On days when Bhai was shooting, the friends would also check with Jamnadasji about when he was expected back at home in the night. If Bhai was going to be home early, they would come for dinner. My duty was to make dinner. The domestic help used to serve them their dinner at 2 a.m. We had a couple of helpers for this at home—Bhai had named them 'Kanda' and 'Batata' because they were as inseparable as onion and potato. They were from the same village. They used to also keep all of us in splits with their innocent antics. Kanda-Batata would forget to serve half the things, so I would watch over them, but from a distance. If Bhai was going to be home late after the day's shoot, the friends wouldn't come because they knew he would sleep directly. Once a week, Bhai would go out to eat non-vegetarian food because that was not allowed at home. That was his indulgence. The rest of the days he would mostly be home. The whole family would sit together and talk. Nikul and he were absolute contrasts when it came to food; Nikul loved sweets (shira, kheer, basundi, gajar ka halwa, doodhi ka halwa), whereas Bhai hated them.

'I remember the Diwali celebrations back then. Bhai also went out for Diwali card parties, either at Raj Kapoor's home or at the famous Sea Rock hotel in Bandra. Bhai was not good at cards, but he would go and play just to give his friends company. I remember Jamnadasji preparing a bagful of money for Bhai to take to the card parties. There would also be the customary puja at home. Nikul and I would sit for the puja and Bhai would watch us do the Dhanteras and Laxmi pujas. While he never actively participated, he would always come forward to take the Lord's blessings.'

3

A Legacy of Respect

In this narration by Uday Jariwala, Hari is referred to as Sanjeev Dada.

I was born on 20 November 1972 in Kolkata. My Nani sent a telegram to inform Baa and Sanjeev Dada about my birth. As the postman arrived at Perrin Villa, he demanded 'baksheesh' (goodwill money) for the news he was bearing.

Baa flatly refused to give him any money, but Sanjeev Dada gladly did so and accepted the good news of my arrival. Sanjeev Dada also came to see me during the time my mother was in Kolkata.

After the customary forty-five-day post-delivery period at her mother's, mom and I came back home. Sanjeev Dada loved the idea of having a cherub around to cuddle. In the initial days, he used to come back home and play with me. It was nothing out of the ordinary—just tickling and hugging and laughing. As I grew up, I used to go to hug him every morning before I left for school and run into his room at all hours, whenever he was around. This was a regular feature of our interaction. My mother taught me to call him 'Dada' instead of Kaka, even though he was my uncle and not my grandfather.

My nickname was Mawwali, which means a spoilt brat. Sanjeev Dada used to enjoy playing with my sister Ekta and brother Prithvi too. We were Mawwali, Dingli and Gotlu, and he loved us dearly. I must add here that Kishore Dada loved us a lot too. Once Kishore Dada was wearing a lungi and kurta, and I showed a great liking for it. He immediately took me to the tailor and got a set made for me too. Both of them pampered us a lot. I have many memories of Sanjeev Dada. As the first-born, I definitely had the advantage of spending more time with him. I remember that during my school days, if he hadn't seen me for a few days in a row, he would make a pit stop at home post his shoot, call me downstairs and spend time with me in his car before he went out for dubbing or other work in the evening. On some days, Dada would wake me up after he came back from work, just to play with me. I was his little appendage and used to follow him around. In those days, a compilation used to come home every month containing all the media coverage received by an actor in that month. I would happily leaf through it. I was in awe of Dada's work!

Initially, I would be surprised at the number of people who used to come home every morning to meet him. By about 10.30 a.m., visitors would start pouring in. Our naughty code word for them was chamchas (sycophants). Only Baa, Jamnadasji and I had a free pass to enter Dada's room. I would prance around in his room all the time. Often, the chamchas would wait all the way up to lunch before he called them in. I used to be surprised—why did they wait and why did Dada allow them to wait? Did they come for the free food? Or had they created a unique symbiotic relationship with my Dada that I couldn't comprehend? I remember that a whole bunch of them tagged along when Sanjeev Dada took Baa to Shirdi too.

People that Dada worked with also used to visit—like Sachin Pilgaonkar, Shatrughan Sinha, Sarita Joshi, Sunil Dutt, Moushumi Chatterjee, and directors like Gulzar or Basu Bhattacharya, for script readings, narrations, discussions, etc. Dada never kept them waiting.

In the afternoon, he would get ready for his shoot. He would be fully rehearsed and raring to go. He was a very inspired performer and used to look forward to his shoots. Sanjeev Dada had one rule—he never entertained his chamchas at work. I heard from Jamnadasji that on one occasion when a chamcha had turned up at the shoot, Sanjeev Dada was livid and lost his cool. Later, he took that same chamcha out for dinner and mollified the man.

A Caring Man

I was about six years old when I realized that Sanjeev Dada was considered rich and successful. Three people used to manage his life—one was Jamnadasji, the second was driver Sharmaji, and the third was Pandit. Sanjeev Dada was a generous employer. In 1973, Dada bought a house a couple of blocks from Perrin Villa in my father Nikul Jariwala's name. Jamnadasji, his manager, shifted into that house. He had just one son, Deepak, about five years older than me. Dada took care of Deepak's education.

When Sharmaji was new in Mumbai, Sanjeev Dada painfully taught him how to navigate the roads (in the pre-GPS days!) In January 1980, when Rishi Kapoor got married, Dada attended the function. When he returned, it was 3 a.m., and he asked Sharmaji whether he had had dinner. When he said no, Dada himself served him food from our kitchen.

Us kids would go with Sanjeev Dada to Gazebo restaurant for lunch on Sundays. Before we left, there would be an important decision to be made—which car must we go in? Sanjeev Dada had five cars—a Mercedes, two Fiats, a Volkswagen Golf and a Volkswagen van which he used to use only for long outdoor shoots. We could choose any one of those, and Sanjeev Dada would himself drive us down. He would sing us songs from his movies and tell us their meaning. But his favourite song was 'Que Sera Sera' by Doris Day, and he used to sing it with all his heart. On one occasion, I remember saying, 'I want to go in a rickshaw' instead of in a car. Sanjeev Dada said 'Okay' without any hesitation. When we reached Gazebo, he realized he wasn't carrying his wallet. He had a running account at Gazebo, and Jamnadasji used to settle the bills monthly. So, Dada called the Gazebo manager and asked him to pay Rs 100 to the rickshaw driver. The fare couldn't have been more than Rs 2! Elated, the rickshaw driver waited till we finished and dropped us back home! Sanjeev Dada had a way of eliciting the best behaviour out of everyone he met. I will never forget the way Dada celebrated my birthdays. There were two fixed parties every year—one on 9 July, his birthday, and one on mine, 20 November. He would invite guests to my birthday with personally handwritten cards. His favourite venue was the Sea Rock hotel.

4

Baa's Death and the Hollow Quietus

'Bhai never believed in God. For him, Baa was God. He was an ideal son and worshipped the ground our mother walked on. There were just two things that rankled Baa: one was that Bhai never visited temples; and the second that she didn't succeed, despite trying very hard, in getting him married,' said Gayatri Patel.

Baa never gave up hope that one day Hari would get married. She fasted every Thursday and also went to the Ambe Mata Mandir until the end of her days to pray for his marriage.

Jyoti remembers Baa very fondly, 'She and Bhai would talk often and for a long time. There were occasions when Baa and he would disagree; let's call this nokjhok. But Baa would go to his room and talk to him with patience and love. I have never seen them shout at each other or get angry in front of me. Even on the rare occasion when Baa would say something to him in front of everyone, Bhai would just smile and go away. Nikul and

I were too scared to venture our opinions when Baa and Bhai were speaking. I often felt it would be a case of *chota mooh badi baat* (youngsters must not interrupt when elders are talking). It was Baa who trained me to think of Bhai as my father-in-law, because he took care of all of us like the head of the family.'

Baa accepted Hari fully, as mothers often do with their sons. Here is an extract from Subhash Indori's interview to Anil Chitre in the July 1980 issue of *Cine Blitz.*

> Throughout his struggle, his mother was his only source of inspiration and encouragement. She provided him with moral strength and guidance, in everything. Sanjeev used to lie to her, take some money and go out and drink. Eventually, his mother realised what he was up to. One day, Sanjeev with one of his many stock of excuses, was setting out on his usual jaunt. His mother stopped him, went to the cupboard, brought out a bottle of whisky and handed it to him saying, 'If you must drink, do it here in the house. That way, you won't spoil your name and if you do fall because of excessive drink[ing], it will be here in my arms and not in a gutter.

Uday still remembers Baa's silver paan ka dabba. 'She would keep it with her and sit for hours, talking to Sanjeev Dada and listening to him as well. She used to sit and cut the supari, put it in the betel leaf, apply white chuna, a mixture of elaichi and laung and relish the taste. Sanjeev Dada never liked this habit of hers. But he could never dissuade her from it.'

Whatever the hour, Baa would give her precious Haria company while he was drinking, serve him food, and sleep only afterwards. She would also ensure that Hari's drinking companions left at a reasonable hour. Baa never left him alone ... but as Kahlil Gibran said, 'Love knows not its own depth until the hour of separation.' Baa's death in 1979 was a big blow to Hari. In fact, Hari was in Hyderabad on the day Baa breathed her last. For a man utterly devoted to his mother, it remained a regret that he was not by her side when she passed away.

Gayatri said, 'In November 1979, I had planned a trip to Mumbai to attend my brother-in-law's wedding—it was my brother-in-law from my husband's side of the family. At the time, Baa was not keeping well and was admitted in Nanavati hospital. When I landed, Nikul was at the airport. I saw his sullen face, and I started to cry. Instinctively, I knew it was about Baa! I regret that I could not bid farewell to my mom. All I could do was participate in her prayer ceremony.'

Baa's funeral was a very emotionally charged affair. At her soulful epicedial rites, friends who felt Hari's loss congregated in large numbers. All three brothers, Hari, Kishore and Nikul, bid Baa a heartfelt farewell. In a very philosophical way, Baa had fulfilled all her duties, save for her reluctant sons' (Hari and Kishore's) nuptials.

Hari became even more silent and withdrawn from everyone else after Baa's demise. He rented another flat at Chadda Niwas nearby. Pandit started living there as a caretaker, also maintaining the house. With no one to monitor his drinking, Hari conveniently shifted his night parties to that house. Over time, Nikul discovered that Hari had a legion of foreign friends. They would often visit India and lodge there. But Jyoti remembers that 'Regardless of however late it was, even after Baa's demise, Bhai would unfailingly come and sleep in his bedroom at Perrin Villa. That was his safe space.'

5

Nine Heart Attacks, Ninepins

Hari's heart was off rhythm in more ways than one.

By 1975, Hari had attained the kind of stardom that very few actors can ever aspire to. But his personal life was to go into a tailspin. During the decade post-1976, there were nine heart attacks in the Jariwala family. Baa's in 1978 and 1979; Nikul Jariwala's in 1982 and 1984; Hari's in 1976, 1978, 1983 and 1985; and Kishore Jariwala's in 1986. Four of these were fatal, and the family collapsed like ninepins.

Hari's first heart attack in 1976

Hari was at a party in the Mumbai mayor's bungalow, accompanied by his driver Sharma. Kishore, Nikul, Jyoti, Baa and the kids were at home. Around midnight, they received a call that Hari had had a heart attack, and Baa, Nikul and Kishore rushed to Breach Candy Hospital.

After routine investigations, the doctors prescribed medical management and lifestyle changes. No procedure was needed. The news spread and the whole industry got to know within a day, and visitors poured in.

'While Baa held fort at the hospital, Bhai kept a book for visitors and Jamnadasji used to request that everyone should sign,' remembers Jyoti. 'Dilip Kumar was among the first to visit. Despite all the media rumours of a talent-based rivalry between them, we knew that there was absolutely no animosity between them. They had a very healthy amount of respect for each other and acknowledged openly that they belonged to two different generations. Close friends Sarita Joshi and her husband Pravin Joshi also came to visit. As Bhai's health got better, he started missing my children and so I took them to visit him.'

Hari was in the hospital for fifteen days. When he came home, he was pensive for a while, but his natural disposition of being happy and ironing a smile over all problems came right back. Friends like Jeetendra, Shatrughan Sinha and his wife Poonam, Sachin Pilgaonkar, Sunil Dutt and Gulzar came home to check on his health.

Jyoti recollects, 'Bhai's health was both a congenital issue and, later in life, a factor of his habits. Bhai didn't like sweets, but because of his eating habits he had diabetes.'

Second heart attack in 1978

Film shoots took Hari all over the world. In 1978, Kishore Jariwala accompanied Hari on a shoot to Los Angeles. This was for the film *Suraag*. As was his habit, whenever Hari shot in the US, he would ask his sister Gayatri and her family to join him. They all stayed at the Beverly Hills Hotel. It was like a small reunion of sorts.

After the shoot got wrapped up, Hari went to stay with Gayatri in Houston for a week. Gayatri said:

> I remember this very well. I was pregnant with my daughter Artee and Bhai had come to stay. I was scheduled for a C-section and it was Bhai who dropped me on 12 June 1978 to the hospital. Artee was born the next day. After the delivery, I was fast asleep. When I woke up, I was waiting for Bhai to come and see Artee, but he did not come. I wondered why. Unknown to me, post the delivery, there was an announcement on the hospital PA system for my husband: 'Mr Patel, you have an emergency.'
>
> Bhai had his second heart attack the day Artee was born! My husband did not tell me as I was quite weak after my delivery. Our close friend Mr Dalwadi took Bhai to Dr Virendra Mathur at the Texas Heart Institute, who treated him. Even when Jamnadasji called on the hospital line from Bombay and asked about Bhai, my husband lied to him, saying, 'Sunil Dutt has come to Houston, so Bhai's busy.' A day later, Jamnadasji called again and spoke to me. He had caught the lie because Sunil Dutt was in Mumbai.
>
> That's when I got to know that Bhai too was admitted in the hospital! When I got discharged after a week, I first went to see Bhai. He recovered well, stayed at our home for another ten days and then left. Bhai was even more clear that he never wanted to get married.

Third heart attack in 1983

Hari had taken his nephews Uday and Prithvi for an overnight stay to his friend Major's empty bungalow at Janki Kutir in Mumbai. Major was an army man who lived in Dubai.

In the wee hours of dawn, Hari complained of a gripping chest pain. Pandit, who was always by Hari's side, alerted Sharma. The latter drove them both to Nanavati Hospital, which was barely five minutes away. Nanavati was like a second home to the Jariwalas and Dr M.J. Gandhi, who practised there, was cardiologist to the whole family.

It was Nikul who got the early morning call from the hospital. Once again, Hari was admitted for almost two weeks. By now, Nikul had also had his first heart attack. It was a distressing time for the family as the threat of death loomed large. This time, the prescription for Hari was to stay off alcohol and spicy food completely—benign prescriptions, but those that did not fit into Hari's manner of living!

Fourth heart attack in 1985

Hari's reckless lifestyle coupled with the genetic cardiac disease was a ticking time bomb. Nikul's health was also now in question, so Hari decided to book heart surgery for Nikul at the Texas Heart Institute. While they were arranging a passport and visa for Jyoti to accompany Nikul for his surgery, the latter succumbed to a fatal heart attack in September 1984. Nikul breathed his last in the new house Hari had rented at Chadda Niwas. Nikul's death was like a thunderbolt, a projectile that pierced Hari's conscience. What would become of Jyoti and her three kids? She would be all alone as Kishore and Prafulla had already chosen to live separately.

Jyoti's family came from Kolkata for the last rites. Her father Hasmukh Patel asked Hari whether he should take Jyoti and the three kids back with him to Kolkata. Hari told him, 'Jyoti is my daughter-in-law and my responsibility. Nikul's children are like my children. I will provide for them, don't worry.'

Now that this promise was made, Hari decided to go to Texas and get his own bypass surgery done to remedy his blockages once and for all. His friend Ravi Walia hopped on the flight from Dubai and accompanied him. Once he landed in Texas, Gayatri and Ashok Patel took his guardianship locally. Dr Denton Cooley was a legendary cardiac surgeon, best known for performing the first successful human heart transplant in the US (1968). He declared that Hari was living on 10 per cent of his heart's capacity and advised cardiac surgery. The surgery was successful, and by all accounts, it seemed that Hari was well and truly on the road to recovery. Jyoti and her kids joined the family in Texas.

When Hari returned to India, he had lost a tremendous amount of weight and was much leaner. Jyoti took a mannat for his health and kept a Mahamrutyunjay Jaap (a ritual dedicated to Lord Shiva for resolving health-related issues). Despite the advice of rest that he had been prescribed, Hari wanted to live as intense a life as possible and started working multiple shifts again. At the same time, he couldn't give up smoking and drinking. His body withered under the double whammy, and he passed away on 6 November 1985 in his favourite place, his bedroom at Perrin Villa, of a massive cardiac arrest. Kishore, too, died just six months later.

A poster of Hari's film *Badal*, which released in 1966.
Courtesy of RJ Anirudh Chawla

iest films were
Mukhtar. This
e such movie,
Smuggler.
Anirudh Chawla

6

Jyoti Relives Baa's Journey

A first-person account by Jyoti Nikul Jariwala.

When Bhai died, I didn't know what to do. He was the mainstay of our lives. With Nikul also not around, I felt abandoned and lonely. I thought of Baa, who had raised four children by herself. I, too, had to raise mine. The first jolt came soon enough. Our lawyer informed me that I had to pay Rs 6 lakh to probate Bhai's will.

Somehow, with the existing reserves and help from my family, I put the money together. Boney Kapoor was the first person to come forward and return his debt—he gave me the Rs 2 lakh that he had borrowed from Bhai to make *Hum Paanch*. Boney's father, Surinder Kapoor, was Shammi Kapoor's assistant, and Bhai and Shammiji had a very close bond. Then the other Shammi—the veteran actress—came and gave us Rs 50,000, which she owed to Bhai. Raj Kapoor also returned some of the money he had borrowed. There was some income from Princess Restaurant in Bangalore initially too, but this stopped after a while and became a legal tangle.

When the will was read, I was relieved that it took care of my children and Kishorebhai's family and that there was a proper division of the assets. Jamnadasji gave us some details about whom Bhai had loaned money to. The list of debtors was mind-boggling; the sum was in crores! We appealed to the Indian Motion Picture Producers' Association IMPPA (for recovery of the money), but not much came out of it. To tell you the truth, we still haven't recovered that money.

In 1980, Bhai had started a twenty-year annuity income plan with LIC for some tax benefits and to secure an income for the family. There was a monthly payout for us, and a part of it was to be given to Kishorebhai's wife (to be stopped only if she got married to someone else). This was the only promised income I could count on.

The house was full of perfumes, watches, clothes, cassettes—all of which I gave away to Bhai's friends and our loyal helpers. I think that's what he would've wanted us to do. We gifted the apartment in which Jamnadasji lived to him. That was the least I could do for his countless years of service to Bhai. I must say this—I cannot highlight enough the need for education among women. As I studied the will and all the papers made available to me and took stock of all the properties that were part of our ancestral family wealth, my head was spinning. Then there were the never-ending lawsuits of which I had no history. It was not easy, and it took ten painstaking years for me to clear the cobwebs. I learnt new ways to communicate, whom to trust and how to survive … all after Bhai's death.

A pensive Hari. According to Paresh Rawal, he had the ideal actor's face: plenty of space for expression and an excellent sense of proportion.

V
H
a

Some of Hari's ea
with actor Sheik
is the poster of

Courtesy of RJ

A pensive Hari. According to Paresh Rawal, he had the ideal actor's face: plenty of space for expression and an excellent sense of proportion.

Veteran artiste A.K. Hangal with Hari. He directed Hari in several plays and was his friend, philosopher and guide.

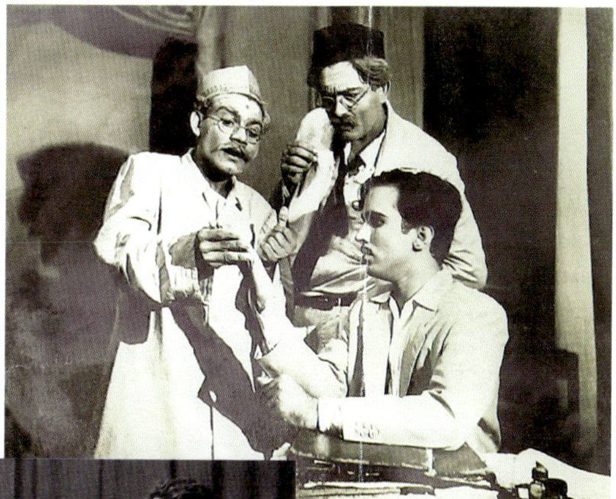

Some rare pictures from Hari's theatre days. He was not even thirty, when he started playing much older characters onstage.

A poster of Hari's film *Badal*, which released in 1966.
Courtesy of RJ Anirudh Chawla

Some of Hari's earliest films were with actor Sheikh Mukhtar. This is the poster of one such movie, *Smuggler*.
Courtesy of RJ Anirudh Chawla

Hari receiving an award from Chief Minister of Gujarat, Ghanshyam Oza, for *Koshish* in 1972.

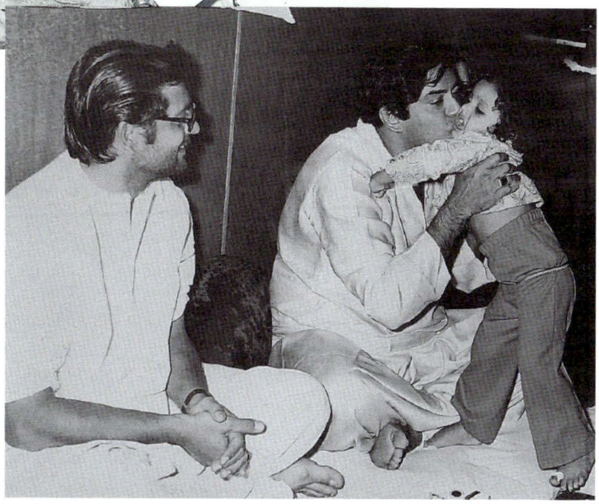

Gulzar looks on as Hari cuddles Uday Jariwala.

In the '70s, it was common for brands to contact a production house and use a still from a film as an advertisement.

Hari's youngest brother Nikul and his fiancée Jyoti on their engagement day.

Nargis Dutt, along with her children Sanjay and Namrata, attending Nikul and Jyoti's wedding reception.

Nikul, Gayatri, Ashok and Kishore with Jethalal Jariwala's framed photograph up on the wall.

Nargis Dutt talking to Baa during Gayatri and Ashok Patel's wedding.

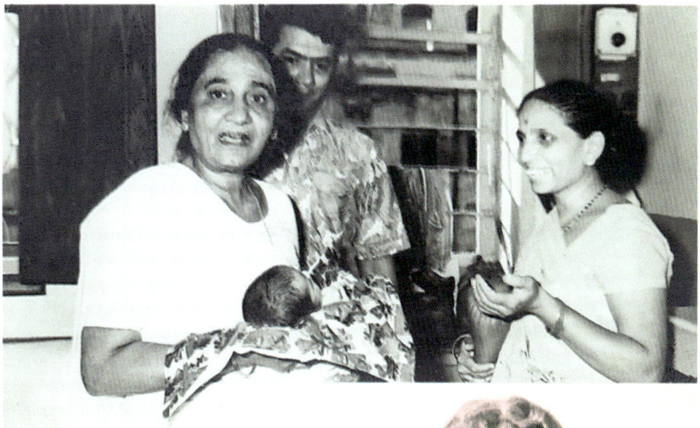

Baa, Nikul and Jyoti's mother Pushpa welcome the newborn, Uday Jariwala.

Hari with his sister Gayatri Patel, who passed away in 2021. She was devoted to him.

Hari with Gayatri, holding her children Alex and Artee in his arms.

The happy family: Gayatri, Kishore, Ashok Patel, Hari with Artee and Alex.

Hari lighting his mother's pyre.

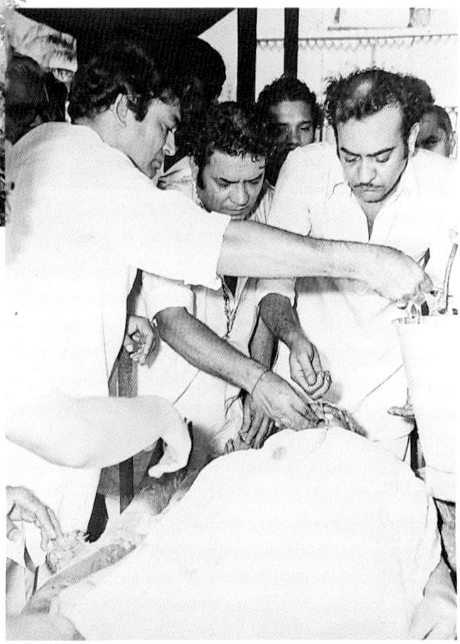

Hari, Nikul and Kishore performing rituals and bidding the final farewell to Baa.

Hari with his brothers during the funeral rites for Baa.

Hari with Rajmata Gayatri Devi at a royal wedding, accompanied by friend and actress Suchitra Sen (extreme right).

A.K. Hangal, a family member, Kishore, Hari and Yash Chopra carrying Baa's body.

Raj Kapoor visiting Hari to express his condolences after Baa's death.

Baa, Hari, actress Rehana Sultan and director Rajinder Bedi with the National Award for their film *Dastak*.

Hari and Tamil star Sivaji Ganesan celebrating the success of *Manchali*.

Actor Mahmood and his wife Tracy Ali with a gift for Uday Jariwala at his birthday party.

To be able to deal with everything, I sent Prithvi and Ekta to Panchgani and retrieved Uday from the Bhonsala Military School in Nashik to stay with me. He was older and more knowledgeable by then and aware of things. Bhai's close friend Subhash Sanas was a great help during those times. When the dust settled, as a token of gratitude, I founded the Sanjeev Kumar Charitable Trust, and later Uday founded the Sanjeev Kumar Foundation.

'I have never held a girl's career against her, as long as a girl is prepared to give it up after marriage. There are women who can do that, who after marriage are able to make their home into their career. I would prefer to marry such a woman because I cannot visualize or accept a situation for myself where my wife and I would both be working and the home is neglected.'

Sanjeev Kumar
Stardust, March 1980

SECTION IV

Love, Loss and Buoyancy

An Account of Hari's Love Life

1

An Account by Bharathi S. Pradhan

My career in journalism began in 1972–73, when I was still in college. Since films like *Khilona* had been released, Haribhai was a known name by then. Our first meeting was when I used to write for *Free Press Bulletin*, a well-circulated tabloid in the 1970s.

He was easy to interact with and have a conversation with, also pretty forthcoming about himself. During a long interview that I once did with him for the *Bulletin*, he freely talked about the Nutan incident where she had publicly slapped him on the sets of *Devi*. It was an incident that had happened before I became a journalist. But he didn't hold back his punches and told me that he had her letters to him—she was going to walk out on her husband to marry him. There was also some talk about him adopting Nutan's son Mohnish, who was a kid during *Devi*.

Those were the days when we had access to and got all our stories directly from the celebrities. There were no PRs and managers acting as filters. I knew Nutan too and she didn't contradict anything that was in Haribhai's interview.

Over the years, I met Haribhai several times. Sometimes at his home on Pali Hill or at a private party in a photographer's house or on the sets of his films where we were always welcome. I remember an occasion where he had distributed pens to all the journalists at a party prior to the release of one of his films.

By and large, we had a cordial, professional relationship. However, there was one occasion when he was miffed with me. I was working with *Star & Style*, a popular film fortnightly, at that time. He was shooting for a Ravi Tandon film at Rajkamal Studio and had asked me to meet him. However, when I reached there, he was icy cold and didn't entertain me at all. I was genuinely surprised to see his evident discomfort with me.

I had no choice but to walk up to him and ask him, 'What's your problem?'

He told me, 'When I called you over, I didn't know that you had written a story saying that I have proposed to Sulakshana Pandit. I've read it now and I'm upset.'

'I wrote it because Sulakshana herself told me that you have proposed to her,' I explained. 'Why would I not write it?'

'Oh, she told you?' he queried, looking surprised. 'But I have never proposed to her,' he clarified. 'And if she told you that then I can't hold it against you,' he added, mollified. We went on to do another readable interview after that.

When I look back, I can confidently say that he never came across as a heartbroken man. Direct, simple and fun-loving. Never down in the dumps and seeking sympathy. There was so much written about his relationship with Hema Malini back then. Hema's mom had famously said about him, 'Hari's too fat for my slim, beautiful daughter.' But he bounced right back to work even after that.

To me, his first love seemed to be food and liquor and, of course, his work.

This personal piece by Bharathi S. Pradhan is the perfect introduction to the women in Hari's life.

2

Phases of Hari's Love Life

'Courage is like love; it must have hope for nourishment.'
—Napoleon Bonaparte

Hari's love life can be divided into three distinct phases. The first phase is when he was a young, ambitious man in his twenties who did not want to get married before he achieved something substantial.

The second phase is when he achieved recognition as an established actor, worked alongside beautiful women, was open to love and interested in marriage. If there was any time in his life when he could've got married, it was this period.

The third phase was after the first heart attack in 1976. He became conscious of the transience of life and the brevity of his own. Some would say that he was disillusioned with love, but his stardom and his bachelorhood both ensured that he enjoyed unbridled female attention. After Baa's death, he openly declared that he was not willing to commit or settle down.

Let's now delve into each phase of his love life.

Hari's early engagement is already described in detail by Gayatri Patel earlier in the book. The great love of his life came after he started working in cinema.

Hari said in an interview with Bunny Reuben for *Star & Style*'s June 1973 issue:

> Till the age of 26, I have never touched a girl. The first time I first fell deeply and seriously in love, was around that time. I wanted more than anything to marry her. I would've married her. But she was a Muslim girl. If I was the youngest son of my mother, I would've said to hell with the world and married her ... She has gone through hell raising four children without my father.'

In another interview as a successful star, Hari has narrated in an uncredited article, 'Years ago, I travelled by bus to meet my girlfriend and I think my return journey by bus was the most beautiful trip of my life. I was so full of her—it didn't matter that I was in a bus.'

Now, Hari worked extensively with Muslim actresses Kumkum and Nazima in his early days. However, there is great speculation that this woman who stole Hari's heart and expanded his world was Saira Bano. This was around the time when Hari played a small role in Joy Mukherjee and Saira Bano's *Aao Pyar Karen* (1965), which starred Mac Mohan, Manavendranath and Haribhai as friends and supporting characters to the lead.

Sarosh Mody has spoken about this in the December 1982 issue of *Stardust*:

> Every woman whom Sanjeev loved and yearned for, ditched him, leaving him high and dry. His ego is terribly hurt. Sanjeev is suffering from some kind of a complex. Luck has never been in his favour. He loved them all. Saira, Nutan and Hema. Maybe with Saira, it was just an infatuation and he misunderstood her.

Later in life, Hari has spoken about some affection between him and another Muslim girl, Shabana Azmi. He said in an interview with Vijaya Irani in the December 1979 issue of *Star & Style*:

> I knew Shabana for a longer period than I had known any other girl in films. Earlier, I had worked on stage with her mother Shaukat. When I first knew Shabana, she was not yet in films. What she felt for me that time must've been mere puppy love, but it could have culminated in an alliance with me if my mother had not put her foot firmly down. My mother, tolerant in other respects, was adamant about her refusal to accept a Muslim bahu—if I had married Shabana, I would've had to move out of the house and that's something I'd never do!

Uday Jariwala recollects, 'I have gone to Shabanaji's house as child for the Holi parties that she would host. She was also a regular at our home. After Dada's demise, we gathered all of his memorabilia and put them into cartons. Years later, when I perused through it I found that among all the fan mail, Shabana Azmi's affectionate letter to Dada had also been preserved.'

Was it Baa's anti-Muslim stance when it came to the matter of his marriage that came in the way of Hari's happiness? Could it have helped Hari in the long run if Baa had been truly unconditional in her love for him?

3

Hari's Heartbreak with Nutan

In the late 1960s and early '70s, Baa continued to hunt for a good Gujarati bride for her son. Sadly, it seemed he wasn't interested in a simple bride—he was looking for a woman who had an identity of her own and yet had an honesty about her.

'I had received a proposal from a nice girl in no way connected with films. But at the time, I was too busy involved with a top star, who was married. After the big slapping incident, I was neither here nor there. Today, the only regret I feel is not having accepted that girl's proposal. She would've made an ideal wife,' says Hari in the same interview with Vijaya Irani for *Star & Style*.

The slapping incident is a reference to the beautiful Nutan Samarth. Nutan married Naval Lt Commander Rajnish Bahl in 1959.

Hari and Nutan met on the sets of *Gauri*, which released in 1968 and then worked together again on the sets of *Devi* (1970). They had been shooting together for almost three years in a row. Now, Nutan was an exceedingly beautiful woman and a well-established artiste, leagues ahead of Hari at the time. Hari was awestruck by her beauty and refinement. Senior scribe and columnist Vithal C. Nadkarni describes Nutan's beauty:

> My sister-in-law lived in the same tower near Colaba Post Office as Nutan Samarth. Nutan had an electrifying aura, a double whammy of a Grace Kelly with a dash of Audrey Hepburn; she came across as absolutely cultured and beautiful. And when she spoke in impeccable French, she did indeed seem like some seraph from an entirely different stratospheric world far above us mere mortals that encountered her in the lift! So one could easily relate to why any man would fall in love with her.

Hari and Nutan's relationship on the sets of *Devi* developed slowly, and the media started writing about the hint of an affair. It is alleged that Nutan slapped Hari publicly during the shoot after she read the news about their affair in a magazine on the sets. It is believed that she did so upon the insistence of her husband.[12]

The Illustrated Weekly, Vol. 107, published in 1986, carries an article titled 'Seven scandals that rocked tinseltown', which mentions that Nutan's husband demanded that she 'humiliate Hari before the unit'.

In the February 1972 issue of *Stardust*, titled 'Best of Stardust', Nutan clarified her stand to journalist Uma Rao:

---

12 https://www.bhaskar.com/entertainment/bollywood/news/nutan-death-anniversary-know-some-interesting-facts-about-the-actress-128248624.html

> Imagine my shock when a reliable associate of mine revealed to me that Sanjeev himself was responsible for such talk. And I had no reason to doubt his information. After all, he had been a witness to Sanjeev's manoeuvres. He even had the nerve to confess that I was living with him, that I wanted to marry him and that we were both wondering if we could get custody of my child. Utter rubbish! What did he think, that I would ever leave my most wonderful husband for him? Sanjeev isn't even worth his toenail!

Harsh words there!

Three years later, there was another article by Uma Rao on Hari and Nutan in the January 1975 issue of *Stardust*. It talked about how the director of *Devi* decided to mediate a truce between Nutan and Hari. Over a few drinks, Nutan's husband Rajnish Bahl said to Hari, 'What is this? You're on your first peg and I'm already four pegs ahead of you? You can't keep up with me, you're SLOW.'

Hari quipped, 'I'm slow but I'm also steady.'

The director wanted both the actors to sign a letter saying they would resume shooting for the film. Hari refused to, unless Nutan tendered him an apology. Nutan refused to apologize, and it started to look like a stalemate.

Rajnish Bahl stood up gruffly and offered an apology. Hari faced him squarely and said, 'Mr Bahl, I don't want your apology. You didn't slap me. If you had, the story would've been entirely different.'

Devi finally released in 1970.

Over time, it was suggested that there might have been much more to this slap. To start with, Bharati S. Pradhan's account shared earlier paints a very different picture of what happened. Also, in the June 1973 issue of *Star & Style,* in which Bunny Reuben wrote: 'Like Dilip Kumar, Haribhai survived intense heartbreak with a married woman. Each heartbreak has made both the actor and the man grow up a little bit.'

Several accounts seem to indicate that Nutan's husband imposed restrictions on her. In the August 2012 issue of *The Indian Express*, journalist Subhash K. Jha interviewed character artiste Shubha Khote, who said:

> Nutan and I were very close. I acted in my first film, *Seema*, with her. I immediately warmed up to her. Nutan made me feel comfortable when we worked together. We became inseparable friends ... After Nutan got married, we could not spend much time together. She was not allowed to receive calls. That did not stop us from being friends. Whenever we were shooting, we'd meet.[13]

In the March 1992 issue of *G-Junior*, Shobhana Samarth, Nutan's mother, pointed to Nutan being under some pressure after marriage. She says, 'I could read her like a book. All this changed once she got married. We grew distant ...'[14]

Bunny Reuben has the last word on this episode. Writing for *Star & Style* in June 1973, he said:

> After all the tom tomming, all the fanfare and all the noise attendant on this episode died a sudden death, in the gossip

---

13 http://archive.indianexpress.com/news/the-tramp/994860/4

14 https://www.cinemaazi.com/feature/nutan-a-flashback-the-daughter

columns and magazine headlines, the poignant aroma of it lingered on, permeating the psyche of the actor with a deep emotionalism and widening his calibre as an artiste with depth and understanding. Today, Haribhai is embarrassed if anyone refers to that particular episode. Even in private conversations, he steers clear of it. Yet, to one who sees clearly beyond the headlines and beneath the surface, it is evident that the love affair has left its scars.

In the December 1979 issue of *Star & Style*, Sanjeev Kumar finally spoke about this in the context of Baa coming to know about the incident:

> My mother suspected something about this married actress. When the slapping incident occurred, she questioned me about it as soon as I came home. I brushed the whole thing aside, explaining that it had been a rehearsal for a film scene and nothing else. But she made inquiries from Jamnadas however and made her displeasure known.

Needless to say, this was another liaison Baa disapproved of intensely. Uday Jariwala says that in defence of Hari, Shammi Kapoor had thrown a party to make light of the slapping incident. Both Shammi Kapoor and Rajendra Kumar were extremely fond of Nutan too.

The ironic truth is that if it were not for the slap, there might have been no records of this relationship at all.

4

Enchanted by the Dream Girl

When Hari started shooting for *Seeta Aur Geeta* (1972), he met another ambitious and beautiful woman. That was Hema Malini. The role of the protagonist in the film, a double role, was originally offered to Mumtaz but was finally performed by Hema Malini.

Gayatri Patel confirmed that in 1971, Hema had started visiting their home occasionally. She said:

> Just before my marriage, Hema had started coming home. She was very close to us and a very beautiful, polite and dignified person. My mom and I have gone to her house in Mumbai as well as Madras and there was a lot of cordiality between us. On every birthday since 1972, Hema used to call my mother and say, 'Mataji, give me your blessings, it's my birthday.' Baa also reciprocated wholeheartedly and loved her a lot.

This made perfect sense. Hari himself told Bunny Reuben much later in the 1979 issue of *Star & Style:*

> The bride that my mother had chosen, Hema Malini and her aunt had come over for dinner. My mother reacted more instantaneously and more favourably to this girl than she had ever done to any other guest—male or female. She told me she admired her simple charm and asked me why I didn't propose to her. Being from within the industry, knowing the profession, she would understand me, my work and behaviour better and her homeliness would make it easy for her to settle down into a good bahu ... so my mother pointed out. She also sensed Hema's nature which obliterated all fears of my being dominated or pushed around. Hema was the daughter-in-law my mother had virtually set her heart on. Seeing her keenness, I who had signed two films with her approached her with a straightforward direct honest proposal, besides which there was a growing fondness on my part too. When I told Hema's mother of my intention, I sensed a certain disapprobation. The consequences of the whole episode are well-known now, including the break-up.

There's some context to this. According to the book *The Greatest Show on Earth*, it was Hema Malini's mother who broke up her affair with Hari: 'While Amma [Hema's mother] was successful in squashing the Haribhai affair, she did not find the going so easy this time [referring to Dharmendra].'[15]

---

15 *The Greatest Show on Earth: Writings on Bollywood*, ed. Jerry Pinto (Penguin India, 2011).

Hema never denied the affair. According to her biography *Hema Malini* by Ram Kamal Mukherjee:

> Falling in love and marrying Dharmendra was possibly the only time Hema had rebelled against her parents. Till then, not only were her mother's words as good as gospel for her, she was also her most trusted confidante. Even something like the Sanjeev Kumar affair—where hardly anyone knows till date what happened—was known to Jaya [Hema's mothers name was Jaya Chakravarthy]. In an interview to *Stardust* in June 1974, Hema had said, 'It's become a habit with me to tell everything to my mom. I can't remember having lied to her at any time. When I got involved with Sanjeev Kumar, I needn't have told her about it. But I didn't hide anything from her. She had nothing to do with the break-up. There were other reasons involved, reasons too personal and complicated to be disclosed.'[16]

There's a lovely picture of Baa in the family archives, feeding Hema Malini cake on Hari's thirty-fifth birthday in 1973. The family confirms that during this period, Hema Malini's make-up lady used to come to the house—Hema and Hari used to exchange letters through her.

It wasn't just Baa; everyone loved Hema.

Gayatri and Hema kept in touch. Gayatri said, 'When Hema Malini visited New York for a play, she knew I had got married and moved there. She called me and I went to see her. Later,

---

16 Ram Kamal Mukherjee, *Hema Malini: Beyond the Dream Girl* (HarperCollins India, 2017).

when I moved to California in 1973, she called me again but this time we could only speak on the phone.'

Jyoti Jariwala pitches in, 'Uday was born in 1972. I had delivered in Kolkata in my mother's home. I got to know that Hema had come home for dinner. I came back in February 1973 and Hema came home again. She talked to Bhai and went away after a cup of coffee. She was extremely cordial with all of us and is a nice person. If she had left her career, she would've made a great housewife as she was genuinely gracious and soft-spoken.'

Jyoti also recollects a visit by Hema a couple of years later, around 1974, when she and Hari spoke in private, and Hema left pensively. This seemed to be a temporary pause in their story. The news of their break-up spread quite fast.

During the period 1974–75, both Hema and Hari were extremely successful artistes. Hema was a hit machine. Her name alone sufficed to ensure a film's box office glory. Heroes wanted to work with her, and for Hari's friends like Jeetendra and Shatrughan Sinha, it became difficult to take sides when the break-up was announced!

Hari himself is quoted in the August 1979 issue of *Super*: 'I was busy romancing Hema instead of signing a dozen films with her … Manipulation, calculation, those are the qualities that should be called a star material. But I don't want to be a star.'

An article that came much later, dramatically titled 'Betrayed by his women, friends and family—why Sanjeev Kumar cannot trust anyone anymore', in the October 1982 issue of *Stardust*, says that when rumours of the Sanjeev-Hema break-up were making the industry rounds, both happened to be shooting at the same studio in Madras. Sarosh Mody says, 'In spite of all this,

Hema sent across a note to Sanjeev, saying that she would like to meet him alone in the privacy of his make-up room and asked Sanjeev to request me to leave them alone. I myself was quite stunned and extremely puzzled by her behaviour.'

According to Hema's biography, her parents were upset about her romance with Dharmendra, who was already married. Hema Malini's mother, Jaya Chakravarthy, thought of getting her married to someone else and immediately thought of Jeetendra. So, in the year 1974, a hush-hush wedding was planned in Chennai at Hema's house.

The book also has a quote attributed to Jeetendra. A close friend of Jeetendra remembers him saying, 'I don't want to marry Hema. I am not in love with her. She is not in love with me. But my family wants it, so I might as well. And she is such a good girl.'

An evening daily got a whiff of the impending Hema-Jeetendra wedding. Dharmendra received a jolt. He rushed to Shobha Sippy's house, and the two took the next flight to Chennai. After a lot of drama, Dharmendra, who was at first physically pushed out of the house by Hema's father, got to talk to Hema alone.

When Hema finally came out, her voice quivered as she asked everyone if they could wait for a few days. Jeetendra's parents declared that that was not an option. The marriage had to happen now or never. As everyone waited desperately for an answer, Hema quietly shook her head. This insult was too much for Jeetendra to bear, and he stormed out of the house with his parents.

Jeetendra and Shobha Sippy got married in October 1974. An anecdote in the January 1975 issue of *Stardust* reveals that

Jeetendra invited Hari to a special showing of his film *Khushboo*. After the screening, he asked Haribhai, 'Don't you think, yaar, that Hema's different in this film?' But Hari replied, 'To me, yaar, she always appears indifferent.'

Hari had let the Hema episode go, but Baa never really gave up on Hema. According to Gayatri, 'My son Ashish was born in September 1976. Baa came to live with me in the US after my delivery. I was meeting my mother after five years. We had a lot to talk about. One of the biggest items on Baa's agenda during her trip was to buy a gift for Hema. She was hopeful that things would work out one day between the two of them. She knew that Bhai had made his views very clear to Hema—that he did not want a working wife. But Bhai also knew that Hema was a very ambitious person and that she would not meet his condition.'

But the story wasn't over yet!

Gayatri Patel further said, 'In early 1977, I visited Mumbai. Jaya Chakravarthy aunty came home. We were all surprised. She and Baa tried to get Hema and Bhai together. Jaya aunty was not happy at all that Hema was going to marry a man who was already married. Baa loved Hema a lot—but both the mothers could not convince Bhai or Hema to marry. Baa felt very bad about it—on the one hand, Bhai was not getting married. On the other, he had also had his first heart attack by now.'

Hari attributed the break-up to Hema. In an interview with N. Bharathi in the March 1977 issue of *Star & Style*, he said, 'The problem with Hema is that she's very confused. She doesn't know whom to listen to,' Hari reminisced. 'We broke up because I wanted her to quit working after marriage.'

N. Bharathi's interview format was interesting. She posed questions to Hari and Hema side by side. She also referred to another article in which Hema allegedly told a journalist that Hari was after her money! N. Bharathi asked Hema whether she had said so. Hema was livid, 'The interview was written by a journalist I have never met in my life ... I was furious when I read it.'

About a patch-up, Hari said, 'I am told, Hema's mother regrets the past.'

Hema Malini, however, denied that there was any attempt by her mother to broker peace between Hari and her. She told N. Bharathi, 'I met Sanjeev ... when he was in hospital. I am not hostile towards anybody but it is certainly not true that my mother has been sending feelers to his place. ... My mother will never do anything behind my back.'

A couple of years later, after Baa's demise, Hari observed in the December 1979 issue of *Star & Style*, 'In spite of all this, my mother still refused to accept it. Veiled hints, constant suggestions even after our break-up indicated how much she had wanted this girl to be her daughter-in-law. I believe they continued to maintain a cordial relationship.'

Hema Malini and Dharmendra got married on 2 May 1980. Thankfully, Baa wasn't around to see that!

Sarosh Mody said, 'Even though Sanjeev had maintained a cool and calm exterior when Hema got married to Dharmendra and was equally unruffled when she gave birth to her baby, he was actually quite hurt and upset.'

Both Hema and Hari distanced themselves from each other thereafter. After Hari's demise, when Jamnadasji went to Film City to meet a producer, Hema Malini happened to be shooting there. She saw him, called him over and they spoke for a long time about Hari. They agreed that his passing was too sudden and soon and hoped things had ended differently.

Media Plays Cupid

As news of the Sanjeev-Hema break-up spread, magazines in the mid-1970s started getting obsessed with getting Hari married. To put it simply, Hari's nuptials were to the media in the 1970s what Salman Khan's marriage was to the media in the 2000s.

The magazine *Cine Blitz* played cupid in May 1975 in an article credited to a writer named Crish and titled 'Wanted, a bride for Haribhai—will you be his saathi?' It speculated thus:

> Who'll be the lucky one? Girls, can you picture yourself as the Jariwala bride? Do you think you can be the ideal one in his life? If yes, send us your picture in profile and full figure. Write to us about your family background, educational qualifications, accomplishments or aspirations, age, hobbies and so on …
>
> Sanjeev has a fascination for girls who are utterly charming, in the finest sense of that term—neither lean nor amply loaded. He has a weakness for a NAME, that is, a girl who had some accomplishments to her credit.

Rather objectifying of women, one would say today! Clarifying that neither Haribhai nor his mother knew about the article, the magazine called their appeal a friendly social service, asking marriage brokers, agents and astrologers to keep off.

In another piece, circa the mid-1970s, in the form of a photoshoot, *Stardust*'s photographer B.J. Panchal shot Hari with seven different brides, as per seven different religious rituals: Prema Narayan (Christian wedding), Ranjeeta (Punjabi wedding), Smita Patil (Maharashtrian wedding), Bindiya Goswami (South Indian wedding), Simple Kapadia (Gujarati wedding), Begum Zaherra (Muslim wedding) and Rita Bhaduri (Bengali wedding). After each ceremony, the bride did kiss Hari on the cheek in good faith. Hema Malini lent her own Kanjeevaram saree to Bindiya Goswami for the South Indian wedding shoot!

In 1978, Haribhai told journalist Mangala Chandran from *Film World*, 'I don't have the urge any longer to get married. In fact, marriage is an obsolete word.'

In the August 1979 issue of *Super* magazine, Hari expressed his consternation about the media's obsession with his marriage: 'Why is everyone interested in my getting married? This problem seems to be taking on an international dimension. Would you believe that on a recent Canadian trip, the press and people also started off on this subject too!'

Hari became even more pensive after Baa's death. In a June 1980 interview with *Filmfare,* he said, 'I wouldn't get married impulsively. If I was the type, I would've got married more than 10 times. I fall in love at first sight and by the time I've made up my mind, the moment has passed.'

Asked about his ideal woman, he said: ' ... someone who is not selfish. Someone who would do things for others when she could, even at inconvenience to herself. Someone like me.'

Every interview that Hari gave in the 1980s makes it evident that he had given up all hope of marriage. In one to Indu Gupta for *Filmfare* in June 1980, Hari said this about relationships: 'The nicest part is the beginning and the worst is the end. No, the worst is when you feel it shouldn't have happened, when you regret it's happening.'

Popular radio jockey and presenter Anirudh Chawla, who has interviewed many colleagues of Hari's, has pieced together his own interpretation. Almost every conversation is meticulously recorded and archived by him. According to him, both Leena Chandavarkar and Moushumi Chatterjee thought that Hari would've lived a lot longer had he got married. And despite the coverage given to the Hema Malini-Hari affair, it was someone else who was his true love. There is scant reference to that, but those closest to him always knew this, says Chawla.

5

The Love That Wasn't Meant to Be

The October 1982 issue of *Stardust* quotes Sarosh Mody as saying: 'It is not that Sanjeev was left high and dry after Hema left him. There were a whole lot of film and non-filmy women who were competing with each other to take Miss Malini's place. And even though Sanjeev himself was flattered by the attention and even played up to them, he had no intentions of marrying them.'

Hari adds in the same interview, 'I will never get married because I don't trust women anymore. Women are the most unpredictable and untrustworthy species on earth … the only thing I like about a woman is motherhood. That's the only predictable and definite thing about her.'

With this mindset, it was obviously very difficult for Sulakshana Pandit to make any headway with him. In a public blog on *Cineplot.com* in 2011 republished from a 1996 interview credited to Shubha Mini and now available on BollywoodShaadis.com, Sulakshana Pandit revealed how she felt about Hari.

> It was during the film *Uljhan* (shot in 1973–74) that I fell in love with Haribhai. We had struck a wonderful rapport with each other. He was madly in love with Hemaji, during those days. So, naturally, he would come to me with all his problems! I felt terrible but I used to console myself, thinking this was just a phase! Once he got out of it, I wanted to tell him how I felt about him. But I never did get the chance. My co-artistes would tell me, 'Sulakshana, you are what this man needs! You will change his life.' [Baa did not disapprove of Sulakshana at all, according to media reports at the time. She had reached a stage where she would've been elated to just see him settle.]
>
> Sanjeevji and I shared a lot in common. He was a Cancerian like me and was also a very emotional human being … We acted in seven films. Sanjeevji was basically a lonely man. He was destined not to marry. I firmly believe that marriages are made in heaven and Sanjeevji's marriage was not destined to be. I have never loved anyone as much as him. At the time I was involved with him, his doctor told me, 'Don't care so much for this man, I give him just two years to live.' But what can you do when your heart is involved?[17]

Hari and Sulakshana had a common friend in Sardar Kulwant Singh Kohli, owner of the Pritam restaurant in Mumbai. True to

17 https://www.bollywoodshaadis.com/articles/sulakshana-pandit-love-for-sanjeev-kumar-8566

her name, Sulakshana was very attractive, highly accomplished and cultured. She was also extremely hardworking. She had been singing since the age of nine. Her father, Pratap Narain Pandit, died on the day of her very first stage performance. But even after she heard the news, she insisted on finishing her performance before proceeding to pay her last respects to her father. 'He would never want me to abandon my singing or my audience,' she said.

After the death of Sulakshana's father, Kulwantji supported the family. She was both talented and hardworking and took the responsibility of being an anchor to her family. She had proved her vocal genius, singing duets with celebrated singers like Lata Mangeshkar, Kishore Kumar, Mohammed Rafi, Shailendra and Yesudas. She had a reputation as an actor-singer and had a promising career.

Hari was fully aware of her affection. Hence, after his first heart attack, he sent a message to Sulakshana through Kohli, 'No man in my family has lived beyond the age of fifty. My first heart attack has already come—death has sent me a message. You will suffer if you marry me.'

'But Sulakshana waited. Unrequited love, that is sincere and true, is not something that we see only in films. We all saw it in Sulakshana's devotion to Hari. But Hari did not want to burden Sulakshana and abandon her as a consequence of his heart disease,' says Kohli in his self-published book *Ye Hai Mumbai Meri Jaan*.[18]

---

18 The Marathi book, *Yeh Hai Mumbai Meri Jaan!* consists of written work and narrations by Kulwant Singh Kohli and has been penned by Prof. Nitin Arekar.

RJ Anirudh Chawla, who has also interviewed Sulakshana Pandit, says:

> During our interview for AIR in 1999, she was extremely emotional. She started crying during the interview. She told me that every time she was asked to sing a song that was about broken hearts, it would tug at her heartstrings and remind her of Hari. I could understand her emotion—whether it was '*Bandhi re kaahi preet, piya ke sang, anjaane mein*' for *Sankoch* or '*Maana teri nazar mein, tera pyaar hum nahin*' in *Ahista Ahista*, the emotion in the songs made her eyes well up with tears.
>
> We had to take unscheduled breaks during the airing of the programme. I remember playing '*Apne jeevan ki uljhan ko kaise main suljhaoon?*' and taking a moment to calm her.

Hari was genuinely appreciative of Sulakshana in more ways than one. In a 1980 interview with *Stardust*'s Indira Albuquerque, Hari said, 'I don't think I'm irritated at all by Sulakshana. In fact, I appreciate her frankness in the entire matter. At least, she hasn't, like other girls, tried to make it out as if I am madly and badly in love with her.'

While having the grace to admit that he was attracted to her, Hari clarified: 'I suppose she has reached that age and stage where a girl has to think seriously of marriage and settling down. And thanks to STARDUST and the press, I have been made out to be a guy who is just dying to get married to anybody.'

Gayatri Patel added relevant context, 'During the days after my mother's death—we used to get daily tiffins for all the guests from Sulakshana's house. I knew about her, and Baa had told me about this "nice girl who had started coming home all the time". When Nikul used to go to return the tiffins, he would always joke, "I am going to my bhabhi's house". It was very understandable why Nutan, Hema and Sulakshana liked Baa so much. My mother was a kind soul and she knew how to make people comfortable.'

Hari was a different person each time with the ladies who won his heart. When he fell in love with Nutan, he was full of hope and he looked up to her. When the Hema episode happened, he was very successful himself and perhaps looked at her as an equal. By the time Sulakshana came into his life, he had given up on marriage.

Hari admitted that after Baa's death, the number of feminine callers was massive: 'As if I'd get a guilt complex and jump into an overnight marriage with them! As the saying goes, strike while the iron is hot, but the iron has never been as cold as it is now,' he said to Vijaya Irani of *Star & Style* for its December 1979 issue.

'Sulakshana was okay after my brother died. She was definitely upset but she was a strong woman and she had made peace with his death,' said Gayatri, who remembered meeting her at Hari's funeral. "I really loved your brother," she had told me. After Bhai's death, Sulakshana came to Houston for a show. I found out about it and went to see her show. I requested the people backstage to allow me to meet her. She was happy with the way her career was progressing and the opportunities she was getting. She hugged me warmly and said, "It feels like I got to hug Hari today. Hopefully we will get united in the next birth."'

Sulakshana Pandit's sister Vijayeta Pandit remembers meeting Gayatriben at the show in the US. She says, 'It wasn't just Gayatriji who was fond of Sulakshana. Baa, Kishore uncle (he made Sulakshana sing in Gujarati films) and Nikul (he made the film *Do Waqt Ki Roti* with her) also wanted Hari uncle to marry Sulakshana. Today, when I look back, I can confidently say that Hari uncle was afraid he would leave my sister a young widow. That's why he never married her.'

The two sisters live together today—Vijayeta lost her husband Adesh Shrivastava in 2015. Talking about what brought her sister and Hari close, she elaborates, 'Sulakshana and Hari uncle used to talk a lot. He would confide his heartbreaks to her and she would console him. Gradually, it developed into a very deep love.'

Vijayeta was barely eight years old when she witnessed their friendship. 'My parents loved Hari uncle too. When he came home, my mother who knew about his heart problem, would bless him and say "*Bhagwan tumhe lambi umar de*". We were vegetarians but my mother would organize mutton biryani for him from a specialist cook. He was shooting for *Sholay* at the time and he would regale us with stories from the sets.'

What about all the stories of heartbreak and depression? 'My sister was definitely heartbroken, but she gathered the courage to face life and the world again,' says Vijayeta. 'She wanted to focus on her singing career. Much later in life, she had a hip bone fracture that resulted in a few surgeries. Other than that, she is absolutely fine. She is like a mother to me and I'm privileged to take care of her. We live a simple life, enjoying music and films.'

An enduring memory she has of Hari is his laughter.

I was accompanying Sulakshana and Hari uncle to Kashmir for the shoot of *Uljhan*. Now, my sister was thirteen years older than me, but a completely innocent person. Hari uncle told me that he was going to pull her leg.

Hari uncle: Where's your boarding pass?

Sulakshana started panicking.

Hari uncle: Give it to me. Otherwise, how will we get out of the airport?

Sulakshana: I think I kept it in the seat pocket by mistake.

Sulakshana was petrified.

That's when Hari uncle and I started laughing and she realized what we were up to. Hari uncle was a great man and a great performer. What happened between him and my sister was just unfortunate. Hari uncle was the first and last man in my sister's life and her devotion to him is as astounding as it is inspiring.

6

Other Influences

There was a time in Hari's life, after the Nutan Samarth and Hema Malini episodes when he was looking for a mature friend. Suchitra Sen was this friend. She was someone who was known to ask directors to make changes in the script if she didn't like a particular scene or incident. They were also seen together in public, such as at a royal wedding alongside Maharani Gayatri Devi. They expressed a desire to work together.

Saba Mahmood Bashir's book *Gulzar's Aandhi* describes an incident:

> There's a story behind the selection of Suchitra Sen. J. Om Prakash, the producer, had called me [Gulzar] for a story, which he wanted me to direct. Written by Sachin Bhowmik, it was a thriller set in a hospital or something, and he said that we could cast Sanjeev and Suchitra, and Sanjeev was, in any case, very keen to work with her. So Sachin Bhowmik had written the story accordingly, keeping the two actors in mind. In that meeting, Sachin Bhowmik, Sanjeev and J. Om

> Prakash were all present. I didn't particularly like the story – it was ordinary, a typical Bambaiya plot. So, I said that it wouldn't be right to call Suchitra Sen all the way to Bombay to hear that story. Why should she do such a film? The first person in that room to react to my comment was Sachin Bhowmik. He said, 'You are right, absolutely right. This is Bombay, you can call many actors from here, but if you call Suchitra Sen, the story has to be something different.' When he said this, everyone else in the room agreed.[19]

Anju Mahendru remembers this period in Hari's life well. According to her:

> Hari evolved with time. During *Aandhi,* he met the very sagacious, sophisticated and self-assured Suchitra Sen. She was the antithesis of everything Hari was—he was a simple quiet man who put others first. He used to flow with the tide. But Suchitra Sen epitomized confidence! During the shoot of *Aandhi*, she was put up in Sun-n-Sand very close to my house. Her daughter Moon Moon Sen would hang around with us often, when Suchitra Sen used to be busy with the film's shoot.
>
> I am certain that though Hari never spoke to me about Suchitra Sen, she impacted him greatly and they formed a very deep friendship. He had never met any co-star as mature and infused with self-worth as she was. In her company, he too came of age and became more independent-minded and capable of taking care of himself.

19 Saba Mahmood Bashir, *Gulzar's Aandhi: Insights into the Film* (HarperCollins India, 2019).

7

What Friends Say

After 1975, Hari was both rich and successful and lived his life king size.

Anju Mahendru has an interesting insight into Hari's attitude towards women: 'Whenever Hari was serious about a woman, he would never belittle her. I knew he was not serious when he used to talk about women in numbers. There was a point when, whenever he was seeing a girl, he'd share the "number" with me. We had numbered his girlfriends 1, 2, 3 … He'd call up and say, "Number 1 called me up today and number 8 said this, etc."'

Friends Sharmila Tagore and Moushumi Chatterjee confirm that Hari's favourite topic of conversation was always the 'imaginary' planning of his own wedding.

However, there might have been more to this. Mac Mohan, his friend of twenty-five years, told *Silver Screen* magazine in November 1985, after Hari's death:

> People have this impression that Hari was not successful in his personal love life. I don't think so. It's just that he found it difficult to trust the women he met. He suspected that a woman would marry him for his money, that she would love Sanjeev Kumar the actor and not Hari Jariwala the man …
>
> Hari was basically not a womaniser but at one stage, he did indulge in a hell of a lot of womanising. Maybe he did it out of vengeance at those times when he felt frustrated in his love life. I never questioned him about his personal relationships, though I always knew who was his girl and so on. That's one thing he appreciated about me. Sometimes he himself would tell me about his girls, which I wouldn't want to discuss because it was too personal.

Moushumi Chatterjee, however, comes to his defence, 'Hari was not a womanizer at all. He was always very clear about his intentions. He had just made up his mind not to marry within the industry.'

Moushumi also talks about the many women who would send dabbas (food tiffins) for him to the sets, believing that the way to Hari's heart was through his stomach.

There were local suitors too, Jyoti says: 'In Marine Apartments, the building next to ours, there was a Christian girl who used to come home a lot. Her father had a garage which Bhai bought; that's how she first met Bhai. She was barely twenty-two when Bhai died; even after his death she kept coming home to commiserate. She was a very nice person and remained single all her life until her recent demise. There was also the lady in Bella Vista, another building close to ours. She was a very persistent stalker. If there was one person who got the worst of Baa's temper, it was this lady because she would either keep calling on the home phone or turn up and ring the doorbell, hoping to meet Bhai.'

Gayatri Patel remembered that Jayshree T., Nanda's sister-in-law, also liked Hari. Jayshree was candid when she spoke of the late Sanjeev Kumar. In an interview published in 2012 on Cineplot.com (republished from an interview with journalist Ranjeeta in 1999), she said:

> There was a big age gap between us. To me, he was a friend, philosopher and guide. I respected him a lot. Today I realise, it was more like puppy love from my side. We worked together in many films and he was, very nice to me. He was very fond of eating and would tell me to bring him home-cooked food. However, our association was blown out of proportion by the Press. A lot of stuff concerning us, was fabricated. We stopped reacting to it, after a point.[20]

Apparently, the entire issue began when a journalist asked Jayshree whether she would marry Sanjeev if he proposed to her, to which she responded, 'Yes, why not, he's such a nice person.' The next day, there was a huge hoarding which read, 'Jayshree T. wants to marry Sanjeev!'

Then there was the very classy Gujarati lady Pallavi Jaikishan, who, as many well-wishers were suggesting to Hari, was the right match for him. Pallavi's husband, music director Jaikishan Panchal of the duo Shankar–Jaikishan, had passed away in 1971. An article by Vijaya Irani in the *Star & Style* issue dated December

---

20 https://cineplot.com/jayshree-t-jayshree-talpade-interview/

1979, however, clarifies Hari's stand, 'I could only think of her as Jai's wife, a Bhabhi.'

Hari was by no means the only great artiste who remained single. One of India's most celebrated writers, Sagar Sarhadi, who died in 2021, has famously said in an interview, 'When I was young, I couldn't afford marriage. And by the time I began doing well for myself, I discovered that the institution of marriage didn't suit me.'[21]

Hollywood actor Hugh Grant has long professed his love for his single status. 'I'm not a great believer in marriage as an institution, or even in very long-term relationships. I'm not sure we're built that way.'

And perhaps the closest to Hari's ilk as a performer, Al Pacino, also single, has said in an interview with *The Independent*, 'Why I never proposed in the past? I hate to say this, but marriage is a state of mind, not a contract. When I think about the law and marriage, I ask myself, when did the cops get involved?'

As American Humourist Helen Rowland puts it, 'a bachelor never quite gets over the idea that he is a thing of beauty and a boy forever.'

21 Aditya Sharma, 'Sagar Sarhadi interview', Scroll.in, 13 May 2017; https://scroll.in/reel/837484/sagar-sarhadi-interview-if-we-stop-hoping-well-lose-our-will-to-live-and-work

8

Rationalizing His Singledom

Almost all of Hari's friends agree that he was an extremely sensitive person. One of his co-stars in both his Gujarati and Hindi films spoke in confidence about his fear of taking the marital plunge with some nostalgia. According to her:

> Hari's loneliness was his own creation. On the one hand, he wanted to settle, but on the other hand, he always found fault with the women he was considering for marriage. *'Jo ladki aati hai—mere naam ke liye aati hai, paise ke liye aati hai,'* he would lament. I would ask him one simple question—'You should've got married when you were a nobody. Why didn't you? No point complaining now about women getting attracted to your success.' The other thing I would ask him was where his wife would go away with his 'fame' and his 'money'. She would share in it and they would coexist. But he never listened. *Zindagi bhar akela raha*!

How much pain was Hari concealing under the convenient cloak of his 'sense of humour' and jovial nature?

Vithal C. Nadkarni had the good fortune of meeting Sanjeev Kumar at a few events, including a Filmfare Awards dinner. He remembers Hari as a jovial host and elaborates:

> The man I saw in the late '70s had already had his first heart attack—he was a shadow of the glittering presence I had seen on screen. But he was an immaculate performer and used to put on a bravura act for us at the award functions. He used to pat his chest gently and say, 'One has to be careful, na.'
>
> During dinner, he would slur to please us, as if drunk, but I sensed that that was part of his sly performance in which he could say anything once he established the 'fact' that he was inebriated. But the mischievous twinkle in his eyes gave it all away ... he also had a light touch, and of course a perfect sense of timing, traits which are so necessary for top-notch comedy.

Nadkarni, a learned man and a keen observer of human emotions, further adds:

> We journalists knew him as the actor who was crazy about Hema Malini. But I had a niggling hunch that Sanjeev Kumar might 'lose' to Dharmendra because of the differences in their respective temperaments. My uncle, Dr G.A. Nadkarni, who worked as a financial advisor to S.L. Kirloskar in Pune, had occasion to travel to Delhi in a first-class coupe with Dharmendra once, and he was full of praise for the man, as someone who personified the saying *'Atmaiva atmano bandhu'*

(the soul is the friend of the soul) from the Bhagvad Gita, as opposed to Sanjeev Kumar, who was over-sensitive to the point of being his own enemy (*'Atmeva riprutatmane'*). He seemed to be the quintessential good guy destined to bring up the rear!

'Bhai was sensitive,' adds Shabnam Sippy Pillai. 'At the end of the day, he was human. The smallest thing could upset him. But instead of bringing it up, he would withdraw into his shell and just smile. If someone hurt him, he would probably not work with them, but he would never lose his dignity by creating tamasha (a scene)! Only Jamnadasji and Sarosh Mody could see his anger and his venting or his deepest thoughts.'

Hari did have a temper, though. A co-star from Gujarati cinema recounts:

> I had a crush on Sanjeev when we were working on our film *Kalapi*. It was an innocent attraction. While discussing a particular scene, we seemed to have opposite points of view and we contradicted each other. Hari was upset. Unfortunately, on that day we had to shoot a romantic song. When the camera turned on, Hari was absolutely flawless. But the minute it turned off, he would disregard me [as if I was something] worse than a dead rat on the sets! I remember this incident, because he could neither get over his anger nor deal with the difference of opinion in a mature fashion.
>
> His irrational fear of being exploited by women led to tremendous personal frustration. We had a common friend named Asha who was a simple woman and not from the film industry. He was so prejudiced [against her] and irrationally

> scared of her that I realized the matter was much deeper than people realized.

Could this have been a case of self-sabotage? After a point, was Hari looking to find fault with women just so that he could say no?

Hari's relationship with Neeta Mehta is a case in point. Hari was serious about marrying her, going by an interview with *Stardust*'s Indu Albuquerque in March 1980. Hari and Neeta had worked together in films like *Yehi Hai Zindagi* (1977) and *Patthar Se Takkar* (1980). Neeta was a regular at Hari's events. Uday remembers the elders at home discussing the reason the marriage didn't happen. Neeta wanted Hari to separate from the rest of his family and to live with her. Perhaps that's why Hari confessed, 'It didn't work out. After some time, I realized that we were not really matched. Her ideas were different and I suppose I'm still too much of a conservative at heart. I don't know. I don't pause to analyse these things.'

Things ended badly. An article in the December 1979 issue of *Star & Style* says that Neeta did not even visit Hari when Baa died. Which begs the question, had Hari made 'unlucky in love' such a major part of his identity that he didn't want to let it go?

In the book *Manik and I*, Bijoya Ray writes:

> Sanjeev … had us [Manik and Bijoya] over to dinner at his house, where we met his mother, brother and sister-in-law. I realised that Sanjeev loved and respected his mother a great deal. Like all mothers, Sanjeev's mother too was keen that he get married, but since things hadn't worked out with the person he wanted to marry (I won't reveal her name), the

topic had been shelved for the time being. His mother was a nice, warm person, and kept asking us to persuade Sanjeev to get married. Sanjeev, of course, laughed it off. Had he married, he might have been alive today.

At this point, let us rest this chapter. You, the reader, must choose what to make of Hari's love life.

Courtesy of RJ Anirudh Chawla.

[At the Gulzar-Rakhee wedding in 1973, Hari was told to apply mehendi on Gulzar's hand as that would bring him luck and he would get married too. Just as he began to apply the mehendi, the photographer ran out of film and couldn't capture the moment.]

'That's always the story of my life. At the eleventh hour, something goes wrong.'

Sanjeev Kumar

Stardust, January 1975

SECTION V

Waxing, Wavering, Wandering

1

Stardom and Liquid Courage

Coming back to Hari's chronology of films, 1975 saw Hari at the pinnacle of success. But it was 1974 that had set the stage for it with Hari losing himself in his work and submitting to it, enjoying himself thoroughly.

Ten films featuring Hari were released in 1974, which has to be something of a record! But it isn't. In both 1977 and 1987, Dharmendra beat this by being seen in twelve movies in a single calendar year.[22] Among character actors, the late Amrish Puri had eighteen releases in the year 1989.[23]

Hari received appreciation for a nuanced role in *Aap Ki Kasam*. Another landmark film was *Naya Din Nayi Raat*, a remake of

---

22 https://www.imdb.com/name/nm0004429/

23 https://www.livemint.com/Leisure/n47yWjW7ntGx4RmNzyTMCL/Ten-actors-with-the-maximum-releases-in-a-year.html

Sivaji Ganesan's iconic *Navarathri* (1964). Few actors can lay claim to a performance as spectacular as Hari's in it!

There's an interesting story behind that film. When the famous writer-director pair A. Bhim Singh and A.P. Nagarajan decided to remake *Navarathri* in Hindi as *Naya Din Nayi Raat*, they had to find a lead actor who would play nine characters in the film. They first approached Dilip Kumar. To their surprise, Dilip Kumar suggested that there was only one person who could do this role—Sanjeev Kumar. Bhim Singh was shocked. Dilip Kumar was suggesting another actor? How could this be?

In February 1974, Bunny Reuben did an exhaustive article on Hari's nine-role enterprise in *Star & Style* magazine. Hari said in the article:

> I saw the Tamil film first about seven-eight years ago in 1966. At that time, I was shooting with Bhim Singh for *Gouri*, in which I was playing the second lead opposite Sunil Dutt and Nutan. I was inspired when I saw *Navarathri* but was pessimistic for I knew the assignment was out of my reach. I knew that they were planning to remake it in Hindi with Sunil Dutt in the lead. Being a comparative youngster at the time, I had no guts to tell Bhim-Bhai that I would love to play the role. Then the idea of remaking it with Sunil Dutt was shelved and in due course, I heard that they were planning to re-do it with Dilip Kumar. Again I was crestfallen. Little did I know that the project would be shelved and that seven years later, it would eventually come to me, with Bhim-Bhai at the directorial helm of affairs. That is luck!

When the film released, a lot of credit was also given to Sarosh Mody, Hari's personal make-up artist. Sarosh Mody had worked in Hollywood for many years before returning to India; he had done make-up for Bob Hope and many other illustrious American performers. Before his Hindi film assignments, Mody had worked in films like *North West Frontier*, *The Wind Cannot Read* and a few other Hollywood productions shot in India. Mody also did a short stint for *The Bridge on the River Kwai* in Sri Lanka. Speaking about his assignment for *Naya Din Nayi Raat*, in the same article, Mody had commented:

> In India, most of our leading men consider that the job of the make-up man is to prettify them. Very few actors desire to be made up to look the character they are playing. Sanjeev Kumar has always been an exception to the general run of actors. Not only does he insist on perfection in make-up, once he takes up a role, he is adept at losing himself in it and interpreting that role to perfection.
>
> … In this case [one of the nine roles, which was that of a leper] the most important thing I had to bear in mind was that he shouldn't look repulsive on the screen and thereby hurt the sensibilities of people in general and those unfortunates who do suffer from this disease in particular. It is easy to do grotesque or a fantastic make-up. The important thing here was to be realistic.

Deepak Javeri, son of Jamnadasji, remembers, 'My father was inundated with letters from doctors who treated leprosy patients, who complimented the make-up and the portrayal.' Was it that realistic?

Hari himself replied to this question: 'Realistic? Yes! Let me tell you what happened! When I was ready with the leper's make-up on, I came strolling out in the studio compound. There were several people there from outside. None of them recognized me. They all thought I was a real leper who had wandered into the studio grounds from outside. They all shrank from me and hurried away.'

The *Star & Style* article by Bunny Reuben also included remarks by Sarosh Mody on Hari's devotion to getting ready for his part:

> I always got the fullest time and patience from Sanjeev, he is the only hero I have worked with who doesn't object to appearing ugly on screen. For the leper's make-up, Sanjeev would sit quietly for hours. It would take two hours to put on and one hour to remove everyday. So much for effortlessness! Dilip Kumar graciously gave a voice-over at the beginning of the film, introducing Hari's performance and paid lavish tributes to the way in which Sanjeev Kumar interpreted each of the nine roles.

One thing that remained Hari's trademark was that he was a simple man with an 'infectious smile', whose only concern was how well he could play the role given. This is also highlighted in Ashok Raj's book *Hero Volume I*, in which the author says:

> His style was unassuming and had a spontaneity and warmth reminiscent of Motilal, Ashok Kumar and Balraj Sahni ... Sanjeev Kumar, like many other credible actors had a massive following among the viewers. There are two main reasons for his immense success. First, he arrived in

> the post classical period as the antithesis of the prevailing macho, glamorous and stylised hero and this he was easily recognisable as a down-to-earth character among the people. He looked far more familiar, the man next door, who did not need an introduction. In this sense, Sanjeev Kumar was the first to challenge the typical hero-centred basis of Hindi cinema and introduce a definite qualitative improvement in characterisations. Second, Sanjeev Kumar represented, in emotionally charged roles, an innate strength of the Indian personality—outwardly vulnerable and yet inwardly strong enough to face the harsh realities of life ...

Hari was the kind of person who would not react unnecessarily or create an uncomfortable situation with people. He was known to be an easy-going man. He told *Film World* in January 1975, 'Off screen I have a very wooden face. I do not react adversely to anything. I just take things as they come. Later, when I go home, I reflect on them. This habit of not reacting to provocative situations helps me a lot. I keep my peace and concentrate on my work. I have always been able to control myself. This way, I do not spoil the situation.'

Hari's demeanour would lead to people mistaking him for being laid-back. Uday recalls that when Nikul dropped in at Hari's sets occasionally, he was told by many people, 'He is so confident that he becomes laid-back.' Nothing could be further from the truth. Hari always underplayed his intense preparation for every role. Hari's keen observation, deep study of award-winning international cinema and excellent memory constituted the secret force behind his seemingly 'laid-back' performances. Moreover, as mentioned by Paresh Rawal in the foreword, and further substantiated by Sarosh Mody, Hari was extremely savvy when it came to make-up too.

There was some controversy about whether Raj Kapoor truly considered Hari to be a great actor, but this was really a war of words between two journalists, Bunny Reuben and Raju Bharathan. Raj Kapoor said to Bunny Reuben in *The Illustrated Weekly of India,* 15–21 August 1976 issue that Hari was ' … experimenting with this medium, trying to give it more depth and dimension than others are doing. But remember that he is functioning in an era fully conversant with cinema. There is a whole body of world cinema before him. Still, we must give him credit for the fact that he is taking the trouble to study this cinema.'

Raju Bharathan, in the October 1976 issue of *Star & Style* picked up this comment and wrote the essay 'Sanjeev Kumar – A Self-made Actor', citing Raj Kapoor's comments as a glib dismissal of Hari's talents. Bharathan wrote, ' … as if Raj's era was wholly unconversant with cinema!'

A hornets' nest had been stirred. Bunny Reuben used to write for many publications at the time. In a follow-up story for *Star & Style,* he questioned how Raj Kapoor's quote could be considered tantamount to a glib dismissal: 'Where does Raj deny Sanjeev his intrinsic merit and where does he say that Sanjeev is great only because there is a whole body of world cinema before him?'

In an article titled *'Sanjeev is trying to give more depth and dimension to the film-medium'* Bunny Reuben further wrote:

> Sanjeev and I have discussed the films and performances of the world's greatest actors such as Paul Muni, Sir Alec Guinness (that master of make-up), Sir Laurence Olivier

> and Sir John Gielgud and of those American actors Marlon Brando, George C Scott, the late Montgomery Clift and Alan Arkin among others. Sanjeev Kumar has seen the films of these world-famous actors. He has studied their work. He has read books by them, on them and about them. He has studied their make-up. He has studied all that is worth studying in respect of his profession. Last year just before his birthday, I happened to mention to Sanjeev that I had with me the original soundtrack of MGM's fulmination of Shakespeare's *Julius Caesar* – all those memorable speeches by Brando and Gielgud and James Mason. Sanjeev was so keen to have it that I simply gave it to him for his birthday as a present from me.

Hari was, of course, also compared with other actors of the day, like Rajesh Khanna, whose fame was at its dizzying peak. In Gautam Chintamani's book, *Dark Star: The Loneliness of being Rajesh Khanna,* writer Salim Khan recalls how, after he had given an interview hailing Sanjeev Kumar as one of the brightest actors, Kaka summoned him to Mehboob Studios and quizzed him about it. He demanded to know if Sanjeev Kumar was better than him. When Khan replied that it depended on the role, it did not go down well with Khanna.[24]

As his biographer, I spoke with several cine-goers of the 1970s to know what Hari's performances meant to them. Here are some of their responses:

'Sanjeev Kumar's entry scene in any film would be greeted with relief—that things would only get better from there.'

---

24 Gautam Chintamani, *Dark Star: The Loneliness of being Rajesh Khanna* (HarperCollins India, 2015).

'We felt that Sanjeev Kumar was the only actor who could stand up to the hero and own the scene.'

'*Sholay* was not just about Jay and Veeru, but also about Thakur and Gabbar.'

Hari's immense talent was only augmented by the fact that he was universally considered a 'good man'. He would do things for friends that weren't necessarily right for his career. When Shammi Kapoor ventured *Manoranjan,* a black comedy, Hari had no qualms about acting in it despite the fact that the film was a bit too ribald to be accepted at the time and the female protagonist was a prostitute. He also did a favour to Mahmood by playing a small part for him in *Kunwara Baap* in 1974.

2

The High of 1975

Hari had a whopping ten releases in 1975, out of which *Aandhi*, *Mausam* and *Sholay* each featured career-defining performances by him. As an actor Sanjeev Kumar rose to prominence—'Sanjeev Kumar' the superstar was already commanding a massive fan following. Close friend Subhash Sanas also testifies to his popularity, 'He had to find creative ways to leave his film sets because so many women would be waiting to meet him.' Hari was a successful actor and a much-loved star. And with this, three things follow—demand for interviews and magazine covers, endorsements and shows.

Hari graced innumerable covers of magazines in multiple languages—from *Star & Style* to *Filmfare*, from *Film World* to *Madhuri*, and *Cine Blitz* to *Mayapuri*. Hari's placement in the magazine covers and the contexts were versatile. He made it to magazine covers with different cohorts of people. There was the October 1976 issue of *Film World* in which he was featured as part of an 'acting trio' with Girish Karnad and Amol Palekar. He also featured in many Bengali magazines, thanks to being a favourite with Bengali directors Basu Bhattacharya (who was a loyal friend), Satyajit Ray and Hrishikesh Mukherjee, and with actresses Sharmila Tagore, Jaya Bhaduri, Suchitra Sen, Rakhee and Moushumi Chatterjee.

The second thing that came his way were endorsements. In an industry where stars were known to keep their personal life guarded and their public image squeaky clean, Hari never hesitated to endorse what he loved. Commercial brand ambassadorships for Bagpiper whisky (he was the first ambassador for the brand and the money he received was donated to a school in Neol near Surat), Wills 'superstar' cigarettes and Berkeley cigarettes were some of the popular products he endorsed.

Hari was always willing to put his best foot forward for a good cause and would make sure to support UNICEF. In a torn clipping preserved in the family archives, there's a picture of Hari, Hema Malini, Shashi Kapoor and Sharmila Tagore attending a UNICEF function for the sale of greeting cards alongside Nawab Ali Yavar Jung Bahadur, the then governor of Maharashtra, at Raj Bhavan, in the mid-1970s.

The third thing that came his way were international shows, especially in the US, which were lucrative. Uday recollects, 'Every summer, Dada would do a unique stage show that he had perfected—it was a mimicry act, featuring him and a few singers. He would repeat his [well-known] dialogues [from films] and intersperse them with songs. He had also developed this specific solo act, putting on different voices. Thanks to his theatre days, there was nothing he loved more than a live audience. These shows were in foreign locations such as Toronto, London, New

York, Chicago, Florida and Los Angeles. Baa was a constant companion to Sanjeev Dada during these shows. When I was grown up enough to manage myself without help, I joined Dada's travel entourage. I vividly remember the organizer of the shows—we used to call him Mr Coca-Cola—he was a very entertaining, roly-poly Sindhi guy.'

One of Hari's favourite places to visit was Los Angeles, where he would stay with a Parsi lady, Aloo Vaghaiwala, and her husband. Vaghaiwala would cook chicken dhansak and fish patia. All over the world, fans, families and tour organizers used to host Hari, treating him with expensive alcohol and delicious food.

The year 1975 also witnessed the release of Ravi Tandon's *Apne Rang Hazaar*, Raghunath Jhalani's *Uljhan*, Shankar Mukherjee's *Faraar* and J. Om Prakash's *Aakraman*. It is believed that *Uljhan* was to feature Jaya Bachchan and later Zarina Wahab; however, it was Hari who recommended Sulakshana Pandit for the role. *Faraar* with Bachchan also did well but suffered under the shadow of *Sholay*'s stupendous success. *Aakraman* blended a love story amid the Indo-Pak war of 1971 and was Hari's first film with Rekha. There was also the Dharmendra-Reena Roy starrer *Apne Dushman,* directed by Kailash Bhandari; it was a remake of the 1967 Hollywood thriller *Wait Until Dark*.

It was a year that belonged to Hari. It was his most successful year as both a lead actor and a character actor. He was relentlessly in the news—whether it was for his break-up with Hema, the *Aandhi* ban, his performance as Thakur in *Sholay* and why he and Hema did not have even a single scene together in the film, or the media speculating on his marriage. There was never a dull moment.

Several years later, in 2013, when screenwriters Javed Akhtar and Salim Khan came together at the *Sholay* 3D trailer launch, they were asked about who would be the ideal cast for *Sholay* from among the current generation. Salim Khan, an old friend of Hari's, said, 'It's difficult to get the ideal star cast. If you find two boys, you still cannot find Sanjeev Kumar. Somehow, if you find a Sanjeev Kumar, who will play Gabbar? The combination in *Sholay* was unbelievable.'

Hari seemed invincible. Except to God.

3

The Forces of Nature

Every actor has that one big film, the big magnum opus that defines his or her career, a classic larger-than-life movie. Guru Dutt had *Pyaasa*, Dev Anand had *Guide* and Dilip Kumar had *Mughal-E-Azam*. However, such an all-encompassing cinematic achievement was not to come to fruition in Hari's case. The December 1985 issue of *Showtime* talks about Hari's promising film, *Love and God*. According to the magazine, in 1962, flush with the success of *Mughal-E-Azam*, K. Asif had announced his version of *Laila Majnu*.

Love and God was an ambitious project in the mould of *Mughal-E-Azam*, with Guru Dutt in the lead. But in 1964, Guru Dutt died after only twelve reels for the film had been shot. Six months later, Asif sahab decided to cast Hari as Majnu (the lead role). Hari was already playing the villain in Asif sahab's *Sasta Khoon Mehenga Paani*, starring Rajendra Kumar and Saira Bano, which also remained incomplete. During the shooting of this film, Asif sahab felt that Hari's eyes were quite similar to Guru Dutt's. He put Hari on a diet to lose weight so that they could do a photo session. Cine-goers had noticed that Hari had an unmistakable bulge in the middle in the film *Aashirwad* (1968), and Asif sahab was determined to trim Hari back to size. He was the first ever to visualize that Hari could be a main solo lead in a blockbuster film!

Death struck again when Asif sahab died in Hari's house in March 1971. His last words to Hari, as quoted in *Star & Style* magazine's May 1986 issue, were to finish his unfinished work. Legal complications followed. It took some time for Akhtar Asif—Asif sahab's second wife—to take over the film. In 1975, Dubai-based businessman Abdul Wassim put in some money. But in 1976, Hari was hospitalized. By the time Hari was finally able to shoot, cast members Jayant and Nazir Hussain had died. Hari was also by now a plumper version of Majnu, and actors Pran and Nimmi had aged. Amjad Khan was substantially wider in girth too. In 1985, filmmaker K.C. Bokadia infused some money into the film. It coincided with Hari's return from the US after his cardiac surgery. He had lost all his excess weight and tried his best to help. It is tragic that with just a climax song and few linking sequences left to complete the film (as reported in *Showtime*, December 1985 issue), Hari passed away. By the time the film released in 1986, it was a classic case of too many cooks spoiling the broth.

Would things have been different if *Love and God* had released in the early 1970s? Filmmaker Yash Chopra famously remarked in the October 1976 issue of *Film World* about Hari's performance in *Sholay*, 'Sanjeev's performance is great, simply great. But what's the use? He doesn't sell on his own steam. You have to present him with one of the top three, Rajesh, Dharam or Amitabh. These are the only three heroes with star status that the distributors buy.' But when Satyajit Ray made his first Hindi film—*Shatranj Ke Khilari* (1977)—he chose Hari. The filming of this and a couple of other projects was postponed because of Hari's health.

Directors like Ray clearly believed that there were some roles that only Hari could do justice to. Friends like B.R. Chopra showed their faith by offering Hari films like *Pati Patni Aur Woh* (1978), where his comic timing was absolutely priceless. Hari remained a choice, and sometimes the only choice, for complex roles. He was also the only replacement imagined when a role was originally offered to Dilip Kumar, as in the case of his role in *Trishul* (1978). Uday had accompanied Hari to the premiere. It was Dilip Kumar who pulled Hari aside and asked him, 'How did you do this role? What a wonderful job you have done! Nobody else could've done this.'

The August 1979 cover story of *Star & Style* featured Amitabh Bachchan, Shatrughan Sinha and Sanjeev Kumar—about how they had broken the 'Punjabi barrier' to become successful leading men in Hindi films. Hari's earnest gaze on the cover would confound anyone who had a 'set' notion of what a 'hero' should look like. Hari also benefited immensely in the industry because of his good nature. *Surya India* magazine's 1979 issue talks about Basu Bhattacharya replacing Uttam Kumar (the article seems to indicate that he was high-handed) with Hari during the shooting of *Griha Pravesh*. The article says, 'Basu threw out Uttam Kumar from his film and signed Sanjeev Kumar in spite of the fact that he had already spent all his money.' It seemed that despite a challenging personal life, Hari was on excellent professional terms with everyone.

Another attribute of Hari's, not openly discussed, was that he was absolutely brilliant at networking. 'Bhai had friends in every part of the world. Also, his friends responded to him with genuineness. He knew how to maintain relationships. This made his life richer and fuller,' says Jyoti.

Hari's global connections were quite powerful. Uday elaborates on Hari's networks: 'Dada and I were travelling to the US—this was 1981—for one of his shows. We had a layover at London. A very famous lawyer, who was Dada's friend, came and took us to his home. We showered, changed, ate, and then boarded our flight to the US. I remember distinctly that our passports were not stamped with a UK visa. I have no idea how he managed this!'

Uday recalls that the late chief minister of the state of Maharashtra, Vilasrao Deshmukh, was also a friend of Hari's. In the 1980s, Deshmukh was rising up the ranks in the Maharashtra government. On one occasion, Deshmukh had invited Hari to inaugurate a government department. However, Hari was two hours late! Luckily, Deshmukh was familiar with Hari's reputation and had already prepared to wait while keeping himself busy. Over time, they became close friends. Actor and politician Sunil Dutt was a very ardent well-wisher too. In fact, Dutt sahab was convinced that with all the love Hari had, he would make for an excellent candidate for the Congress and even offered him a ticket to become an MP.

Hari also had a taste for the good things in life. At his peak, he showed a natural appreciation for luxury, such as his special brand of Philip Morris or 555 cigarettes, which he guarded quite zealously. He would unfailingly get caviar for Shammi Kapoor on his trips abroad. Hari also had an order-on-demand lifestyle. Jyoti remembers that there was a Sindhi supplier who would provide him chocolates, cheese, alcohol and cigarettes regularly. Imported goods were not so common back then, and whatever the children wanted would appear pronto! Jamnadasji used to settle the accounts monthly. Hari's collection of timeless Hollywood classics was also legendary. He would get them on his trips abroad, and everyone from Yash Chopra to Rishi Kapoor and Ravi Tandon to Shatrughan Sinha would borrow his tapes.

Hari also didn't like to get bogged down by any kind of pressure. It was his nature to forget about the setbacks and set his aims higher, engrossing himself in chasing a new goal. While he remained down to earth at heart, he knew how to walk the talk of stardom. After his surgery, Uday and Hari proceeded to New York, where they stayed at Sushil Malhotra's (Vinod Mehra's friend) house. 'Dada got some elegant tuxedos made on Fifth Avenue, as he had lost a lot of weight after surgery and wanted to look good on his return,' remembers Uday.

He could also manifest the impossible. While recuperating in the hospital, Hari managed to bribe a nurse to get him a cigarette. How the nurse agreed to such inducement is purely left to the reader's imagination!

Uday also remembers going to Canada with Hari. 'We were picked up, hosted well and taken around—all by foreigners. During the trip, I fell sick and had to be hospitalized. There were folks around Sanjeev Dada who oversaw my entire treatment, they treated us like family,' says Uday, who was stupefied to see how everyone waited on Hari.

Hari also knew how to make people feel special. Kadir Pirzada, former mayor of Surat, recalls, 'My friend from Surat, Ashok Patel, and I visited Sanjeevji in Mumbai when he was dubbing for *Qatl* at Prakash Mehra's dubbing theatre, near Kings Hotel in Juhu. When he saw us, Sanjeevji wrapped up quickly and made time to take us around. He would never forget how during his many trips to Surat, Ashok Patel and his wife Sheela used to host him at their house. He would feast on Surti delicacies like handwa, dhokla, ponk and surti ghari during his stay there and tell us about Chandravadan Bhatt, the man who gave him a break in Gujarati theatre.

The charmed life of Hari's stardom is actually best validated by his fans. Hoards of them just wanted a peek of the man! Crowds outside the Perrin Villa gate at 1 p.m. every day was a common sight. The watchman and the drivers would be in great demand for a tip or a confirmatory nod to indicate that Hari was expected to leave within the next fifteen or twenty minutes.

Just a glimpse of him was enough!

4

Well-Deserved Recognition

BY KADIR PIRZADA

When Sanjeev Kumarji won the National Awards for *Dastak* in 1971 and for *Koshish* in 1973, I was a councillor in Surat Municipal Corporation (SMC). Later in 1976, I started serving as chairman of the social welfare committee. During this time, Sanjeevji's graph was rising continuously with hits like *Sholay*, *Mausam* and *Aandhi*.

I was very keen that SMC and the Gujarat government honour him for his achievements. I knew that Sanjeevji used to stay at Moti Sheri, in a house that belonged to his father, whenever he visited Surat. So I approached his neighbour, Prof. Ishwarbhai Jariwala. The gentleman professor was in touch with him and was kind enough to seek a meeting with him for me. Both of us went by road to Mumbai.

When we finally met Sanjeevji, I said, 'We want to honour you. Both the home minister and the information and broadcasting minister of Gujarat will also be present at this ceremony.' Sanjeevji gave us a date, 'Let's keep the function on 9 October. I will ask either Dilip Kumar sahab or Raj Kapoor sahab to come along.' He paused again and added, 'Dilip Kumar was just part of a function honouring me at Shanmukhananda Hall, Mumbai. I think Raj Kapoorji will agree to come along.'

After a few days, we went to meet Rajji, who was extremely hospitable. He agreed warmly and said, 'When you're going to honour Sanjeev, I will be there with Krishnaji.'

We processed all the work needed to pull off this function and, on 9 October 1977, we honoured Sanjeevji at a robust function at the Rang Upvan theatre to a packed audience. The entire coordination was done with Jamnadasji, his PA, who was very reliable and always answered the phone in Haribhai's office.

The mayor had given me a budget for the function, and we booked Sanjeevji and the rest on the Western Express Deluxe train. There weren't any good hotels in Surat in those days, and so we had them stay in the guest house of Sangaramsinh Gaekwad Maharaj, the owner of Baroda Rayon. They stayed in three rooms in the guest house—one for Raj Kapoor's uncle, who came along, one for the couple and one for Sanjeevji. The video of the function is not available, but I still have the photographs. After the function was over, all of them sat down to drink, and it was four in the morning when they ate.

After the event, we both stayed in touch. He would take me to many places in his green Volkswagen like Mehboob Studio, Bandstand, Carter Road and, finally, Gazebo. I was a teetotaller, but he would drink for a long time. His lineage was originally from the Patidar community in Bardoli, which was about a thirty-minute drive from Surat. He had invited me to his cousin's wedding there. It was a very hot area, and in those days we did not have many comfortable AC halls. We were there for two to three hours and enjoyed the food.

I have travelled with Sanjeevji to Niyol (about 4 km from Surat), where he had agricultural land. Every year, he had to pay revenue tax, and the officials used to give him a printout. Sanjeevji used to ask me to accompany him; we would meet the caretakers and spend some time at the farm.

Land, property etc., meant nothing to him; he never rented anything out or tried to maximize his income. He invested in a Bangalore hotel just because someone told him to. He wasn't a smart investor. In Mumbai also, people used to spend his money.

In 1982, when I got married, he stayed with me for a few days for the wedding in Surat. He said to me, 'I have everything, *lekin mera hai kaun?*'

When I encouraged him to find a companion, he would say, '*Jo main chahta hoon, woh ho nahin sakta. Jo doosre chahte hain, woh main kar nahin sakta.*'

This was extremely touching for me because Sanjeevji was blessed with crores of fans. *Log marte they unke peechche* (fans were crazy about him).

Sanjeevji was an emotional person who responded to his friends with great sincerity. I was continuously worried about his health. After 1983, his health deteriorated. He went for his heart treatment in the US, but unfortunately, he died on 6 November 1985. It felt like a personal loss to me. His funeral was a very moving experience because of the sincerity with which people were crying. Both Jayshree T. and Sulakshana Pandit were there.

Amitabh Bachchan, Shatrughan Sinha, Jeetendra and Shammi Kapoor were also there.

All his co-stars, except Dharmendra, were there. He loved his brother Nikul's children like his own. He was particularly fond of Uday.

After his demise, when I became the mayor of Surat in 1988, I approached his Jamnadasji again. I said to him, 'I want to make Sanjeevji's name immortal and build a Sanjeev Kumar Road. Sunil Dutt sahab is our party MP and was a great friend of Sanjeevji, we can ask him to inaugurate it.'

Sunil Dutt sahab agreed immediately, and we inaugurated this road at the same auditorium where we had honoured Sanjeevji so many years ago. We also bought a medical van and called it 'Sanjeev Kumar medical van'—it was Dutt sahab's idea.

In 2001, when the BJP government came to power in Gujarat, I suggested that we should build an auditorium in his name. Fortunately, this also came true, and what a grand auditorium it is! A postage stamp bearing his picture was also released by the Indian Postal Service on 3 May 2013 to honour him.

I am very fortunate that not only did I get to know Sanjeevji in my lifetime, but also that I could contribute in my own small way to make his name live forever.

'All my tensions disappear when I come to visit Shammi [Kapoor]. I'm so much at ease ... whenever I come here, I realize that it's not necessary to stop eating and start reducing.'

Sanjeev Kumar

Stardust, January 1975

SECTION VI

Tales of Friendship

1

A Loyal Friend

Hari's friendship was highly coveted. Talking abou one cannot neglect to mention Subhash Indori— as Uday Jariwala remembers, everyone dismissed as 'ch Jyoti Jariwala, however, endorses the need for Subhas in Hari's life. 'Bhai needed some company to unwind, does,' she says.

While most people tended to dismiss Indori's friend Hari as sycophancy or even parasitic behaviour, Shatrug firmly believes that Subhash Indori's friendship was im Hari in its own way. 'Indori gave Sanjeev Bhai his tim easy,' says Sinha.

Indori, on his part, has always praised Hari's gene dependability:

> Here's an example of his sincerity. The producer of wanted to complete the dubbing of his film. Sanjee

> catch a 1.30 noon flight to Los Angeles the next day for a one-month shooting spell for Jagmohan Mundhra's *Suraag*. That evening, Sanjeev packed his bags. He was up at dawn the next day. He went and dubbed for Beraham until noon and went directly to the airport to catch the flight. And despite his poor health he completed his work for other producers by working around the clock before leaving for Los Angeles. Which other actor would be so considerate? He will harm himself just to safeguard other people's interest.

Hari gifted Indori a Volkswagen, but that was not surprising at all, given his generosity. Uday Jariwala recollects that Sanjeev Kumar also had a protective side to him. Jamnadas had told Uday that when Leena Chandavarkar, his *Manchali* co-star, was going to meet Kishore Kumar, who was known to be a little flirtatious, Hari said in jest, 'Take a rakhi with you.' Even as Hari laughed, the message was conveyed.

Magazine reports from the 1970s reveal that Hari was very fond of Jaya Bhaduri. *Filmfare*, in its January 1978 issue, quotes him as saying:

> Jaya has always been my favourite. I've always enjoyed working with her. From the first day, we established a certain rapport. Over the years we became very friendly. I didn't treat her like a star. The same kind of relationship I had with Tanuja. We were very close. During the 'Tanuja years' I enjoyed working with her. But comparing Tanu and Jaya—Tanu is an extrovert, outspoken bindaas. Jaya is much more

gentle, feminine, fragile. They were two of the best actresses I ever worked with.

Jaya Bhaduri was easily one of Hari's most important co-stars, and it seemed that Hari's fascination for the simple kurta pyjama hooked her too. In her memoir *A Patchwork Quilt*, director Sai Paranjpye takes note of this. She writes that when she went to Sanjeev Kumar's house to narrate the story of her film *Sparsh*, he was wearing an orange silk lungi and kurta. (He didn't do the film, eventually. Naseeruddin Shah got the role.)[25]

Sanjeev Kumar was seen in silk lungi-kurtas often in his films, and in at least two of those films, the heroines wore them too. In *Anamika* (1973), Kumar plays a writer who favours this combination at home. He gives shelter to a mysterious young woman Anamika (Jaya Bhaduri), who, since she doesn't have clothes of her own, wears his silk lungi-kurtas, even trying to seduce him in an orange kurta and yellow lungi while singing the come-hither number '*Baahon mein chale aao*'. But the silk lungi-kurta combination worked. In *Pati Patni Aur Woh* (1978), both Sanjeev Kumar and Vidya Sinha (who play husband and wife) wear it at home. We see Kumar in a bright orange lungi-kurta (clearly a favourite colour) and Sinha in a shimmery maroon silk kurta with matching lungi.

Jaya Bhaduri was also very fond of Hari and reciprocated his warmth. In February 2016, when the team of *Sholay* came together forty years later to launch Hema Malini's new album, *Dream Girl*, Jaya Bachchan was quick to say to the media, 'I am missing Haribhai and Amjad Khan today.'

---

25 Sai Paranjpye, *A Patchwork Quilt: A Collage of My Creative Life* (HarperCollins India, 2020).

Uday remembers an incident involving Jaya's husband, superstar Amitabh Bachchan, too. 'I had accompanied Sanjeev Dada to the shooting of *Khud-Daar*. It was during the shoot that one day, Amitabh Bachchan had knocked on Dada's door. I ran to open it and was both surprised and happy to see him. Over the course of their conversation, Amitji convinced Sanjeev Dada to do *Silsila*. He had said no to Yash Chopra, but he could not refuse Amitji.'

Age was no bar when it came to friendship for Hari. Uday, who accompanied Hari to the shoot of *Vidhaata* in Ooty with Shammi Kapoor, says: 'They got along like a house on fire and thoroughly enjoyed their food and drink.'

Co-stars fondly remember that when the director said 'cut', Hari would say, '*Chalo, chalo, patte baanto*' (lets deal the cards). Hari enjoyed playing cards, and he also liked to keep the environment around him free of unnecessary tensions. He was carefree in that sense. Amit Divatia adds, 'Hari's generosity and gratitude towards those who helped him when he was a struggler never waned. Over time, his status in life changed, but as a human being, he was always humble and approachable. In 1972, Hari was already an established actor and was in great demand. At the time, Chandravadan Bhatt was preparing for the play *Didi* to commemorate his twenty-five years in theatre. He hesitatingly asked Hari, who was by then a star, "Will you act in it?" Without batting an eyelid, Hari agreed. He also helped others with no desire for personal gain whatsoever.'

In the next few pages, there are some essays and conversations with Hari's closest friends who continue to miss him to this day—a glimpse into the man through those who knew him best.

2

Sachin Pilgaonkar

Director Ramesh Sippy sahab wanted Haribhai for the role of Thakur in *Sholay*. But Haribhai told him, 'I will do Gabbar's role. You take Pran sahab for Thakur's role.' During subsequent discussions, they surmised that Pran sahab had done several such strong character roles. The lead roles were also signed when Dharamji and Amitji were signed as Veeru and Jai respectively. Everyone agreed that nobody could play Thakur like Haribhai could.

An Ageless Friendship

Haribhai and I have had the most unusual relationship. He was my friend, philosopher and guide. I used to be known as Master Sachin in those days and was one of the prominent child actors in cinema. I made my debut at the age of four and a half with the Marathi film *Ha Majha Marg Ekla* in 1963, which won me a National Award.

My meeting with Haribhai came shortly after, by a stroke of coincidence. The great Homi Wadia (we used to call him Homi Seth), who was famous for his stunt films like *Hunterwali* featuring Fearless Nadia, selected me for a role. I was approached for a pivotal role in the third franchise of the film, *Zimbo Ka Beta* (1966), I played Zimbo's son. (Homi Wadia made a series of films on Zimbo, a suitably Indianized Tarzan-like character). The mahurat for this film was at ten in the morning.

As it happened, the same banner was making another film by the name of *Nishan*. It featured Haribhai in a double role and Prem Chopra as the villain. The mahurat for that was at around 11.30 a.m on the same day. So we were on the same premises around the same time, and that's how I met him first. I was all of seven years old, and he was in his late twenties. Quite an age gap there! But I was struck by his warm smile. Over time, I got to know more about him; that he was a Gujarati actor and had also done theatre and had had his fair share of struggles. Back then, theatre had immense gravitas; some very illustrious names, both his seniors and his contemporaries, were from theatre.

Haribhai belonged to the stage! His first role in theatre was apparently that of Shaukat aunty's [Shaukat Azmi, Shabana Azmi's mother] husband. For some reason, he was continuously getting roles in which he had to play an old man. This probably made him worry about getting typecast.

Together we did *Bachpan* in 1970, in which Tanuja aunty also featured. This was the time when there was some talk of the remake of my first film *Ha Majha Marg Ekla*, inspired by Charlie Chaplin's *The Kid*. The storyline was thus: a child strikes a friendship with a drunkard who begins to take care of him, but certain events put their relationship in jeopardy. Haribhai was offered the part of the drunkard, and hence wanted to see the original film. After he watched it, Haribhai said, 'Sorry, this cannot be remade. Which kid will be able to do Sachin's role?'

Haribhai had a big heart and never hesitated to praise others. He came to my house straight from the preview theatre in Pali Hill after watching *Ha Majha Marg Ekla* and knocked on my door. My father opened the door. I must have been around thirteen when this happened. By now, Haribhai was becoming a well-known name in Hindi cinema. When he saw me, he was overwhelmed with joy and took my autograph. 'How did you do this role,' he asked? I shared my method with him, innocently. From that day onwards, his approach towards me changed completely. 'You may be having a lot of fans, but I'm your biggest fan,' Haribhai said. I was deeply touched.

That's how our friendship started. He used to call me 'Chachin' and gave me my first Nepali topi—an accessory he was very fond of. Through my adolescence and adulthood, I kept working, getting some big successes as a young hero with *Geet Gaata Chal* (1975) and *Balika Badhu* (1976). Haribhai also rose to become a distinguished name in the film industry. I started visiting his home and met Baa.

Haribhai made many genuine admirers and was always generous with references. He always believed in giving people a chance. During the casting of *Sholay*, Danny Denzongpa was signed on to play Gabbar. However, there was a date clash, and Danny had to opt out as he was committed to Feroz Khan's *Dharmatma*.

When Ramesh Sippy sahab asked Haribhai to recommend someone for the Gabbar role in *Sholay,* Haribhai suggested Amjad Khan, who was a sincere young man and very active in dramatics at the National College in Bandra. The rest, as they say, is history. Haribhai was quite close to Amjad Khan, as the latter was an assistant in the direction department of K. Asif's (lovingly called Asif sahab by all of us) dream project, *Love and God*, in which Haribhai had stepped into Guru Dutt's role.

The friendship between us remained strong through the years. I was witness to his phenomenal rise to stardom. Haribhai definitely did not have the same joie de vivre after he started getting his heart attacks. But he remained a fiercely loyal friend. When my father passed away in 1983, Haribhai was one of the first to come home. When Supriya and I got married in December 1985, we had two pictures on either side of the stage during our reception; one was that of Haribhai, and one was that of my father. Such was his place in my life!

I think Haribhai had a premonition that he wouldn't be able to attend our wedding. Supriya and I had been working together before our marriage too. I had directed her in her debut film *Navri Mile Navryala* in 1984. She had delivered a superlative performance and was all set to win her first Filmfare Award. When Haribhai returned from his open-heart surgery at the Texas Heart Institute in February 1985, the Filmfare Awards team was trying to rope him in to attend the function. He refused as he was not feeling well. But when Haribhai got to know that Supriya was winning the award; he came to the function just to give away her award. Eventually, people came to know why he had changed his decision. Haribhai was as true and loyal a friend as one could ever find. Even though I wasn't present at the function, I was deeply touched by his gesture.

Looking back, Haribhai went through a lot in his life. References to him as 'kanjoos' do not do justice to him at all, as he had a great generosity of spirit and spent carefully to help others. He remained a very helpful and appreciative person throughout his life. Was he insecure at times? Yes, but who isn't? More than that, I felt he was 'emotionally tired' at times. Would it have made a difference if he'd had a life partner and children of his own? Yes, of course. There's a void, a loneliness in your life, when you're alone.

He wasn't a gambler, but his poor eating and drinking routine grew like the chains of habit—becoming too tough to get rid of eventually.

3

Shabnam Sippy Pillai

Two things haunt me to this date!

I did not go to meet him on his last day—6 November 1985—despite his warning that I might not see him again. And that I could not go to the crematorium. We all see many deaths in our lifetimes, but I still grieve for Bhai.

When Bhai and Kapil Dev Won the World

I met Bhai as a rookie on the sets of my father, N.N. Sippy's film *Paras* (1971). He was about thirty-two years old, fifteen years my senior. My job was to wake him up and get him out of his room for the shot. I used to place my hand on his forehead to do that. During the lunch break, I would sneak a little bit of rice into Bhai's plate despite my father's instructions to the contrary. Papa did not want Bhai to eat rice and look bloated on screen. I would chuckle because Bhai didn't care at all about his appearance. He would walk around in shorts all day with no make-up and not care. But when it came to the character he was playing, he would devote himself zealously to it. Bhai believed that as long as he acted well, everything else would fall into place.

Bhai was a superstar with a massive female following. Everyone wanted to feed him, woo him and marry him. But my husband Prem Pillai and I would joke that Jamnadasji was his mother-in-law and Sarosh Mody, his wife!

I remember the time when Baa took him to Surat to see a few prospective brides. He came back open-mouthed! 'The women of Mumbai pale, both in boldness and capacity to enjoy alcohol, as compared to the women in Surat,' he remarked upon his return. Perhaps it was his way of saying that he was looking for someone more traditional.

It was normal for Bhai and me to meet with a warm hug. At the jubilee party of *Devata* (1978), journalist Devyani Chaubal must have noticed our camaraderie. She proceeded to insinuate that Bhai and I were having an affair. I was already a wife and mother by then. But we all sat together and had a hearty laugh. Bhai was a regular at home. He came over for paya and mangoes—his top favourites—whenever he felt like, and often brought a bottle of whisky with him. Another person who came with him often was Sachin Pilgaonkar. We were his young friends—both of us over fifteen years younger than Bhai. I remember that Sachin even wanted to get married on Bhai's birthday, 9 July, in the year 1985, but pushed it a bit because Bhai's health was not so good.

Bhai was known for throwing some really lavish parties. Two popular locations for him were Sea Rock hotel and Pritam. He was shooting for *Hero* with Subhash Ghai when he announced a party at Sea Rock. Everyone said they wouldn't come—India and

West Indies would be playing the World Cup finals that night. Then Bhai announced that he would arrange for the match to be shown on a large screen. Kapil Dev's team won that match! Some members of the cast and crew of *Hero* and close friends like Prem and I celebrated with Bhai that night, cheering loudly for India.

What will remain eternally etched in our minds is that Bhai was a colossal talent. The scene in *Devata* where he wants to reveal his identity to his daughter, but doesn't, has to be one of the finest moments in Indian cinema. His superstardom was unimaginable; he had come such a long way from his first film, *Hum Hindustani*, when he was working for a fee of Rs 35 per day. The director had Scotch-taped his ears behind because he felt they were jutting out. Bhai quietly obeyed. And he was magnanimous. It was Bhai who introduced the visually impaired music composer Ravindra Jain to my father—not because he wanted to show he was powerful, but because he had a genuine appreciation for Jain's talent and wanted to give him a break.

Bhai was also fond of cars. I travelled with him in his sports car once when he drove me back from Mahabaleshwar. I slept through the drive! His other car, an off-white Mercedes, was often used in the movies.

Our relationship was intensely personal; it thrived even when my father wasn't making films with him anymore. Prem and I worried about Bhai's health, his smoking and drinking habits. We knew that his sister Gayatri was also suffering from cancer. Nikul had already died, and Bhai had suffered three heart attacks! We used to try everything—scolding him, explaining to him, even threatening him! But he had a lot of unexpressed grief piled up inside. We were together even on his last night! So many memories came flooding in when I heard about his demise! It was Bhai who had consoled me when my mother had died in 1981 at the age of forty-seven. He had said, 'She was so young. This is no time for her to go.' But look at him! He went early too. I have so many complaints about Bhai. Why did he not give up smoking after his bypass?

When I finally reached his house on the afternoon of 6 November 1985, Sonu [Shatrughan Sinha] and I sat in Bhai's bedroom next to his body. I put my hand on his forehead, like I used to do earlier. This time, it was ice cold.

I still look up at the window on the second floor of Perrin Villa, and sometimes I see him there!

4

Shatrughan Sinha

To understand the legacy that Sanjeev Kumar has left behind, you have to understand a fundamental truth: actors are popular. That's what their profession entails. However, they do not always earn respect. Sanjeev Kumar earned the respect of his audiences and peers with his bold choices and stellar performances. He also earned the personal respect of those he interacted with, thanks to his simplicity and generosity.

Long Live Sanjeev Bhai

I graduated from FTII in 1967, and, like all hopefuls, my struggle to find work in Hindi cinema began. I was trying to meet good filmmakers and writers, hoping for the elusive break.

Luckily for me, a film that I had acted in as an FTII student, *And Unto the Void*, had made it to many an international film festival and was much appreciated. I would go from office to office, carrying the box with the showreel of the film, hoping that someone would see potential in me and offer me a role. After a few months of legwork, lady luck smiled unexpectedly—Raj Kapoor had seen the film at FTII and had mentioned it to others. Word spread that a lanky, talented FTII graduate, all of 55 kg, was looking for a break. Imagine my astonishment when I heard that Sanjeev Kumar was asking to see me. He asked his man Friday Jamnadasji to find out more, 'Who is this boy? Ask him to show me the film.'

Forsooth, I hastened to meet him, taking my showreel to the preview theatre he had asked me to come to. After watching it, he said gracefully, 'I have become an admirer of yours.' One of the leading actresses of our times, superstar Mumtaz, also watched it. I don't know how they managed it, but both seemed to have half a reel each and showed it to as many people as possible. If not for their kindness and generosity, my work would not have become so visible so quickly.

Sanjeev Bhai, as I called him throughout my life, was senior to me in every sense. He was a highly respected theatre actor and versatile film actor. I never knew him as Haribhai; he was already 'Sanjeev Kumar the star' when I was just a neophyte. He was always fikarmand (concerned) about me finding the right break as an actor, and I will always be grateful for that. Around that time, his film with Dilip Kumar, *Sunghursh*, had just released and was very much appreciated. It is one of my favourite films of Sanjeev Bhai's.

Our first film together was *Khilona*, which released in 1970. My role was that of the villain in it. I had the guidance of the director Chandan Vohra and support of the producer L.V. Prasad. Yet, I couldn't give a single shot in the first half because of the atmosphere around me and because the great Mumtaz was the heroine in the scene. I was nervous about my understanding of the character and the manner in which I would have to portray it. I thought they would pack me off. Then Mumtaz came forward and made me comfortable and at ease on the sets. She also said, 'Why don't you take inspiration from Haribhai, whom you have made your friend, philosopher and guide?' Sanjeev Bhai, like a guardian angel, supported me through those times. From that day began my journey of growth, going to a point where people started saying, 'Confidence, thy name is Shatrughan Sinha.'

His habit of coming late was legendary. Perhaps that's why I also started taking it easy on the sets. As the shooting progressed, L.V. Prasadji said, 'Shatru, you're also coming late, why don't you bring Sanjeev Kumar with you?' I readily agreed. I would go and fetch him up from his Pali Hill residence. He used to be sitting in his house, wearing a lungi and smoking. He would smoke a very high-quality cigarette and show me his secret technique of how not to inhale smoke all the way into the lungs.

To set the context of how late we would be, when the call time was 9.30 a.m. in Chembur at R.K Studios, I used to reach Sanjeev Bhai's house at 10 a.m. We would have chai, smoke and chat, and finally leave between 11.30 a.m. to 12 p.m. Upon reaching the sets, L.V. Prasadji would ask, 'What happened?'

'There was traffic in Mahim … or a tree fell on the road in Mahim … or a bus broke down in Mahim,' would be our response.

One day, L.V. Prasadji got tired of our standard 'dog ate my homework' excuses and requested us to at least invent a new place where the breakdowns were happening. He said, '*Roz roz situation nahi sudhaar sakte, toh kum se kum location toh badal sakte ho.'* We were red-faced but incorrigible! But despite the delays, Sanjeev Bhai was always prepared on the sets. He would hold back a little while rehearsing, but during the take, he would flow. I observed him—as to how he used to always know his lines by heart and recite them with flair. It was thanks to his, and of course Mumtaz's, encouragement that I was able to deliver a fine performance in *Khilona*.

When it came to his performance, he would execute his shots single-mindedly with no distraction at all. I don't remember a single occasion when he was lazy or disinterested in his work. But his real 'fun time' would begin after work, when he would bathe, wear his cream silk lungi and cream shirt and step out with his friends for dinner somewhere. He would normally proceed to this Chinese restaurant in Bandra owned by our own actor-filmmaker Sachin Pilgaonkar's friend and have several rounds of drinks and meals there and then some mauj masti! He would relax and stay back. The restaurant owner would never ask him to leave. You could call it gupshup or even the Sanjeev Kumar baithak—but it extended up to 4 or 5 a.m. The staff who used to wait back never complained because he was generous with tips. The same thing used to happen at my home too. The milkman would arrive at the time Sanjeev Bhai was leaving.

He shared a *'masti bhari muskurahat'* (disarming smile) with my mentor Atal Behari Vajpayee, who also happened to be an admirer of his. Perhaps the ultimate measure of this respect he commanded, if I could add tongue-in-cheek, was the massive number of fans he had amassed in the so-called underworld. People who were on parole would come to Gazebo restaurant on Linking Road in Bandra and sit there and say, 'We have come to meet Haribhai.' Having met their favourite star, they would go back to jail.

We share an important date in our lives. Sanjeev Bhai's birthday also became the day of my wedding anniversary. We had gone to seek Puttaparthi Sai Baba's blessings for the wedding, where we decided the date of our wedding to be 9 July. For many years afterwards, I used to host his birthday party along with my anniversary at Sun-n-Sand hotel.

When I heard Sanjeev Bhai was no more, I felt terribly lonely and disconsolate.

Poonam, my wife, was also distraught with grief. Sanjeev Bhai was the favourite uncle to our children Luv and Kush. His reticence to get hitched stemmed from doubts as to whether the lady would be kind to his mother; he also feared that she might perhaps love him just for his money and fame. Whenever I met him, he would share his private matters with me. As for his being surrounded by so-called 'chamchas', let me assure you that sycophants have their place in every celebrity's life. Every celebrity has trust issues of their own, and we need people who can give us unconditional time, who don't have early morning commitments and can give us company till 3 … 4 … 5 a.m. They leave their families to be with you; they don't ask you uncomfortable questions; they laugh with you; cry with you; spend time with you. How can you undermine their importance in your life?

As for Sanjeev Bhai's drinking, let's not forget that many people drink. I know of people who used to drink even more than he did! His health problem was genetic.

Like every relationship, ours had its share of misunderstandings. Once, he had been instigated by some cronies into believing that I had done something to hurt him. I got a sense of a burgeoning rift and started avoiding him. It is his greatness that he couldn't keep it that way. One day when we were shooting on the same premises, Sanjeev Bhai reached out. He called me to his table.

He asked me, 'Why did you do this?' I responded, 'Before I explain myself, how did you believe I could've done that?' And that was that! He hugged me and forgot about it. But I appreciate the fact that he was forthright with me and confronted the problem. On another occasion, when I wanted money for some urgent reasons, many close friends pretended to help, but none were actually forthcoming. Sanjeev Bhai promptly sent the money with Jamnadasji. When I asked about returning it with interest, he mentioned, 'I'm not a professional moneylender to charge interest, take it as a friend. If I need it, I will ask for it.'

Sanjeev Bhai's 'jeev' (life) was pure and exalted. I feel his hand on my head to date. Love, and long live Sanjeev Bhai!

5

Anju Mahendru

In the 1970s, Hari was extremely sought after by the womenfolk. With Shashi Kapoor already married, Vinod Khanna married in 1971, Kaka and Bachchan's marriage in 1973, and Jeetendra's marriage in 1974, Hari was the only successful bachelor left at the time. I introduced him to a Gujarati woman whose husband had passed away. She was very classy and wealthy. Somehow, that was not Hari; his comfort level was something else.

We first met at Ravi Tandon's wedding in May 1966. I was twenty then, and Hari was twenty-eight. I was part of a large group and was sitting with them. At our table, there was buzz about Hari and the fine work he was doing. So, I went over to him and asked him, 'May I have your autograph?'

He looked at me with a twinkle in his eyes … then started writing. He took so long that I had to tell him, 'I asked for your autograph. Hope you're not writing a love letter!'

We hit it off instantly, as Hari was just a simple, jovial guy! He happened to come home soon after. It was Raksha Bandhan day and my mother, Shanti Mahendru, decided to tie him a rakhi. We were truly taken in by his simplicity and honesty, and this was the beginning of a lifelong friendship. He used to come home and have dinner very often. He would place his own request for what special non-vegetarian dish he wished to eat—bhindi gosht was one of his favourites. But after two drinks, he would keep his mouth shut, not trusting himself to speak anymore. He would just nod or smile.

My grandfather Rai Bahadur Chunnilal owned Bombay Talkies and was also a partner in Filmistan Studios. He was the president of IMPPA for fifteen years. My mother was born into wealth. We had a huge British-style home with antiques, crystals and stunning artefacts. I think Hari was impressed and inspired to have his own home like ours someday. My mother used to deal in antiques. Hari loved buying them and keeping them all around his bed; he would buy them by the truckload! His home was very simple, and despite his success and acquisition of a home next to Chetan Anand's in Juhu, he lived in a rented place all his life.

In 1969, I started tying him a rakhi too. Once, I told him, 'Chal Hari, I'm not going to take anything stupid, give me a sari! He threw his briefcase at me, playfully. I thought I would make the most of it and hurriedly took a wad of money from his briefcase and ran gleefully down the stairs. When I reached the ground floor and looked up, Hari dangled my gold lighter at me from his balcony; to my dismay, I noticed that instead of picking up a Rs 100 bundle, I had picked a Rs 20 bundle! What a tragedy! Reluctantly, I had to go back and pick up the lighter, but

I refused to return the money I had taken. Something was better than nothing, I guess! On occasion, I would gift him colognes and cut-glass vases.

I was very close to him. We have done two films together, *Dastak* (1970), which released, and *Airhostess*, which didn't. All his secrets were safe with me because I was a sister and a buddy. The only women about whom he would be absolutely quiet were those he really liked or wanted to be in a serious relationship with. For instance, he never spoke to me about Hema or Nutan, even though there were so many media reports about them at the time.

One has to understand that for a successful actor there is no dearth of female attention. His girlfriends would keep coming over for lunch; many of them would either bring lunch or send it, imagining that the way to Hari's heart was through his stomach. I wish they knew how little that mattered to Hari. I'd like to go one step forward in Hari's defence and say that despite being single, Hari was not chasing women. If he was actually involved, he wouldn't talk loosely about the person in question.

Many of the names that were linked with him at the time are no more. For every actress who makes it big, there are hundreds who don't! They end up doing small roles. Several of them are not very ambitious and are looking to settle down. Hari was a happy-go-lucky guy with a heart of gold, and perhaps many considered him a soft target. Several other lead actors just had innocent crushes on him.

When I broke up with Rajesh Khanna in 1972, Hari and Basu Bhattacharya were the first to come home. Hari had no words of wisdom to offer. All he said was, 'Chalo, get up. Let's go to this party.' Hari was always a dependable friend. He never knew what it was like to be rude or scheming.

He had a hereditary heart problem and was acutely aware of it. After his first heart attack in 1976, we started drifting apart, for no reason at all. Perhaps it was not possible to stay in touch. But whenever we met, it was as if time had stood still, and we used to pick up from where we had left off. I used to tell him to take a chance and get married. However, he knew his life was short, and he wanted to secure his family's future, especially that of Nikul's wife Jyoti and her three kids.

After his surgery in 1985, he withdrew from everybody. When we lost him, I was shattered.

6

Sharmila Tagore

When we were shooting for *Griha Pravesh* in 1976, he had his first heart attack. One particular scene in the film was very intense and demanding. There were a few retakes before we got it right. Although it exhausted him, he was absolutely brilliant in the final take, which Basu okayed. But in the laboratory, somehow that take got damaged. By then Haribhai was in the hospital, and re-shooting of the scene was impossible, so Basu made do with another take. Haribhai never got to know.

An Effortless Performer

I don't quite remember when I first met Haribhai. It was probably on the sets of *Shaandaar*. He was already a big star. Our working equation began on a note of mutual respect and friendship. *Shaandar* was shot in 1974 in Chennai. The film industry there is extremely disciplined and strict about the language. Since Hindi is not their native tongue, they are very hesitant about changing even a single word of the dialogue that is sent from Bombay.

In one of the scenes, I had to say, '*Mera dil huk uthega.*' This to me sounded overly dramatic. I couldn't identify with its sentiment. I got into a vehement argument. The director and the assistants tried to convince me that I had to say that line, but I wouldn't listen. In those days there were no mobile phones, so they couldn't get in touch with the dialogue writer in Bombay to suggest an alternative. Being a Bengali, I couldn't come up with better suggestions either. This stalemate continued for a couple of hours at least.

Finally, Haribhai came up to me and whispered, 'Rinku, (my nickname) do you want to stay here all night? It doesn't matter, whatever the dialogue is, if you say it with the right emotion, I am sure you will sound convincing, and the scene will also work.' I understood the wisdom of his words and did just that. That day I learnt an important lesson from him—that to make a scene work, one needs to cooperate. As long as you deliver your dialogue sincerely the audience will also believe it.

Although I loved Haribhai to death, he had one very irritating habit—he just couldn't make it to shoots on time. At one time, I was doing a double shift, *Faraar* in the morning and *Mausam* in the evening. In both the films, Haribhai was my co-star.

Those of you who have seen *Mausam* would know I played a double role in the film. On my first day's shooting as Kajri, I was extremely excited, and all keyed up. I was portraying this kind of a character for the first time and was really looking forward to the day's shoot. I was ready with my make-up and dialogues by 2 p.m., and guess at what time Haribhai came? 8 p.m.! I had been waiting for about six hours, and by the time we went to the set

I was exhausted and livid. I was so angry that I had a meltdown and said very nasty things to him, which had absolutely no effect on him. He remained totally calm, and that made me more angry. Finally, Gulzar sahab, in a very conciliatory tone, said, 'Can we at least take one shot?' Haribhai had no problem doing the scene. He did his part perfectly, and I, on the other hand, kept giving retakes after retakes. I don't remember how the day ended, but again I learnt a valuable lesson—that you shouldn't allow your temper to get in the way of your performance. We continued to work together for fourteen hours a day, for *Faraar* in the morning and *Mausam* in the evening, but I refused to talk to him. I was still very angry.

Ten days went by, and I went to see *Aandhi*. I loved the film, and particularly Haribhai's performance. The next day, when we were shooting for *Faraar*, I went and knocked on his dressing room door and told him, 'You really are an awful person and very irritating but because you are such a brilliant actor I would like to shake hands and make up. Just one request, if you're going to be late, please let me know so that I can adjust my time as well.' He heard what I had to say calmly. If he felt anything, he didn't show that, and of course, he didn't apologize. But he had a twinkle in his eyes. I think our friendship became stronger from that day on. I had accepted him the way he was.

Haribhai and Basu Bhattacharya shared a great friendship. Basu was a gregarious and affectionate man. When Haribhai was admitted to the hospital, he would visit often. Once, I visited with him too. Basu and Haribhai both loved non-vegetarian food. That was the basis for their bond. Haribhai would drink himself silly, and though I never saw Basu drinking, I can only guess that he offered his silent company.

Haribhai had fantastic timing, a charming presence on screen and impeccable dialogue delivery with a perfectly modulated voice to match. Though he mostly stayed quiet on the sets, nothing really escaped him. Hari loved working with Basu Bhattacharya, Satyadev Dubey and, of course, Gulzar. Somehow, I got the impression that he didn't enjoy working with Satyajit Ray, though he never told me as such. Just once, he reluctantly admitted that Ray would allow Saeed Jaffrey to improvise any way he wished, but with Haribhai, he told him *exactly* what to do. Even if he lifted his elbow an inch more, Ray would say, 'It's spoiling my frame, don't do that!'

Once I visited his home. When I went to his room, I was so taken aback. It didn't look like a 'star's' room at all. Every inch of his bed, every chair was stacked with either his clothes or his papers; there was no place for me to sit. Finally, I asked, 'Haribhai, where do you want me to sit? On the floor?' So he transferred some clothes from one chair to another and made some space for me. This was his lifestyle. He was comfortable anywhere, whether in a cramped room or working with an annoyed co-star. Puffing away on his cigarette, which couldn't have done him any good because there was a genetic cardiac problem in the family, he always managed to stay at peace with himself.

On many occasions, he came to our house. Tiger liked him very much. They would drink and chat, and sometimes Haribhai would have one too many. I remember that, on one occasion, Haribhai had to hold one hand with the other to ensure that the spoon of food actually landed inside his mouth. He loved his alcohol. But he would ring up the next day to ask if he had misbehaved in any way. And I would tell him, 'You only wiped your hands on the curtain. But not to worry, I will send you the laundry bill.'

On another occasion, I forgot his birthday. The next day at a shoot, I apologized to him for my lapse and wished him a belated happy birthday. One of our co-stars made a snide remark, 'This is a very convenient excuse.' But Haribhai instantly checked her and spoke in my defence, 'If Rinku says it, she means it. She doesn't make up stories like you.' Which still makes me smile. I knew then that he really liked me.

He was extremely devoted to his family, and his mother meant the world to him. In between shots, among other things, he would discuss his marriage plans with me. His mother was looking for a bride for him, but he didn't agree with his mother's choice. He wanted someone who was beautiful and dignified and would understand and appreciate his work. In that context, he mentioned a couple of co-stars, but nothing ever came of them.

As I look back, I can see that there has been tremendous appreciation for Haribhai and his immense talent. Recently, I saw one of his songs with Jaya, '*Bahon mein chale aao*'. His utter ease and nonchalance were so enchanting. He was a gifted actor and commanded respect. He was a good human being. He was a star without any trappings of a star. His connection with theatre was very strong. He had friends from all walks of life. Once, even Haji Mastan had come to meet him. When I asked him, 'What are you doing with him?' He looked straight at me and said, 'What's wrong with him? Why are you interrogating me?'

He had a tremendous sense of humour. Once at the airport a fan came up to him excitedly and asked him how his day was. He instantly put his arms around the man and started on a long explanation about his health. How he had not slept well because of something he had for dinner and went on to describe at length what it was and how that adversely affected his morning ablutions. How even now his stomach was cramping, and asked the fan if he had any medicine that would give him some relief. By this time, the man was struggling to escape, but Haribhai held on tightly and carried on and on in the same vein. Finally, I had to intervene. The poor man made a dash for his flight, never to look back!

After his second heart attack, I didn't see much of him. Basu stayed with him till the end and really looked after him. Haribhai made for a very loyal friend, and I remember him with much fondness. The memories of our shoot together in *Mausam* and *Namkeen* will always remain very special to me.

7

Moushumi Chatterjee

One day, on the sets of *Swayamvar* (1980), I told Hari, 'Because of your late-coming, the producer and director don't give a lunch break, and the staff and technicians suffer. They are not able to eat. Do you want their bad wishes to reach you?' This was in Chennai. I can say that after that day, at least he tried to come earlier and always enquired as to whether the staff had eaten. He never wanted to harm anybody.

A Man with a Conscience

I got married in class ten. My aunt had terminal cancer, and it was her last wish to see me married. After my Bengali film debut in 1967, I came to Mumbai in the 1970s. I was only twenty-two then.

I don't remember when Jariwala and I first met—must've been on the sets of our first film. But his open, honest smile and simple manners immediately told me that he was a man with a conscience in an industry where it is rare to have one. As I got to know him better, I was convinced that I had gauged him correctly. There were three reasons for that: he never interfered in other artistes' work; he could see other people's point of view; he was very kind-hearted.

Jariwala was very comfortable with me. I was new and did not know the ways of the industry. He always treated me like the 'Little Red Riding Hood' and made me aware of things and told me about industry politics. He used to call me 'Moush'. During the shoot of *Kachhe Dhaage*, my director Raj Khosla told everyone, 'Moushumi is a lamb. When it comes to her, either it is 8 or 80. She does not understand anything in between.'

Our first film together was *Zindagi* (1976), where I played his daughter. This was later remade as *Baghban* in 2003. During the period when we were shooting for the film, he once telephoned me at home at 8 a.m. Here's how our conversation went:

> Jariwala: Are you going for a shoot? Can I visit you at home for ten minutes?

I had already got ready, so I went to his house instead. Knowing him to be perennially late, I didn't want to take the risk. I climbed the two floors to his flat in Perrin Villa and found that lots of people were seated in the hall. Jariwala had a toothbrush in his mouth when I spotted him.

> Jariwala: Come and sit in my room. Give me a minute to freshen up.

I did as told.

> Jariwala: Have I ever misbehaved with you?
>
> Me: Why?
>
> Jariwala: Why are you going around telling producers to remove Haribhai and put Vinod Mehra in my place.
>
> Me: What!
>
> Jariwala: Did you say this or not?

By now, he saw the expression on my face. I was in shock because I didn't even know that I could speak like that, let alone actually do it!

> Jariwala: I was quite sure that you would not know. Your secretary is playing you for a fool.

I realized then that Jariwala was saying the truth, and I had to fire my secretary. On another occasion when Jariwala confronted me, he also allowed me to clarify the matter with the other person. 'You can use my name as the source,' he said. In a politically expedient world, Jariwala's candour and honesty meant a lot to me. We became very close friends after that.

During the ten years that I knew him, I had seen him in at least six different relationships. I also saw that many other women used to love him ardently. I remember the actress Neeta Mehta in particular. Jariwala would enjoy female attention; any eligible bachelor would. But as far as his emotional involvement was concerned, he had made up his mind after his second heart attack that he was not cut out for that kind of relationship.

I also knew that he had bounced back from two serious relationships that had gone completely wrong. He had formed the opinion that most women could not be trusted. I tried to get him out of it, but he didn't really care beyond a point. He was an easy-going man who was not in it for the chase. He didn't want the headache of constant explanations, clarifications and justifications.

Dinners at my home were common, and he had made friends with my cook. So even if my husband and I weren't at home, it didn't prevent Jariwala from having a meal at my place. He would often come with his nephew, whom we called 'Bhindi' because that's all the boy wanted to eat. But when he started coming home very late, I fought with him and told him that it was easier to send him a dabba than keep waiting for him!

I am very lucky to have been his friend. Because Jariwala fought for his friends. I had to leave the film *Koshish* because of simple disagreements with the director. Jariwala knew that it was not my fault, that it was a misunderstanding. So he resolved that the same director and I would work again. This came true during *Angoor* in 1982.

Maybe because I was not from the film industry, lots of people, especially Jariwala and Vinod Khanna, saved me from difficult situations. Once when I was shooting in New Jersey, I needed a few thousand dollars. Jariwala was not even in the same city, but he sent me the money.

He did not know how to be glamorous and stylish. And if I can be blunt, many of the leading actresses in those days used to find him simply unfit to be romanced. He was not a handsome hero, just a great actor. One day, on the sets of a film, a successful senior actress had come to meet him. He also liked her, and there were definitely some sparks between them. But in front of her, he asked the security guard on the sets, 'Do you have a bidi?'

That was it! The woman was horrified by his lack of sophistication, and this budding romance died a young death.

Towards the end, there was a lot written about Sulakshana Pandit. Jariwala was not into her at all. Neither was he into Jayshree T. or Yogeeta Bali. These were just rumours because in those days, with due respect to all the ladies, media was obsessed with wanting to get Jariwala married. In 1983, he got involved with another talented Muslim actress. I found out because I saw her letter in his fan mail. I don't think Jariwala even knew it was there; otherwise, he would've hidden it. However, he knew that marriage was not on the cards at all.

When it came to commitment, Jariwala was a very mature man. He knew what he was doing. He loved his family, and their financial security was a very big motivation for him. He allowed a part of him to die emotionally, much before he died physically. But that was his choice. He could've got married any number of times because women from the ages of seven to seventy were in love with him.

But when he faced his own heart disease and Nikul's death, he prioritized the family's safety over his selfish love. Till the end, he had a will to live. He did not want to live his days eating food he did not like or spending time with people who would not matter in the long run.

8

Ravi Tandon

When Hari had his third heart attack and was admitted to Nanavati in 1983, I offered my house to him to stay. This was Tandon House, Juhu. He occupied the first floor of my bungalow for a month, and I moved my wife and kids to the second floor, so he could be comfortable.

'I want a place where I can stay alone,' he had said to me.

Hari was Lucky For Me

My friendship with Hari started in Filmalaya Studios. P.D. Shenoy used to teach the acting classes at Filmalaya and Hari used to attend. At the time, I was a runaway dreamer from Agra and was trying my hand at various roles. When I heard that R.K. Nayyar (who went on to become a renowned producer and director) was starting work on *Love in Simla* with Joy Mukherjee, I started assisting him. Later, when Joy Mukherjee and I were making *Aao Pyar Karen*, we needed to cast three friends in the film. I suggested Hari's name, along with Manvinder and Mac Mohan.

From here on, Hari went from strength to strength. But he never forgot his old friends. Much later, when I had a subject ready, I told Hari about *Anhonee* (1973)—it was a mangled plot in which the protagonist initially seems crazy, but at interval, he turns out to be a police inspector. I was a new producer and this was also my first film as a director, but Hari did not hesitate one bit. '*Gudh ki beli and sawa rupaiya* (a symbolic gesture) will be my fee,' he said lovingly. With the support of R.K. Nayyar, Manoj Kumar and Gullu Kochar, who backed me, I cast Leena Chandavarkar and Kamini Kaushal also in the film. The music was composed by Laxmikant–Pyarelal. Luckily for me, *Anhonee* became a big hit. So, Hari had a lot to do with my successful entry into the film industry.

I retained my style of making films with twists and turns. I made *Majboor* and *Khel Khel Mein*, and cast Hari again in *Apne Rang Hazaar*. Our relationship was special. In those days there was a theatre named Sumeet outside my home, and it had a dubbing studio. A road led from my home to the theatre, and whenever Hari was dubbing there, Jamnnadasji used to ask me, 'Are you at home? Bhai wants to come.'

Hari would promise to come by 10 p.m. but reach only by 11.30 p.m. He could not stop himself from drinking, and he could not stop himself from eating. The revelry would continue till 3 a.m. Over time, I was unable to give him company at that hour because I would be through with my dinner and all set to retire. I think both of us realized that our personal paths were diverging—he was addicted to the 'single life'—his visits became less and less frequent. But our friendship and professional work continued unabated.

He was absolutely irreplaceable when it came to challenging roles. So when I wanted to make *Zindagi* (1976) and break the 'thriller' mould I was known for, I approached Hari again. Mala Sinha came on board as the lead actress. The two of them played an old couple in the film. During the narration, Mala Sinha had asked me, 'Is there any flashback to when we are young?' But Hari was not one to bother about the age or looks of his character.

In some ways, perhaps he lost out on the glamour of being a superstar; however, on performance alone, there was no one to beat him. He was so sharp that he never asked me to give him a copy of the dialogue. His way to prepare was to say, 'Just read it out to me.' He would listen and then deliver the dialogue flawlessly, with an instinctive understanding of the setting. In those days, the entire industry knew that 'Haribhai is the best actor!'

He never said things like, 'Give me a good song.' It was all about the quality of the role. When Hari spoke on screen, it was the character, not the actor speaking. He was always ready for a good script. I was disappointed when, despite its very good subject, *Zindagi* didn't do well. Thankfully, Hari was never bothered about such things. In 1982, when we made *Khud-Daar*, Hari was one of the only bachelor superstars left in the industry. Women used to be crazy about him! We also started work on *Professor Ki Padosan* in 1981, but it eventually released (with suitable modifications) only in 1994.

Marriage was an important subject for him—more from Baa's point of view than his own. Once, he had gone to Surat and found a girl and had even agreed to marry her, but eventually, it didn't work out. He had also gone to Baroda and seen a few prospective brides. Somehow, he was always disappointed. We also spoke about this very good friend of mine who had a sister whom Hari was almost ready to marry. But after his third heart attack, he decided against it. Despite all this, I always saw that he was a very happy man. He was never heartbroken—he was always aware of what he was choosing in life.

Our families knew each other very well, and we would often go to Hari's house for Gujarati food cooked by Baa. My kids would play with his nephews—and there would be camaraderie and conversation. On these occasions, Baa would confide in my wife Veena about his smoking habit and how she wished she could rid him of it.

So when Hari was living at home in 1983, after Baa's demise, Veena wanted to honour Baa's wish. Hari and I would stand for hours and talk in my balcony facing the sea. He used to tell me all about his life. Doctors had given Hari strict instructions for healthy eating and no smoking. Veena being a strict disciplinarian, did not even keep cigarettes at home during that time.

But Hari found a sneaky way. He would tell us that he had important work matters to discuss with Jamnadasji and close the bedroom door. Unbeknown to us, Jamnadasji would sneak in oily, spicy food from the Chinese hotel he loved so much! They would eat clandestinely out of that hideous plastic packaging. The parcels would also contain Hari's beloved cigarettes, which he would puff soulfully in the bathroom.

After he left, Veena and I occupied our bedroom again. Imagine her chagrin when she found copious cigarette stubs outside our bathroom window sill. Hari's entourage was part of this elaborate hoodwinking scheme! I had laughed heartily—Hari was well nigh unstoppable!

Hari was a good friend, and he would always help you if he could. I know many people that he loaned money to. He never cared what would happen to him. Two people who loved him a lot were Baa and Jamnadasji; the latter was a very good friend in addition to being his manager.

The last time I saw him was about ten days before his death. He never gave me a hint that he was suffering. I was not aware of the genetic trait in the family and never thought he would go away so quickly. He was truly one of a kind.

Ravi Tandon passed away on 11 February 2022, a few days after writing this essay.

9

Tanuja

Harry was *seedha saadha*, a gentle soul and a fabulous actor. If he scored twenty in a scene, I'd try and reach twenty-one. We had a competition about who would do a scene better. Both of us would finish our shots in one take. If Basu asked for a retake, we used to ask him why he needed one.

Seedha Saadha Aadmi

Harry was shocked when his younger brother Nikul died in 1984. '*Nikul ko dekho, mere se pehle mar gaya,*' used to be a common remark from Harry towards the end of his life. He could not get over his younger brother passing away before he did. I saw all the three brothers die, in the space of eighteen months. And since Nikul died before him, his death hit him the most—it was a jolt of reality.

Harry, as I used to call him, was a terrific actor. When he infuriated me, I would call him Harihar. He, on the other hand, would call me 'Chota' or 'Chota bachcha', and when he was drunk, it would become 'Sota'!

He never played any role; he became the character. In each and every movie, he was very different. It was Siraj Burmawala, uncle to filmmakers Abbas-Mustan, who had introduced me to Harry. We ended up doing umpteen films together; I don't even remember how many. There was *Anubhav*, *Bachpan*, *Jeene ki Raah* ... I've lost count. I remember that Basu [Bhattacharya] shot the whole of *Anubhav* in my flat in Usha Kiran. Every morning, Harry and Basu would land up in my bedroom, and I'd throw them out! 'Get out of my room,' I would scream.

The making of *Anubhav* was so uncomplicated. Harry and I shot for it whenever we had the time. The film required just twenty-five days of shooting, but it stretched over three years, given our hectic schedules. I remember Sagar Sarhadi penning the dialogues on the sets. We'd tell him what we wanted to express in English and he'd quickly write that out in Hindi. Both Harry and I could speak English well. We just used to warn Sagar, 'Do not write complicated Hindi!'

The thing with Harry and me was that we had a tremendous friendship and chemistry. Both of us were very capable of convincing our audience about the scene we were doing. The way we reacted to each other on the sets was honest and competitive in the healthiest way possible. Harry had no method. He would quote Stanislavski in interviews, but that was not his method. He would just feel a scene and emote it.

Common friends would ask us, 'Why don't you both get married?' because we were really close. But we were close as buddies, and our friendship was really important to us both. He had a terrific sense of humour and was a gullible gully goose!

He trusted everybody—and so many people let him down. He was an extension of his mother's loving personality. All she wanted to do was to look after everyone and feed everybody. I have gone to his tiny Girgaum house for lunch, and I remember relishing every dish Baa used to make. She had a glow in her eyes when she used to look at Harry; she loved him tremendously. But I remember him telling me that there was no space in his house to sleep.

We had an exclusive friendship. We were just us—our crazy conversations had no logic and no context. When Guru Dutt died on 9 July, I would tell Harry that 'My best friend died on your birthday'. Guru Dutt and I were avid readers; I had worked with him in *Baharen Phir Bhi Aayengi*. Harry and I could talk about anything and everything. I was close to some of his other co-stars, too, like Suchitra Sen. She had this amazing make-up man, Shailen Ganguly, whom she would generously offer to me whenever possible.

In terms of work, I was definitely senior to him, but let's just say that that never mattered. We just tried to do our best in front of the camera. Both of us also cared about our co-actors. We were from an era where acting wasn't our whole life. We weren't consumed by it. It was a part of our life, and our decisions were motivated by factors like friendship and concern. The entire crew used to sit and eat together—there was no separate five-star food for the actors—we would've felt awkward and declined it ourselves.

I vaguely remember shooting in Kashmir with Harry. Ravi Khanna was our stunt director, and Veeru Devgan—his first film—was supposed to do a very dangerous stunt. Harry and I felt it wasn't safe for Veeru and we cancelled the shoot. Veeru was our age; Harry and I couldn't see ourselves putting him in danger.

One night, during a shoot, at about 11.30 p.m., there was a knock on my hotel room's door. Harry was fully drunk and leaning against the door.

'Ay Sota,' he said.

'Are you drunk, Harry? Haven't I told you not to drink so much!' I screamed.

'*Lekin wahaan sab log pee raha tha*,' Harry said.

He quietly went back to his room. Harry was unable to stop drinking once he started, but he was not the kind of person to drink and misbehave. If anything, he would go quiet after drinking. I just feel that he got addicted quickly. I was never curious, but he told me everything because he wanted an outlet.

His performances were eternally amazing. No two performances were the same. It's not that he had to look radically different. Just his performance of each character was very different. That's why the mimics can't crack him. All the other actors of that time, they patented a style. Not him. You can never even try to imitate him. Because there is no one Haribhai style, what we have are innumerable credit-worthy performances.

Harry was a good human being with a heart so big that it trusted the whole world! He was able to portray each character in its true form without allowing even an iota of himself to seep in.

As it happens with many friendships, we, too, drifted apart. I met him at Baa's funeral, but after that, he cut off, and we didn't meet as often. In fact, we never went out after Baa's death. He spent more and more time with other friends.

10

Subhash Sanas

Haribhai loved my mother. So much was his fondness for my mother and her culinary skills that once when I was abroad, he visited Pune and asked me to inform my mother in advance so that she could cook something for him.

Securing His Family's Future

Haribhai and I had a very long and affectionate relationship. When he had come to Pune in the 1970s, there were no five star hotels there at the time. I was the owner of Jawahar Hotel, and he had come to stay with us. After we met, Haribhai told me that he wanted to procure a 'Malibu Chevrolet automatic' in yellow. I was able to procure the car for him. This was in 1972.

On another occasion, Jamnadasji saw an off-white Mercedes at my premises. Haribhai always wanted the number 9991 for his cars—the first 9 was for Perrin Villa, and the second one was for his birth date 9 July, and the third for the nine roles he played in *Naya Din Nayi Raat*. To confirm the purchase, Jamnadasji gave me just Rs 500, but with that 'shagun', I transferred the car to Haribhai's name.

I promptly delivered the car to him the next morning and handed him the keys. This was in the year 1974, on the day of the release of *Naya Din Nayi Raat*. He was stunned that I had transferred the car to his name on a token of Rs 500. He invited me to stay for the premiere. After the show was done, when I was preparing to leave for Pune, he told me, 'Take the car and go to Pune. Have it delivered back to me later.'

Once, he came to Pune for my birthday celebrations. He told everyone, 'Subhash is my brother.' He had an incredibly warm smile. Over the years, Haribhai became like a family member to me. Whenever he was in Pune, he would visit us at home. One of his favourite occasions was to come home for Ganpati darshan, and the first question always was, '*Aai kaisi hai*?' Mothers were always an object of reverence for him.

I, too, would visit him often in Mumbai; his brother Nikul's wife Jyoti used to tie me a rakhi. Haribhai wanted to get married, but it was not in his destiny. Yes, the media has written plenty about his relationships, but Haribhai was not the kind of person to feel dejected at that. He was a superstar with a meteoric female following, and he knew how to move on. On the innumerable occasions that we spent time together, drinking till the wee hours of the morning, he never complained about it. He was a superstar with a tremendous fan following and with undeniable mastery over his craft. Several fine ladies would wait for hours outside his shoots to meet him and talk to him. On one occasion, a princess from a royal family in Pune wrote to him, seeking to marry him. He refused politely. Baa was the one who really wanted to see him married, and understandably so. She used to tell me to get a 'Maharashtrian *gharelu ladki*' for him. But to get a woman who matched Haribhai's tastes was really difficult.

Both of us reached a consensus—that our lives are guided by our destiny and that we must accept life as it comes. In those days, I used to run an underground bar called the Umar Khayyam Bar on the premises of Jawahar Hotel, a residential hotel that I owned. It was the first bar to receive a license in Pune. It was a private pad, and so hoards of celebrities would come with their friends—Parveen Babi, Lata Mangeshkar, Jaya Bachchan, Shatrughan Sinha, Navin Nischol, Anil Dhawan … everyone would come.

Haribhai had an exceptional relationship with his co-stars in Bollywood. His best friends were definitely Sachin and Shatruji. He also had very high regard for Shammiji. Once, he brought Shashi Kapoor to Jawahar Hotel in Pune for dinner and we had a small function in his honour. Haribhai was always generous in his praise for his co-stars. Directors like Ramesh Sippy and Ravi Tandon had very high regard for him. He would always clear up misunderstandings with people by talking straight. I happened to be with him when he once tried to clear the air with Vidya Sinha. It was a funny situation, and I was with him in the car. I didn't know what to do because I had no context. All I remember is that Haribhai apologized and went back to his shoot.

Once, when I visited Mumbai, he was dubbing. I reached the dubbing studio to call on him. He saw me and told the producer, 'My throat is not feeling good today. Can we do this another time?' He came out and asked me with a wink, 'Where are you staying?' I was at the Horizon. He promptly decided to stay the night with me there.

After Baa passed away, he was in two minds about spending time in Bangalore, which he often visited for shoots. He used to love the weather there. He set up the Princess Restaurant on Brigade Road in the city with Amar Lulla and a KnockOut bar adjoining the restaurant. I remember that Haribhai had gone to Singapore to buy music systems to make KnockOut as cutting-edge as possible. For the opening, a lot of us had travelled to Bangalore. Dilip Kumar, Randhir Kapoor, Raj Kapoor, Shammi Kapoor … they came on Haribhai's invitation, and we stayed together for three or four days. After the initial excitement, he asked someone to run it for him. However, such arrangements rarely work out, and this venture became a financial mess. After his death, his family exited the business by selling it to a third party.

I've been with him for shoots at Mehboob Studio too. When Haribhai was playing a blind character in *Qatl*, just to lend authenticity to a scene, he told me, 'Subhash, brush the Mercedes against me.' I had to do it!

Haribhai never cared for money or material comforts. When he was going to Houston for his surgery in 1985, he booked my ticket too. When he came back, he spent a lot of time at my hotel. In fact, Haribhai made his will at Jawahar Hotel. During his recovery period and stay at my home, I remember we went to the theatre and watched *Sagar* when it released in August 1985. We took a trip to Shirdi and Nasik too.

When he resumed shooting in Mumbai, he told me that the doctor had asked him not to climb stairs. He had to climb two floors to get to his home in Perrin Villa. So every afternoon, he would go between shoots or dubbing to rest in my flat on Linking Road, Bandra. This, too, was on the second floor, but the building had a lift. He used to take lunch breaks and rest there briefly.

He was also specifically asked to abstain from alcohol. 'The doctor has told me that for six months I can have just one or two brandy shots at best. Cannot have whisky till then,' Haribhai would tell me. But invariably, he would have more than his quota. I would constantly chide him. 'You've taken 4-5 drinks today. You must take care of your health.'

Our relationship was so personal that when he turned forty-seven and hosted a party at Sun-n-Sand, he wrote to me saying, 'Please come; this may be my last birthday.' That was the last time I saw him alive and enjoying himself.

After his death, the industry was plunged in grief. All his co-stars came for his last journey because they loved him and respected the actor in him. It was a sincere funeral where people mourned deeply and genuinely. My mother and I both attended.

There was a lot of unfinished work in the wake of his sudden death. Some who felt that no one could do justice to his roles, like producer Hari Walia, who had shot seven reels for a film with him, canned their films. Haribhai was a legend—no one could fill the gap he left. He didn't have any of the trappings of stardom, despite being a superstar. I continue to be in touch with his family. When we opened one of the best multiplexes in Pune's E-Square in 2003, I was able to offer a small stake to Jyoti bhabhi in lieu of the investments that Haribhai had made with me.

A man so fond of perfumes, Haribhai left the world more fragrant with his love.

11

Randhir Kapoor

Harry had a wish: to get a chance to work with my father during his heydays. He truly admired Raj Kapoor sahab. There was even some talk of him working in *Ram Tere Ganga Maili*, in Saeed Jaffrey's role.

Footloose, Food and Booze

Harry and I met on the sets of R.K. Nayyar's *Inspector Daku Aur Woh* in 1980. Ranjeeta was to be our co-star. Harry had just lost his mother, and that was the context I knew at the time. We didn't exactly make waves with our first film together! Producer N.P. Ali died (while the film was still incomplete) and the film never saw the light of the day.

I came into Harry's life very late. He was Sanjeev Kumar the superstar by then, and I was a great admirer of his art, his terrific sense of humour, and we were bonded by our common like for great food and good booze. I have not seen his struggle; I have only seen his superstardom.

Harry used to drink since his days on the stage. The plays used to end at night; they would've been rehearsing non-stop all day, and a drink was their way to unwind. I think he truly understood and mirrored my 'easy living' philosophy. To appreciate this, you have to understand that he was a truly talented man. Only an artiste of his virtuosity could have truly relaxed like he could. He had nothing to prove and nothing to hide. I don't think he was ever serious or sad. Three things I could certainly say about him—he was never in a hurry, he was always late everywhere and he was so simple that it was beyond him to scheme or plot or even discuss vicious things.

We came together again for *Sawaal*, and that's how our friendship grew. I remember we were offered a lot of films together, but we couldn't, obviously, do all of them.

Our favourite hangout place was the Gazebo oriental restaurant in Bandra, where we used to enjoy Chinese food. There would always be a few friends from his struggling days with him, and he never seemed to mind. I particularly remember Subhash Indori. The other side to him was that he was a great family man. He was single, but he wasn't one to crib or need a shoulder to confide in. He was a *mast maula, jiyo aur jeene do* kind of guy!

He was also very close to my uncle Shammi Kapoor. The three of us have also had good times together. We were a formidable threesome when we got together to drink, sometimes at my house and sometimes at my uncle's house. Harry never entertained at his home because non-vegetarian food was not allowed there. My only exposure to his family was Nikul, who used to come to meet him on the sets.

As the puff of Harry's 555 cigarette wafted in the air, melting away to become nothing, so was his own approach to life. Harry had famously said, 'I'd marry Daboo, because he wouldn't bring his tensions home' in *Super* magazine in the year 1978. I think that defines our comfort and our friendship. We met to have a good time, and that's probably the best reason to meet!

12

Amardeep Singh Kohli

Sardar Kulwant Singh Kohli, owner of Pritam Hotel in Dadar, Mumbai, was a close friend of Hari's. His memories of Hari have been immortalized in his memoirs Yeh Hai Mumbai Meri Jaan. *Amardeep Singh Kohli, son of Kulwant Singh Kohli, offers here memories of their friendship.*

Ki Gal Hai?

My father, Kulwant Singh Kohli and Haribhai were great friends. But it was my grandfather Prahlad Singh Kohli who could match Haribhai's potomania glass for glass and keep up with his appetite for delicious non-vegetarian food.

It was Prehlad Singh Kohli and his wife Har Kaur (my grandmother) who set up Pritam restaurant in 1942. In those days, the entire film industry was centred on Dadasaheb Phalke Road. All the studios were a stone's throw away from the

Director K. Asif and Hari on the sets of *Love and God*.

Hari seen here with singer Mohammad Rafi.

Hari with filmmaker B.R. Chopra and his son Ravi Chopra.

Hari with his Pune-based friend Subhash Sanas.

Courtesy of Subhash Sanas

K. Asif shares a laugh with Hari.

Director S. Ramanathan and producer N.N. Sippy bond with Hari at the success party for *Devata*.

Hari with director-producer Ravi Tandon and his wife Veena.

The inimitable Jamnadasji, the Jeeves to Hari's Wooster.

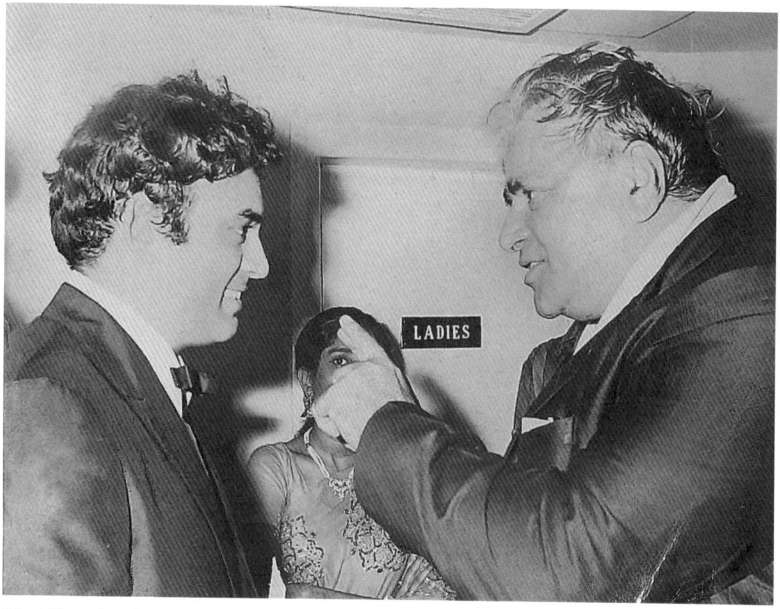

Hari listening intently to Prithviraj Kapoor at a party.

Hari with close friend Shammi Kapoor.

Seen here with screenwriters Salim Khan and Javed Akhtar.

Hari, Shabana Azmi and Protima Bedi gathered for a card game at Perrin Villa.

Hari was an absolute favourite with the magazines.
Courtesy of RJ Anirudh Chawla

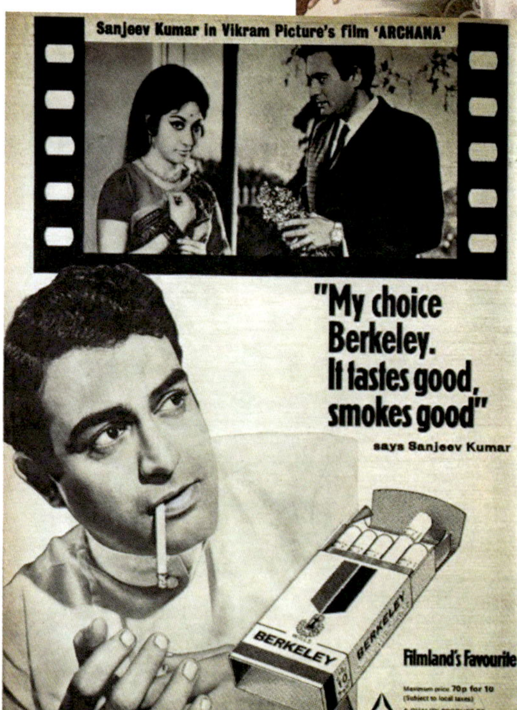

Another still from one of Hari's films converted into an advertisement.

The great obsession of media, in those days, was to get Hari married. His relationships, marriage plans, Baa's preferences, etc. were a hot selling point for the press.

Courtesy of RJ Anirudh Chawla

Hari with underworld don Haji Mastan, who enjoyed showing off his film industry connections.

Hari seen here bonding with Dharmendra.

Hari with Raj Kapoor and friends Praveen and Sarita Joshi at a film's muhurat.

Neila Devi, Hari and Shammi Kapoor at the launch of Hari's Princess Restaurant and KnockOut Bar in Bangalore.

Shatrughan Sinha and producer Pahlaj Nihalani at the launch in Bangalore.

Hari in conversation with Yash Chopra.

Raj Kapoor and Dilip Kumar also attended the launch.

Hari revisiting his Bhuleshwar home, with camera in tow, as crowds throng for a glimpse.

On their wedding day, Supriya and Sachin Pilgaonkar placed Hari's photo on the dais and sought his blessings posthumously.

Courtesy of Sachin Pilgaonkar

restaurant—Shree Sound Studio, Ranjit Studios, Kardar Studios and Rajkamal Studios.

In the 1950s, the entire film industry, not just the actors but also the crew, were predominantly Punjabi. Many used to live on R.P. Masani Road in Matunga, also known as 'Punjabi Galli', barely a kilometre from Pritam restaurant. The Kapoor family—Prithviraj Kapoor with his sons, Raj, Shammi, Shashi, and their sister Urmila, stayed there. Producers, directors and actors such as Madan Puri, Trilok Kapoor, Manmohan Krishna, K.N. Singh, Jeevan, Jagdish Sethi, J.K. Nanda ... they all stayed in Punjabi Galli.

Thanks to their proximity to the restaurant, they knew about our food and used to come regularly. Occasionally, they would invite us to cater too. However, our family's relationship with the industry grew deeper when we became producers ourselves. In the 1970s, my father Kulwantji formed Sangita Film Corporation. Our first film was *Pakeezah*. It took us quite long to make it, and we were looking for a distributor. Shankar B.C. was one of the biggest distributors in those days, and he verbally agreed to buy the film. We organized a screening at the Embassy theatre. But there was a power cut due to an Air Force tracer net atomic energy drill. We all mistook it for an attack, and Shankar B.C. backed out of distributing the film. He wouldn't budge, despite our entreaties. We had to open our own distribution to screen *Pakeezah,* and the rest is history.

The film fraternity was beginning to get familiar with us in a whole new way. From being asked to cater at film parties, we were now guests at these same parties—hobnobbing with the stars. Kulwantji was now a regular fixture at Bollywood dos, and that's how he first met Haribhai, who was already the famous actor Sanjeev Kumar. They were introduced to each other by filmmaker B.R. Chopra at his residence. The friendship that started at B.R. Chopra's home continued till Haribhai's death. To his credit, Haribhai did not give Kulwantji any starry vibes—he was a humble man who knew how to speak to people with respect. He always referred to Papa as Kulwantji, as he was four years older than him. Kulwantji would refer to him as Haribhai or Sanjeev.

Chopra sahab and we Kohlis were family friends—we would always find reasons to meet. But Chopra sahab was a teetotaller; he had no vices. And whenever Haribhai and Kulwantji met at B.R. Chopra's home, Haribhai would watch the clock for the evening hour and slyly quip, 'Chopra sahab, won't you offer Mr Kohli a drink?'

Chopra sahab would indulge him, knowing fully well that it was Haribhai who wanted to drink. He would tell his son, 'Ravi, go get a Black Label. It's time for his drinks.'

Interestingly, Haribhai's introduction to Kulwantji was as the head of Sangita Film Corporation. It was only afterwards that he got to know about Pritam restaurant. The floodgates to the foodie in Haribhai now opened! He was both discerning and insatiable and had a fine knack for sifting out quality food. Haribhai started coming to Pritam. The stars were so aligned that Haribhai met my grandfather Prehlad Singhji at Pritam and discovered to his joy that they shared a birthday—9 July. Now, Haribhai was a charmer and a superstar. My grandfather, too, was gregarious and basically 'Punjabi' in his demeanour. Both got along like a house on fire! Haribhai went on to make a special place in my grandfather's heart, and they celebrated several birthdays together.

Haribhai was also demonstrative. One year, on 9 July, he came with a band and a music procession. He had brought along a troupe to sing for Prehladji. 'Papaji, come down and give me your blessings,' Haribhai sent word for Prehladji, who was sleeping at the time. Haribhai persisted, 'How can he sleep so early? It's our birthday. Either he comes down or I will go up!'

Prehladji finally came down, blessed Haribhai and took everyone up with him to the third floor where our residence was. What ensued was bacchanalian revelry, with drinks and food and good cheer. Haribhai was in a particularly good mood, pulling everyone's leg and having fun.

Haribhai was loyal. He never tolerated misdemeanour, however inebriated the person was. In hindsight, what aided the friendship between my grandfather and Haribhai was that Kulwantji was a one-drink man, but Prehladji had a far heartier appetite. Whenever Haribhai came, it was Prehladji who would give him company till the wee hours of the morning. The ladies of the house didn't mind as the revelry was happening at home.

Haribhai would always come with a few of his friends. There was Johnny Whisky, the comedian, Subhash Indori, the poet, Salim Khan, the writer, etc. The more he drank, the quieter Haribhai would become. But he was a keen observer of people and would be quietly making mental notes of how people behaved in different situations.

Kulwantji recalls what A.K. Hangal told him about a conversation the latter had with Hari:

> From the very beginning, Hari belonged to the school of natural acting. He would understand the character sketch very well. He would delve deeply upon the arc of every

character; their evolution in the story, the nuances of their behaviour and the manner in which their situation could be best conveyed, were important to his study and preparation. I was spellbound with his performances. He was convinced that he was born to play the central part in any script. So, when I offered him the role of a father of six boys in a play called *Damroo,* we had a conversation that went thus:

Hari: Dada, you give me elderly roles to play again and again.

Me: That shouldn't matter, Hari. All you need to do is work. Don't focus on what the role is. Focus on how you will play it.

Hari: But Dada, in my youth, people will mistake me for an old man.

Me: You have to play the roles you get. I know you're young; I also know that whatever role I give you, you will elevate it with your talent. Focus on your work. When you become an established actor, you will have a co-actor playing your love interest in one film, daughter in another and mother in a third. You will emerge more sensitive as an actor out of this experience.

Hari: Okay, Dada. I'll do as you say.

Over time, Kulwantji and Haribhai got to know each other more deeply. Sanjeev Kumar the actor also grew in stature. He was a rare gem in cinema, a true friend with deep sensitivity and a blithe, happy-go-lucky man. You could ask him for an inch, and he would give you a mile. But if you asked him to harm another, chances were that it would spell the death knell of your relationship with him. Hari never believed in harming another human being. The only person he tormented mercilessly was himself.

Kulwantji was concerned about his friend's nocturnal binging. He asked Haribhai about giving up alcohol. Haribhai jestfully said, 'I can leave alcohol, but alcohol won't leave me!' And that was that—he never took this conversation as seriously as he should have.

Haribhai was fond of cars. He used to keep buying new models. But he did not like to see anyone else owning the same car as he did. Kulwantji was fond of cars too, and this mutual fondness for cars led to some awkwardness. On one occasion, Haribhai filled a government tender and bought a small Datsun sports car. Kulwantji liked the car too. There was another tender after six months; this time Kulwantji applied and got the same car. It was parked outside Pritam. Haribhai saw it and remarked, 'Kulwantji, you've bought the same car as I have. Are you copying me? You should've told me at least. I would've given you my car.'

Kulwantji maintained a smile. 'I bought it in a tender,' he said. But Haribhai couldn't bear to see another person in possession of the same model of the car he had. Haribhai's artlessness and petulance could be quite a handful! Haribhai made him an offer: 'Let's do this. I bought the car for Rs 40,000; you take it from me for Rs 20,000.' Kulwantji smiled and dropped the conversation.

Haribhai was an eager conversationalist. You asked him a question and he would provide elaborate and genuine answers. He also spoke freely about his struggle—'Kulwantji, I did my first film *Hum Hindustani* in 1960. It featured Asha Parekh and Sunil Duttji. I played the part of an inspector in the film. When the movie was released, it was so embarrassing for me! Even the dog in the film was given title credits, but not me. The next four to five years were a period of intense struggle.' Later, when *Nishan* released, the producers took the credit for 'introducing' Sanjeev Kumar.

Whenever Kulwantji visited Haribhai at his home, he would be sprawled on his big bed. There was a cupboard next to the bed, and there were at least 200 perfumes inside that cupboard.

Kulwantji would ask, 'Haribhai, why do you keep so many perfumes?'

'Kulwantji, whoever comes to see me, I like to spray their favourite perfume on them. Tell me, which is your favourite,' Haribhai would reply. He would then proceed to spray one of those perfumes on Kulwantji.

In 1978, B.R. Chopra produced the superhit *Pati Patni Aur Woh* with Haribhai in the lead. The movie played on Haribhai's sense of comic timing. The stars of the film and the Kohlis gathered at B.R. Chopra's home to celebrate its success. Haribhai was in full flow at the party, and the conversation flowed thus:

> 'Chopraji, the film was a hit but you've allotted the roles incorrectly.'
>
> Chopra sahab asked, 'What happened, Haribhai? Why do you say so?'
>
> 'In the film, Vidya Sinha plays my wife. She's married to someone else in real life. You should at least give me a wife in real life.'
>
> Mrs Chopra said, 'Haribhai, you're very funny. The ladies who want to marry you, you're not even looking at them.'

But Haribhai was insistent, 'Bhabhiji, don't say this. Either you change my heroine or you get me married.'

Mrs Chopra smiled, 'Both are difficult, Haribhai.'

It is well-known that Haribhai was a generous man. When director Khalid Akhtar's project *Ladies Tailor* was stuck for funds, actor Pran sahab asked Kulwantji to see if we could step in and help. We immediately agreed because Pran sahab was a senior actor and we took it not as a request but as a command. Haribhai was the hero, and the project also had Reena Roy and Amjad Khan in pivotal roles. Now, Khalid Akhtar had been an assistant to K. Asif sahab since the *Mughal-E-Azam* days. He was a good man. As soon as Haribhai knew that we were helping out Khalid, he called for a meeting of the film's actors. 'Let's finish the film and then take the money,' he urged all of them. Then Haribhai himself went a step further. He told Akhtar, 'Pay me only if the film earns.'

Destiny timed Kulwantji and Haribhai's heart surgeries in tandem. They would discuss their ailments with each other, share their experiences. Bypass surgery wasn't very common in India in those days. Both decided to go to the US for surgery—Haribhai chose Texas Heart Institute, and Kulwantji chose Los Angeles. We had family there and a house in LA. Kulwantji asked Haribhai to accompany him and live with him in LA. But Haribhai preferred Texas Heart Institute. Their bypass surgeries happened four days apart. Both were asked to take six weeks' rest. But Haribhai was not one to listen.

While Kulwantji got discharged eight days after his surgery, Hari was asked to continue in the hospital for another four weeks. He was very curious to know how Kulwantji got discharged so quickly. Kulwantji once again entreated him, 'Come and stay with me [in LA]. I have family here. We will recuperate together. Take it easy for six months.' But Haribhai didn't listen and went back to India after one month. He started working again. His weak body couldn't take the strain. He died before Kulwantji got back to India.

Eventually, Kulwantji found the courage to pay Haribhai's home a visit. The cupboard with the perfumes was missing. Haribhai must've taken all of them to ask God which one to spray on the Lord Almighty!

And let us be certain that Haribhai has made the heavens more fragrant too. Haribhai was family; he attended my grandfather's funeral and bhog in January 1983, he was there at my wedding to Dimpy (Anita Kaur) in 1977 and my sister Jasdeep Kaur's wedding in 1979.

What remains with me is the conversational Punjabi that Haribhai had picked up in my father and grandfather's company. His *'Itthe aa'* to the staff members who waited upon him lovingly and *'Ki gal hai'* to start a conversation are etched in my memory.

'A star cannot live without glamour. It is an essential part of his career. Teenagers are mad about him. The day his craze with the teenagers ends, his stardom also ends.

'A star is not necessarily adept at acting. The success of a film or two makes one a star. A star has market value. An actor has artistic value. A star is more concerned about maintaining his image, his dialogue delivery. He keeps on repeating himself, film after film. He does not grow as an actor. He does not play the character in the film, he plays himself. Every new film becomes a question mark for him; not a challenge. Will he be able to keep his fan following? Just the reverse is the case with an actor. His popularity is not dependent on the craze of teenagers or on market fluctuations. An actor is a mature artiste. He understands the character he has to play; then moulds and shapes it according to the requirements of the script.'

Sanjeev Kumar

Film World, January 1975

13

In Conversation with Gulzar

This is an interview of Gulzar with the author, with some sections of it in first-person narration.

'Haribhai was a true friend and an irreplaceable actor. He never asked me for a script. "I know you will never waste me," was what he told me. So, we would work together without any terms of understanding being reached. He trusted me wholeheartedly from the time when neither of us had entered films. Our friendship was not because of the film industry, but because of our struggle and learning.'

Dheela Aadmi

It was Padma Shri Sarita Joshi who first spoke about the directors who admired Haribhai. 'Mahesh Bhatt used to say, "Kitna talented ladka hai", and Gulzar loved him. After Gulzar touched his life, there was nothing left for anyone else to do,' Joshi says.

Gulzar brought out the best in him—propelling Haribhai into an orbit of excellence, where his impeccable craft was placed amid emotional vistas in which would triumph. Gulzar himself admits that thanks to the body of work they have done together, he has been hounded by the media on Haribhai's birth and death anniversaries for quotes and anecdotes. His relationship with Haribhai was both intense and heartfelt.

'We met during our theatre days,' he says. That was a time when Gulzar used to be a regular at Bhulabhai auditorium. He first saw Haribhai when the latter was playing the father in an adaptation of *All My Sons*, a play by Arthur Miller. It was directed by P.D. Shenoy. Hari was twenty-three at the time. He was playing husband to Leela Chitnis, a very senior actor who was in her fifties at the time, and father to Manavendra Chitnis, who was about the same age as he. 'I was stunned to watch him pull off the role with ease. It was such a beautiful performance,' says Gulzar.

'Now, Papaji (Prithviraj Kapoor) had come to watch the play. He had been invited by P.D. Shenoy. After the play, we were all standing together—Papaji, Sagar Sarhadi (who went on to write *Kabhi Kabhie*), Haribhai (who had then removed his make-up) and I.'

'Papaji ended up asking Haribhai, "Who was that old man who played the part very well?" Haribhai laughed, and Papaji was shocked to know it was him.'

Gulzar recalls that there cannot be a bigger compliment. Such observations about Hari's acting were made time and again, and this aggregate regard and appreciation is what Haribhai carried with him.

It is well known that Gulzar and Haribhai were very close. Their first project together was *Sunghursh* (1968), a film starring Dilip Kumar, produced and directed by Harnam Singh Rawail. Gulzar wrote the dialogues for the film.

Gulzar remembers the first scene Haribhai shot for *Sunghursh*. It was a game of shatranj (chess). 'He had a dialogue, "*Chaal to hum chal chuke*". Dilip Kumar sahab saw the way the dialogue was delivered by Haribhai and paused. He was clearly acknowledging the actor's brilliance. He enquired about Haribhai with the director Harnam Singh Rawail, who plainly said, "I found him in theatre".'

Gulzar had two professional anchors in his life—Haribhai and R.D. Burman. He would always first put both of them in his projects and then look for the rest of the talent. They did a lot of work together, including great films like *Parichay* (1972), *Koshish* (1972), *Mausam* (1975), *Aandhi* (1975), *Angoor* (1982) and *Namkeen* (1982).

Gulzar says that he would read an entire scene with Haribhai, rehearse it and then start shooting it. From there he would leave it open for Hari to take it to the next level. 'Haribhai could take a simple dialogue and add so many nuances into it that I needed to say nothing more to him. The scene would turn out to be exemplary.'

He adds, 'Once I told him, "*Bas kar*, stop playing old men in films." He said, "Look who's talking!" True enough, I did write roles for him that aged him; the younger bits came only in flashbacks.'

Over the course of their many shoots, Gulzar recalls that Haribhai was a favourite with the women. 'He was a simpleton, they would often come forward to help him dress better, choose a different-coloured tie, etc. Also, another aspect of Haribhai's brilliance, often ignored, is the natural ease with which he would lip-sync and picturize his songs.' Gulzar especially recalls the song '*Beeti na bitaayi raina*' from *Parichay*.

'Haribhai comes down the steps and joins the song mid-sentence. He picked up the mood of the song so flawlessly, so viscerally, that I was stunned. When I saw his take for the song, I told him, "Ask what you want, *jo mango doonga.*"

'He said, "Will you? For sure?"

'For a minute, I pondered, "What could he possibly want?" But then, he told me, "*Paan chod do.*" I wasn't aware that he hated my habit of chewing paan. I gave up paan from that day. Such was our friendship.'

Naturally, there were several personal dimensions to the relationship as well. Gulzar was very fond of Haribhai's manager Jamnadasji. Food was often a common conversation topic for both Hari and Gulzar. 'I was very fond of the patra, a Gujarati dish that his mother used to make. She would often send it for me. Haribhai, on the other hand, was very fond of non-veg food. He would come to my place; there was a phase in our life where standing orders were given to my cook—to be ever ready with a hearty meal for Haribhai! I had to wake my sister up to cook for him. Haribhai would tell me, "I will come anytime. I need Black Label. If you cannot afford it, I will leave a bottle here with you." He was a "*dheela aadmi*", a happy man who loved to relax after a hard day's work.'

It was evident to all how close Gulzar and Hari were. Sharmila Tagore recalls distinctly how Gulzar's sister would sit down to peel green peas and join them in their pre-dinner conversations. Gulzar corroborates, 'With every film that we shot together, there was one understanding—after the last scene of a schedule or the last shot, we would pack up, come home sit down with food and drinks. After Hari's mother passed away, we sat down and watched *Dumbo*, a movie about a mother elephant and a baby elephant, on a few occasions. He would cry. When his heart problems began, I encouraged him to go to the best of doctors so that he could get better soon. Finally, when he went for his surgery in 1985, he kept telling me that he wanted to change his house and that he was finding it difficult to climb the two floors to his house. Somehow, that never happened. Perhaps he was too attached to Perrin Villa.'

Gulzar adds, 'Our last interaction was when I spotted him standing next to his car, during one of my walks. He was standing and talking to someone.

'*Dil ka kya haal hai?*" I asked after his health.

'*Per ke neeche se nas lagate hain—dil ko laat maarneki adat ho gayi hai,*" he said. (The doctors have inserted a tube through the leg to the heart, so the heart has got into the habit of getting kicked!)

'Such a sense of humour about a disease that was all set to take his life! Haribhai lived courageously and was a bright and happy young man. He could see the funny side of his own impending death—what could be more courageous than that?'

SECTION VII

Hurricane Hari

1

Waning, Wining and Dining

After Baa's demise, Hari's drinking became uncontrolled. Tanuja says, 'Baa would feed him food at home after his drinks, and at least put a full stop after a point. After Baa passed away, he started going out to drink and there was absolutely no one he would listen to. After he got drunk, he would do exactly what he wanted to do. He ate like a glutton! He had no self-discipline and there was no one who imposed discipline on him either. Was all that excess filling some void? He was a very private person and he never showed what was deep inside. The truth is, he was drowning in his own emotions. Sometimes, I think I was the only person whom he could've confided in. And I wish he had, fully. It can destroy you, when you cannot share your innermost thoughts.'

Despite their good intentions, Hari's well-meaning successful actor friends from the industry had family commitments, and they couldn't give Hari time, night after night, to keep him company. Hari had no wife to go home to. All he was left with was his gang, led by Subhash Indori.

An article by Anil Chitre in the July 1980 issue of *Cine Blitz* talks about how Hari did not know when to stop drinking. At Rajkumar Kohli's silver jubilee party for *Jaani Dushman* (the film released in May 1979), when Hari boozed till the early hours of the morning, hardly aware of his surroundings, it was Subhash Indori who stood stoically by his side. Indori is famously known to have never left Hari's side, regardless of how 'drunk' Hari was.

Indori said to Anil Chitre, 'His close friends Satpal Verma and I used to dissuade him from drinking and smoking, but the problem was that he doesn't like anyone telling him not to drink and smoke. He hates being fussed over and is aware of his health. He has accepted the fact philosophically.'

Sulakshana Pandit disagrees. In her earlier mentioned blog on Cineplot.com, she has written, 'His friends, who were also drunkards, took advantage of him. Had I been with him I would have thrown out all his bottles, one by one.'

Fellow actor Moushumi Chatterjee also discouraged Hari's nightly revelry. 'I had asked him why he was gathering "yes men" around him ... *woh tumhara daru peete hain, pakoda khaate hain,*" I told him. I also remarked pointedly that they were not capable of true friendship! Jariwala told me, "Maybe I have a little complex. An inferiority complex." Jariwala was an excellent judge of character and always knew what he was doing. I warned him that one day this behaviour would take his life. When you abuse your health, your health abuses you right back. But he remained naive about this, and poured his heart and soul into his performances. He had no energy for seriousness in any other part of his life.'

Uday Jariwala, too, is in broad agreement with the observation that people used Hari for their own gains. Hari somehow seemed to be aware of this. In an interview with *Filmfare* in 1980, Hari had said, 'I don't have a friend or a companion. Sanjeev Kumar has many friends, but Harihar Jariwala doesn't have any.'

Younger brother Nikul's position became awkward. Uday explains, 'It's logical to ask, did none of us try to stop Sanjeev Dada from his addictive drinking? But the age difference between my father and Sanjeev Dada was quite a bit. My father's position was very awkward as he had grown up under Dada's shadow and found it very difficult to question him or stop him. So I never saw my father confronting him about his drinking habit or joining him during his sessions. My mother Jyoti too could never muster the courage to discuss his lifestyle with him.'

The family, however, spoke to Jamnadasji about it to enlist his help. But Jamnadasji also had given up. *'Kya karoon? Peene ke baad, ek kaan se sunta hai, doosre kaan se nikalta hai.'*

During the shoot of *Daasi*, Hari told reporter Jyoti Venkatesh, as reported in *The Free Press Journal* in December 1980, 'My doctors have advised me to give up liquor and cigarettes, but I've been unable to give them up because I'm addicted. I've cut down on my intake, but I've not been able to give them up altogether.'

Friends Subhash Sanas and Kadir Pirzada confirm that on several occasions Hari did try to give up alcohol, but found it too difficult. In 1985, Ram Advani and R.K. Nayyar—producers of the film *Qatl*—hosted a party for Hari in which he met the press after his return from surgery. In a clipping of an article titled 'Director's Headache' available in the family archives, where neither the publication nor the journalist's name is visible, Hari had said, 'My hands used to be around a whisky glass, now I don't know what to do with them.' It is well known that Hari could not stick to this resolve and went back to drinking.

'The prescription for him was always no alcohol, no cigarettes, no spicy food. But he never listened,' says Subhash Sanas, who spent many evenings with Haribhai. 'To add to this, food was his weakness. He would eat several meals in a single night, completely surrendering to the sin of the moment.'

Hari was definitely prone to excesses on the food front. Randhir Kapoor says, 'I remember one incident distinctly. During the shoot of *Biwi-O-Biwi* at Chandivali studios, we were all having lunch. Now, R.K. was the banner producing the film, and we always made our own food. Harry and I had just got up after a full meal. Even dessert was done. Harry was about to wash his hands when a boy came in and said, "Ek tiffin aaya hai." Harry promptly sat down again and had a second lunch! He was that fond of food. Again, this was 1980 and Harry had already had two episodes with his heart. I knew he didn't take his heart problem seriously enough because he knew it wasn't in his hands. I think he knew he was dying—I could sense that he wasn't vested in the idea of recovering himself fully.'

Fellow actor Parikshit Sahni, who was very close to Hari, said in an interview with Bollywood Hungama:

> We often shared a drink in the evening, and he could drink anyone under the table. He could guzzle up a bottle of Dimple Scotch as though it was a bottle of Pepsi. One could rarely tell that the booze was having an effect on him, it was usually well past midnight before food would be served, and

he could polish off an entire handi of payas, mutton curry, a couple of tandoori chicken, kebabs and other delicacies with the help of half a dozen naans! But even that was nothing compared to what I witnessed when Haribhai and I were shooting in a casino in Las Vegas for a film by Jagmohan Mundhra called *Suraag*. We were shooting till two in the morning and Haribhai was hungry. So we made our way to a nearby Chinese restaurant that was open all night.

Haribhai took a fair amount of time ordering food. After he had placed the order, the waiter politely asked him when the rest of the diners would arrive. 'Who others?' Haribhai asked in surprise. 'Surely this food is not just for the two of you?!' the waiter remarked. 'Yes, it is!' Haribhai replied nonchalantly. The waiter left, looking totally dazed.

When the food arrived, the table creaked under its weight. It was enough for an army platoon. I had ordered a plate of jumbo prawns and rice for myself. When Haribhai started to eat, the entire Chinese staff of the restaurant stepped out and stood against the far wall to see how two people could possibly finish off so much food!

They couldn't believe their eyes when Haribhai ate with relish and finished off the entire spread with consummate ease. He didn't even spare the plate of jumbo prawns that I had ordered for myself. And I got to eat just one prawn! I heard one of the Chinese chefs saying, 'Indian people velly stlong people, velly stlong people!' as he returned to the kitchen.[26]

---

26 https://www.bollywoodhungama.com/news/features/parikshit-sahni-talks-about-his-best-friend-sanjeev-kumar/

Perhaps Hari's liquid and gastronomic courage was literally just that—a way for him to briefly forget his hereditary heart disease; a little giggle juice for a troubled soul!

Was there a self-destructive streak in him? He was pushing the envelope as an actor—but did he also want to see how much he could push God?

2

Stardom, Interrupted

It was the 1980s, and times were changing not just in terms of Hari's physical and emotional decline but also in terms of competition. A new crop of heroes was in the fray—Mithun Chakraborty, Sanjay Dutt, Anil Kapoor, Jackie Shroff and Sunny Deol.

Hari's slew of heart attacks had some people backing out of projects to which he had committed. Other high-quality projects did not materialize. In 1980, the Telugu superhit *Sankarabharanam,* starring J.V. Somayajulu, was released. There were talks that Sanjeev Kumar would reprise it in Hindi. That role would have added to Haribhai's repertoire of priceless roles.

A few like Gulzar remained loyal and wrote *Angoor* for him, which was a resounding success. The July 1982 issue of *Film World* had Sanjeev Kumar on the cover, calling him the 'Killer of Superstars'. His co-star in *Angoor*, the respected comedian Deven Varma, also said in an interview:

> I enjoyed working with Sanjeev Kumar the most. People think from my surname Varma that I am Punjabi. But I belong to Kutch so I speak Gujarati and Kutchi. Sanju and I got along well. We spoke in Gujarati on the sets and we ate the same kind of food. He had no ego; he never tried to cut down your scene or do something to upset the shot or take the focus on him. He would appreciate others' work too. There were lots of actors who would get your scene cut from the movie.[27]

As said earlier in the book, Gulzar and Hari were great friends. Hari used to share all his worries with him. Hari's kidneys were in bad shape, and it was during the time they spent together during *Angoor* that Gulzar persuaded him to get his kidneys treated or get a transplant and also to get a proper heart surgery done.[28]

But *Angoor* was an exception, not the rule. Most fans will agree that less than five of his best films released post-1980. Barring *Angoor, Silsila, Shriman Shrimati, Khud-Daar, Qatl* and *Namkeen*, the sixty-odd films featuring Hari that released in this period were qualitatively just not what people had begun to expect from Hari.

Hari himself was quoted as saying in the June 1980 issue of *Filmfare:* 'Being considered the greatest actor is the biggest joke I've played on the film industry.'

What could have made him say this? Hari's staff could feel his pain. 'Sanjeev has helped not only upcoming and new producers

---

27 https://www.rediff.com/movies/report/sanjeev-kumar-had-no-ego-ashok-kumar-had-a-feminine-voice/20141202.htm

28 https://www.filmfare.com/features/actor-for-all-seasons-sanjeev-kumar-5000-12.html

but sometimes even the established ones by working free of charge for them. And yet, it was the same people who without any scruples visited Sanjeev at the hospital and informed him of being dropped from their movies. Tell me, how much more suffering can a man take?' Sarosh Mody said with anguish in the December 1982 issue of *Stardust*.

Close friend Subhash Indori echoes this sentiment and vouches for Hari's magnanimity. 'He would say, "Don't cancel the shooting for the sake of money. Take it from me." He has given money to Raj Tilak for *Chehre Pe Chehra* (1981), Satram Rohra for *Ghar Ki Laaj* (1979) and Arun Verma for *Heere Jawaharat* (which never released).'

One might understand that the producers were being cautious—an unfinished film is a bad investment. Besides, Hari's expanded girth, his severely combed hair attempting to hide his bald patches and his puffy face weren't helping either. It almost seemed like Hari was telling filmmakers, 'This is how I am, take it or leave it.' Even Meryl Streep has famously said, 'I think the most liberating thing I did early on was to free myself from any concern with my looks as they pertained to my work.' Hari seemed to have done the same from a very early point in his career.

There wasn't much cheer in his personal circumstances either. In 1982, when brother Nikul had his first heart attack, he was shaken. Uday recalls, 'I had never seen Sanjeev Dada angry. But when my father had a heart attack, Sanjeev Dada was very upset. My mother was inundated with work, at the hospital and at home, and for some reason I was being difficult to manage. I also hit someone in the building and they complained to Sanjeev Dada. Dada confronted me and slapped me very hard for not understanding what my mother was going through. I saw stars in the daylight and cried all the way from home up to Nanavati hospital where my father was being treated.'

The pressures of his responsibilities and his loneliness were building up. Kadir Pirzada says, 'I was worried about his health and also that he wasn't a smart investor. He put money in a Bangalore hotel just because someone told him to. In Mumbai too, I could see how other people used to spend his money.'

As quality work dried up, the normally easy-going Hari became quieter. In Sarosh Mody's interview in the December 1982 issue of *Stardust*, he observed, 'Sanjeev's nature had undergone a tremendous change too. He's become more serious, irritable, moody and less open to suggestions. Till sometime back, anyone could go to Sanjeev and he would listen to them with an open mind. He would laugh and talk with anyone and everyone. But lately, I've seen so many people trying to make conversation with Sanjeev, while he just sits silently, with a blank look.'

Hari agreed with Sarosh Mody's observation in the same interview, 'Yes, I do admit that I have changed a lot. I have mellowed down and become more serious. If I wanted to survive in the industry, I couldn't just go on being the way I was. The industry is a tough place and one has to learn how to adapt and change to be able to take things as they come, without breaking down.'

Tanuja says, 'Harry was a good human being with a heart so big that he trusted everybody. But so many people let him down.'

To his credit, Hari continued to find character roles in the 1980s, too, though they weren't as memorable as his earlier roles. For example, he worked with Jackie Shroff in *Hero* (1983), with

Mithun Chakraborty in *Hum Paanch* (1980), with Sanjay Dutt in *Vidhaata* (1982) and with Anil Kapoor in *Humare Tumhare* (1979). Several actors who were prominent in the 1970s were struggling during this period to establish longevity and continuity.

But Hari's professionalism ensured that filmmakers continued to bet on him. The superhit film *Hero*, which launched Jackie Shroff and Meenakshi Sheshadri, features a qawwali filmed on Sanjeev Kumar. Uday recalls, 'Sanjeev Dada had a few costume changes in the film and the shoot for the day had wrapped up. It was then that the director Subhash Ghai remembered that there was some part still left to be shot. He rushed to Dada's dressing room and requested, "*Thoda sa hi baaki hai.*" '

Now, Hari had changed fully, and his mood had switched, all ready for his nightly revelry, which meant he was wearing his trademark lungi and kurta. But he had a golden rule—he would finish his work for the day; he would not call it a day till the director was satisfied.

Without so much as a whisper of protest, Hari nodded, changed his top and finished the song. In fact, getting ready for the shot took much longer than the shot itself, which he nailed with precision.

3

Forgettable Films

Even a cursory look at Hari's last few films before his death reveals that a few of them cannot be defended or endured even by the most ardent fans!

Rusvai, starring Hari and Ranjeeta, never released, and this was confirmed by the leading lady herself. That makes *Zabardast* the last film of his to release before his death on 21 June 1985. Its rating of 5.3 (on IMDb) could be considered generous. Even Hari is over the top in the film as he screams uncontrollably and collapses, clutching at his heart! The film sank without a trace, despite being a Nasir Hussain film and featuring a young Sunny Deol. Reading the various reviews available online, one could say that the story sagged under its own weight and lacked in content.

Ram Tere Kitne Naam released on 15 February 1985. Starring Hari in the lead with Rekha, the project was originally launched in 1974 with Rajesh Khanna. This was director P. Madhavan's remake of his own award-winning Tamil film *Raman Ethanai Ramanadi* (1970), starring Sivaji Ganesan. Hari is rather uncharitably named 'Petu Ram' in the film; he plays a big actor who is unlucky in love. The story is spookily close to Hari's own life and flopped at the box office.

Mera Dost Mera Dushman doesn't seem to have a release date. An action movie with an abysmal 5.2 rating (on IMDb), the film is not even available for viewing on the internet. However, the songs are available, but they do not appear to have any redeeming quality. The song *Goli Chacha Ko Salaam Karo* rendered by Hari seems like a force fit that even Hari does not seem convinced by.

Dasari Narayana Rao's *Yaadgaar* starring Kamal Haasan and Poonam Dhillon with Hari released on 20 July 1984. This is the only venture that Kamal Hassan and Hari did together. A well-mounted project, the film is a social commentary on whether behavioural change is indeed possible, especially when people are perceived to be of a certain type. Hari plays a superstitious rich man, the evocation of which happens in comic style, and is in fine fettle. The last scene in which Hari breaks down and yet manages to laugh for a dying Kamal Hassan is a veritable manual that can be prescribed to students of acting.

Lakhon Ki Baat came days before that. Released on 6 July 1984, three days before Hari's forty-seventh birthday, the film is a remake of the delightful *Fortune Cookie*. The original film starred Jack Lemmon as a cameraman who is injured while filming a football match. His brother over-projects his injury to make a big legal claim. In *Lakhon Ki Baat*, Farooq Sheikh plays the photographer, and Sanjeev Kumar plays the lawyer. Hari and Farooq Sheikh are together for the second time after *Shatranj Ke Khilari* (1977). Fresh from the success of *Chashme Buddoor* and

Kissi Se Na Kehna, Farooq Sheikh was popular in the comedy genre. The film was received reasonably well. About a couple of other films, the less said, the better. Released on 1 January 1984, *Bad Aur Badnam* was such bedlam that Hari, Shatrughan Sinha and Parveen Babi together couldn't bring any order to the proceedings. A review says: 'The heroes seem past their prime and in need of better belts to stop their paunches from running ahead of them.'

Pakhandee, also released on 1 January 1984, begins promisingly, but the editing has holes wider than islands. In one scene, Hari is speaking to Ranjeet, who is playing the villain, wearing a green jacket and with frizzy hair. Ranjeet wants to show Hari something, and they go to see it together. But when they reach their destination, Hari is wearing a shiny red jacket and has neatly swept-back gelled hair. The editing is simply incomprehensible. Announced originally in 1974, it took nine years to ready the film for release—the effort and the patchwork are both uncomfortably visible.

What is worse about this period is that Hari's voice had changed, and his dialogue delivery started following a pattern. Mimics, who had been struggling to find a weak point in Hari's performances, were now quick to pick up these patterns. Doppelgängers hammed away to a supposed Hari impersonation, wearing a white kurta and dangling their arms, a la *Sholay* mode.

4

A Legacy All His Own

BY BHARATHI S. PRADHAN

If Haribhai wasn't the top box-office hero of his time, it was because he tended to prioritize his role in a project over its saleability.

In his days, there were be no monster weekend collections and hurried pronouncements about the fate of a film. We would allow a movie to settle for about ten to fifteen days before the trade gave its verdict. And the truth is that some of the films featuring Haribhai as a solo hero didn't do well. On the other hand, there were films like *Pati Patni Aur Woh,* where he powered the show and did exceedingly well.

I do believe that it was a conscious decision on his part to not pursue being a conventional romantic hero. If he had wanted to be a hero, he wouldn't have let his waistline expand unchecked. He would've been more careful. But his acting overshadowed his physique, and that's why he was so well-respected as an actor.

Whenever he teamed up with another hero, he would bring energy into the film. In an era where Amitabh Bachchan wouldn't share screen space with Rajesh Khanna anymore or had problems with Vinod Khanna during the shooting of *Muqaddar Ka Sikandar*, everybody willingly worked with Sanjeev Kumar; probably because he wasn't in competition with anybody for the tag of No. 1 hero or superstar.

Anybody who says that Sanjeev Kumar was in a rush to do as many films as possible because he had a premonition that he had a short life would be quite off the mark. In the 1970s, all actors did multiple shifts in a day. Shashi Kapoor would show me his schedule for the day where he'd have allotted a few hours to a film before rushing off to shoot for another. Kapoor, like many others, would do three or even four shifts in a day. That was the time when Raj Kapoor famously called his brother a taxi, and yet Shashi had a long life. So, I wouldn't equate Haribhai's early death with wanting to pack as much as possible into a short life.

There are two ways to interpret his legacy. One is when an actor who aspires to be a hero says, *'Arre yaar, mere ko Sanjeev Kumar nahi banna hai.'* Here, actors did not want to become a Sanjeev Kumar because he epitomized the character artiste with a wide range of performances and not just as the conventional hero. Another way of looking at his legacy is the way people compare an Ayushmann Khurrana with Sanjeev Kumar—by which they mean an actor who makes unafraid, bold choices.

The best way to illustrate Sanjeev Kumar's courageous choices would be to look at the ease with which he played Jaya Bhaduri's husband in *Koshish*, her parent in *Parichay* and her father-in-law in *Sholay*. Those were times when actors played safe and didn't tamper with their 'hero' image. I'd say this was what set him apart from the rest.

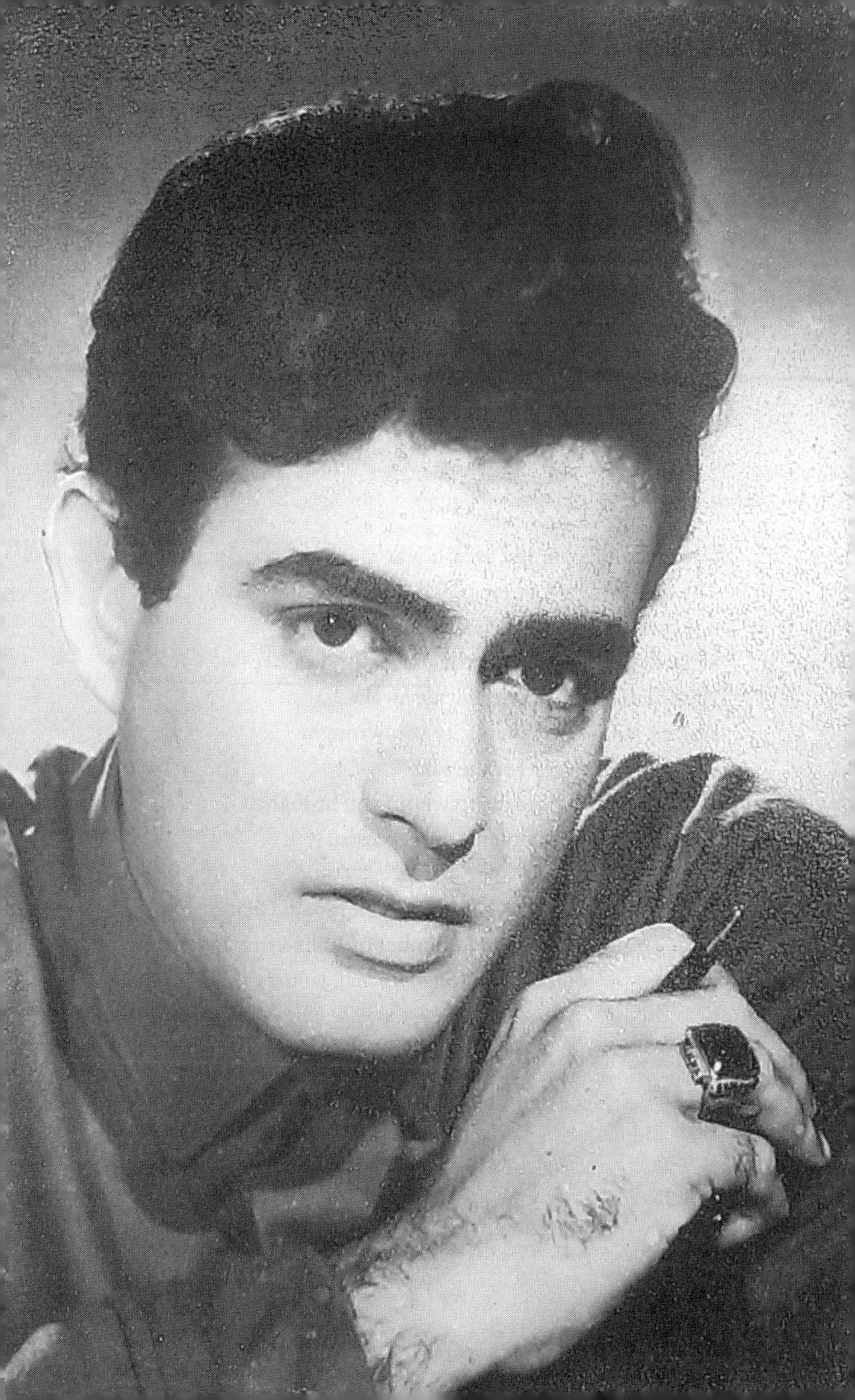

A Tribute to Hari

The heave of your last breath was
The first heave of a new ocean touching a new sky
It is sheer ignorance for us to grieve
Since deathless ones like you can never die!
Your memory in us keeps wide awake
Master! With what simplicity you wrought
Rare historic magic for the sake
Of millions of your fans to whom you brought
Enormous entertainment, unsurpassed.

—Dr Harindranath Chattopadhyay
Poet and Member of India's first Lok Sabha
Cinema India-International, January–March 1986

SECTION VIII

The Last Lap

1

The Thronging Crowds

The Morning after,
Voices lost cheer.
A solemn moment
Antithetical, unclear.

His breath no more
But spirit thrives;
Must we mourn
Art that survives?

—Reeta Ramamurthy Gupta

On Hari's final journey to his maker, fans expressed their grief publicly. The crowds at Perrin Villa stretched out over a kilometre from the building, and police had to be called to manage the situation.

Close friend Kadir Pirzada remembers, 'Haribhai's funeral was a moving experience because of the sincerity with which people were crying. There was utter shock and disbelief. People had not had enough of him. Along with his brother Kishore, Amitabh Bachchan, Shatrughan Sinha, Shammi Kapoor and I held the four corners of the cot that held his body, on the way to the crematorium.'

The journey from Perrin Villa to the Santa Cruz Hindu Crematorium was of less than fifteen minutes, but that day it took hours! As the flower-laden truck with Hari's smiling photo made its way down the roads, the crowds wanted to somehow express solidarity with Hari and their loss.

'Everyone attended Bhai's funeral,' remembers Jyoti, who was in a daze during those few days, suddenly finding herself all alone with three children. Her son Uday performed Hari's last rites amid an overpouring of grief for a much-loved man. Uday, Jamnadasji, Kishore Jariwala and Ashok Patel went to Allahabad to immerse Hari's ashes at the Sangam. The flight was via Lucknow. When the ground staff got to know who they were and why they had come, an elaborate meal was arranged for Hari's family at Lucknow airport. It was as if Hari's death was personal to everyone who loved him!

Shatrughan Sinha remembers, 'When I heard on the final day that Sanjeev Bhai is no more, I felt terribly lonely and disconsolate. I reached Perrin Villa at about 5 p.m. and stood at his side till midnight. I was in shock. His embalmed body was calm and peaceful. As memories chased before my eyes, I was reminded that even though I am the youngest in my house, it was Sanjeev Bhai who had been a true elder brother to me. He was my first and last friend, philosopher and guide.'

Actor Parikshit Sahni, too, had a very emotional moment during the funeral. He says, 'Haribhai and I shared a very close bond. When I acted in my first Hindi film *Anokhi Raat*, I knew very little about acting (having just returned from Russia after doing a course in film direction). I was not well-versed in Hindi and delivered my lines atrociously. The producer tore his hair whenever he came on the sets and wanted to boot me out of the film. Haribhai, my co-artiste, a newcomer himself, taught me correct diction and the importance of pausing during dialogue delivery. … At his funeral, I pushed my way to his pier through the milling crowds and touched his feet before his body was consigned to the flames. I wept bitterly, as I had lost one of my best friends.'[29]

Even those who couldn't attend the funeral somehow paid him their last respects. Hari's relationship with Amjad Khan was reportedly mercurial. Amjad Khan was on a stage tour with R.D. Burman and Asha Bhosle when the news of Hari's demise reached him. Immediately, he asked the audience to maintain silence for a minute so they could all pay their last respects together.

Contemporaries never hesitated to appreciate Hari, even if only at his deathbed. In the blog *South Asia Daily*, journalist Mayank Chhaya writes:

'I never met Kumar. It is ironic that the only time I saw him was on the day he died, laying down between two slabs of ice on the floor of his apartment in Bandra/Khar neighbourhood of Bombay. I had gone to report on his funeral. I vividly remember talking to superstar Rajesh Khanna who had come to pay his

29 https://www.bollywoodhungama.com/news/features/parikshit-sahni-talks-about-his-best-friend-sanjeev-kumar/

last respects to a "dear" colleague and whom he considered "formidable." "Haribhai was an actor's actor," Khanna told me.'[30]

Uday Jariwala remains emotionally attached to Hari to this day. 'After Sanjeev Dada's demise, I was in denial for a really long time. Every time the doorbell rang in the night, I would imagine that Sanjeev Dada had somehow miraculously returned,' he says.

But the last word belongs to Tanuja, who pays him an exceptional tribute, probably just what Hari would've liked to hear. 'I don't feel sorry for Harry at all. He chose his life and lived his forty-seven years fully. He experienced love, friendship, success, adulation and stardom. There will never be an actor of his calibre again. His legacy is untouchable.'

30 https://southasia.typepad.com/south_asia_daily/2015/11/sanjeev-kumar-deft-light-and-effortless.html

2

The Enduring Music of Hari's Films

WITH RJ ANIRUDH CHAWLA

In 2019, Film and Television Institute of India conducted a two-day retrospective titled 'Smaranjali' for Hari. The students made the event interactive by recreating some of his superhit songs like '*Tere bina zindagi se shikva toh nahi*', '*Khilona jaan kar tum toh*', '*Baahon mein chaley aao*', '*Dil dhoondtaa hai phir wahi*' ...

In India, music is inextricably connected to an actor's memorableness, and Hari was blessed to have worked with composers like Shankar–Jaikishan, Laxmikant–Pyarelal and R.D. Burman, who made the songs he picturized transcend time.

RJ Anirudh Chawla has immense knowledge about the music of Hari's films. A curator of priceless Hindi film-related memorabilia, Chawla owns such a vast array of material that an entire retrospective on Indian cinema is conceivable with his collection alone.

He starts off with a forgotten kind of book—the A5-sized song booklets—which used to be so popular in the 1970s and '80s. Chawla says, 'Song booklets were sold before the release of the film, at railway stations and outside single-screen theatres. They were also given to the media as promotional material, to get them to know more about the cast and crew that was credited for the film. A song booklet typically has about eight to ten pages and features the synopsis of the film, the lyrics in Hindi and in Urdu and the film poster as the front and back cover.'

Chawla is in possession of a variety of song booklets of Hari's films like *Aandhi*, *Pati Patni Aur Woh*, *Qatl* and *Gustakhi Maaf*, preserved carefully. The song booklet of the film *Ladies Tailor* carried an announcement of another film on its back cover, *Hanste Hanste Ho Gayi Baat,* a film that never got made. 'It was common practice in those days to announce two films with the same lead jodi. However, the second film would get made only if the jodi worked,' says Chawla. Mahurats to announce films were also a trend by themselves. For example, the producer or director would invite a legend like Dilip Kumar and announce a film that they intended to make in the near future.

Chawla adds that Hari's memory is eternally etched amongst music lovers because of some truly timeless tunes. Haunting melodies like '*Tere bina zindagi se koi*' from *Aandhi* or '*Meri bheegi bheegi si*' from *Anamika* remain alive and relevant even today.

Chawla layers the music in Haribhai films into phases: 'Sanjeev Kumar's songs straddled three stages. The first, when he had not yet built his persona, such as "*Tumhare zulf ke saaye mein*" from *Naunihal* and "*Tere naam ka deewana*" from *Suraj Aur Chanda*, both sung by Mohammed Rafi.

'The next phase was that of a young, effervescent hero. This was evidenced in "*O manchali, kahaan chali*" from *Manchali* and "*Hawa ke saath saat*h" in *Seeta aur Geeta*. This is the phase when Kishore Kumar's voice suited him best. He and Kishore were completely in sync in the melodious "*Gham ka fasaana*" from *Manchali*. However, even during this phase, a bulk of the songs in Haribhai's films were being sung by the female lead. For instance, in *Anamika*, most of the songs belong to Jaya Bhaduri. A reason for this could probably be that the audience expected dance movements and popular mannerisms to underline songs, both of which Haribhai did not care for.

'The third phase was characterized by maturity, the songs mostly populated by Gulzar and R.D. Burman. By now, Haribhai had become an iconic actor with a language all his own, as evidenced by *Aandhi* and *Mausam*. Whether it was "*Dil dhoondtha hai*" by Bhupinder Singh or "*Is mod se jaate hain*" with Kishore Kumar, it was difficult to mimic Hari because his portrayal of songs comprised dramatic pauses and a very distinctive use of his body. This mature way of delivering songs was aided by the genius of both Burman and Gulzar. Several films back then did not even have a choreographer. *Aandhi*, for instance, does not credit any. It was Haribhai's sense of timing, and how he introduced inflections and pauses, using his expressive face and his body language, that were his unique art.'

Perhaps one could identify another phase, the fourth phase, where he wasn't being considered for songs at all—such as in *Vidhaata* and *Sawaal*.

The other aspect of Haribhai's songs was the manner in which he would lip-sync them. He sang his songs loudly during filming, like Moushumi Chatterjee and Rishi Kapoor. One such song, '*Thande thande paani se*', featured Haribhai displaying his belly in its full glory! His candour and unabashed approach towards his own body were inconceivable. Equally interesting was the gusto with which Mahendra Kapoor, known for his patriotic songs, belted out this number!

It's this kind of behaviour, characteristic of outliers, that made Haribhai stand out. Perhaps in the current generation, Vidya Balan is the only actor who has this kind of gumption. In an industry where north Indian lead actors ruled the roost, Haribhai's rise to fame was purely a function of his audacious confidence. He was also loved deeply by his friends and colleagues. Perhaps one of Haribhai's most eternal friendships was with Gulzar, who often said that he had two eyes—one was Pancham [R.D. Burman] and the other, Haribhai.

'I wonder,' sums up Chawla, 'how it might have been if Sanjay Leela Bansali had directed Haribhai for a song!' A grand thought, that!

3

Qatl: A Redemption

Thirteen films of Hari's released after his death. Out of those, *Qatl* managed to endure the test of time. The movie features the thrilling story of a blind man plotting a heist—a new kind of plot for Indian audiences.

Hari's first posthumous release, *Qatl* opened to audiences on 24 January 1986. The movie credits open with a tribute to Hari. He plays a famous actor who goes blind, trying to save his wife Sarika's life. Ranjeeta plays his nurse. Over time, Hari realizes that Sarika is having an affair. He plots an elaborate murder, using his senses of touch, smell and sound. After months of practice, he manages to murder his wife. He also knows that thanks to his blindness, he would never be a suspect in the case.

Those who have seen *Qatl* can easily distinguish between the portly, pre-heart-surgery Hari and the skinny post-surgery Hari with ease in the film.

Hari's co-star Ranjeeta recalls that she was both nervous and intimidated when she stood face to face with Hari for the first time. It was for a photo shoot for their earlier film *Pati Patni Aur Woh*. 'I was taught at FTII that cinema requires that the actor establish an equation with the camera. This is what I focused on, so as to maintain my composure. I had been told that Haribhai's flawless dialogue delivery can stupefy his co-actors. His prowess was legendary, and just by observing him, I learnt so much,' she admits candidly. 'Haribhai never interfered with anyone else, and he didn't expect you to follow his lead. He just trusted you to do your job.'

Pati Patni Aur Woh went on to become a silver jubilee hit. Two films, *Inspector Daku Aur Woh* and *Rusvai*, which Hari and Ranjeeta shot for, never released (the song booklets are available, though). Then there was *Hathkadi,* which released in 1982.

Hari's last film was the convoluted comic caper *Professor Ki Padosan,* which released in July 1994, nine years after his demise. It had Asha Parekh, Deven Verma and Padmini Kolhapure. Amitabh Bachchan participated in a special segment in the opening and closing credits of the film and offered shraddhanjali to his friend 'Haribhai', with whom he had worked in so many blockbusters.

There were bits of the film that Haribhai had not completed shooting for. Hence, the filmmakers used a cigarette dangling in thin air and a voice-over by Sudesh Bhosle, to give the impression of Hari and patch up the ending of the film.

'Haribhai had an uncomplicated reputation—everyone knew he was a man who loved drinking, smoking and eating. I wasn't friendly with him, but I had massive respect for him. When I attended his funeral, and saw him lying down—serene and quiet—I sincerely wished that his legend would live on,' says Ranjeeta.

4

The Truth behind Hari's Health

Many of Hari's medical reports and diagnoses have not been preserved and are not available today. What was the nature of his heart disease? Dr Ramakanta Panda, one of the world's best-known cardiac surgeons and who runs the famous Asian Heart Institute in Bandra Kurla Complex, has an explanation. He remembers reading about Sanjeev Kumar's heart issue when he was working at Cleveland Clinic in the US in 1985.

> I knew Dr M.J. Gandhi, the doctor who was treating him, well. There are a few important things to understand about Sanjeev Kumar's case. He had a strong family history of coronary heart disease, with many family members suffering from it. In Sanjeev Kumar's case, like those with strong family history of coronary heart disease, even though he had no symptoms in early years the cholesterol deposits start to

build up slowly inside the coronary arteries to be manifested in thirties and forties.

Medically speaking, there are many things we know today that we didn't know in the 1970s. For example: firstly, the protective effect of aspirin in preventing heart attacks was not known. Secondly, cholesterol medicine wasn't there in the 1970s and '80s—statins came in the '90s. Hence, doctors had limited options to manage heart disease and recurrences were common. Thirdly, only vein grafts were common in those days in cardiac surgery. It was only in 1986 that the world knew that arterial grafts are better than vein grafts. Even the best surgeon at the time—and I mean Dr Denton Cooley who operated on Sanjeev Kumar—would've had limitations in terms of how to manage the case. Today, we know that arterial grafts improve the outcome of cardiac surgery much better. Finally, the contribution of sedentary lifestyle and poor habits in making cardiac disease worse weren't fully understood then.

One can also say that in those times, the idea of family history in coronary artery disease may not have been understood or documented. Traditional joint families had poor food habits and were prone to a significant amount of overeating. Sanjeev Kumar himself was known to eat and drink in excess.

But how do you explain the gluttony? Modern psychologists concur that food is often used as a 'numbing' strategy. In the words of Dr Amanda Baten, a nutritional psychologist, 'Food is a distraction strategy in the same way that people might use alcohol or drugs or sex or TV as ways to create a buffer between themselves and whatever difficult feelings they might be experiencing.'[31]

Here it is useful to remember that Hari always had to be strong for his family, given that his father passed away early and the responsibility of settling his siblings fell on him. He was not comfortable showing his vulnerability. He was accustomed to suppressing what he felt.

Hari was aware of his early, impending death. Isn't it logical then to surmise that he was in fear of this? Was his sense of humour his armour? It can be difficult, trying to know exactly how much time you have left and not knowing exactly what's going to happen to you and when! So he was looking for people who would support his 'numbing strategy' of food and alcohol. It was Subhash Indori, Satpal, Arun Verma, Dilip Dutt, Johnny Whisky and K. Razdan who gave him company. And vastly unlike a wife, they did not ask uncomfortable questions! Hari probably felt a faux safety in their company.

What was the influence of the company Hari kept on his life and his mind? As the heart attacks kept coming, everyone knew that his time was limited. Did the sycophants who were close to him try and influence him or build a rift between the brothers? In the 1980s, media had started reporting that the brothers were not getting along. Such misunderstandings are quite common in India's joint families. But Indian families are known to stay together and stand together during tough times, despite individual differences. Who seeded these stories to the media?

---

31 Jamie Ducharme, 'Here's Why You Stress Eat—And Why You Should Stop It', *Time*, 31 July 2018; https://time.com/5347612/how-to-stop-stress-eating/

Was anyone else hoping to inherit Hari's wealth? It's a fair question.

Hari's close actor friends have spoken about his suspicion that the women who professed their love for him could have been after his money. This may have played on his mind and actually prevented him from walking the last mile. Could the company he kept have fuelled this suspicion—in their own interests?

This is quite believable. We know that married people take fewer risks, eat better and maintain healthier lifestyles, on average, compared with single people. There is also evidence that married people tend to keep regular doctor's appointments and follow doctors' recommendations more often than single people. Did Hari keep his doctor's appointments and have his medicines regularly? Did he try alternative treatments and therapies? We can never know.

What we do know is that Hari wrote his will in a hurry, all alone, cooped up in a room in Jawahar Hotel in Pune, owned by his friend Subhash Sanas, who treated Jyoti like his own sister. He was not under anyone's influence at this time. This was immediately after returning from his cardiac surgery in 1985.

This brings us to the elusive and tricky word called 'freedom' and every person's interpretation of it. In his forty-seven years, Hari had earned enough money and provided for his family more than adequately. He was free to love and be loved by many women. This freedom itself is quite seductive, and he may not have wanted to give it up. Hari's friends absolutely insist that he lived freely and as he chose to. He had enough female attention to last a few lifetimes. It was his choice to remain single; maybe it was one pleasure that he didn't want taken away when life itself threatened to be taken away from him!

At last count, I was informed of about eight serious marriage proposals that were brought to him by friends and family, other than the ones mentioned in the book. Those are left out of the book, as the ladies in question have either died and cannot defend themselves or are happily married. They include princesses from royal families, artists and even other actresses. I have even come across two extremely intimate love letters written to Hari by actresses who were much younger than him and who are happily married today. These are part of the family's personal collection. I contacted both the ladies for their comments and they declined. Respecting the fact that they have moved on in their lives, their letters are not being reproduced here.

But here's the thing: anyone who thinks that Haribhai died of heartbreak is so far away from the truth. It's time to rewrite that narrative. In line with the patriarchal mindset of the time, Hari was very traditional-minded when it came to what kind of a woman he wanted to marry. It is understandable that Gen Z would be offended by the idea that he 'insisted on a housewife' or that 'the women of the house should give up their career after marriage'. These are not ideas that find favour today.

Haribhai died early, not unhappily. He clocked about six films a year during the twenty-five years that he worked. The friendships he cherished must've had some quid pro quo embedded in them. Hari remained an unattached bachelor who carefully refrained from commitments. He had fulfilled too many.

5

Sanjeev Kumar Foundation

Uday Jariwala runs the Sanjeev Kumar Foundation in memory of his late uncle. It is a national level development organization (NGO) that directly helps children and their families every year, mainly focusing on education, healthcare and culture.

The foundation has adopted a government school in Surat and named it 'Sanjeev Kumar Primary School'. Students here are given books, study materials and computer bags on Hari's birthday, 9 July, every year.

From 2015 onwards, the foundation has also been the sponsor of the annual Sanjeev Kumar Drama Competition held by the Surat Municipal Corporation during a ten-day period between the festivals of Ganpati and Diwali. The awards and cash prizes are given in memory of Haribhai to the best actor, actress, director and backstage technician every year.

The Sanjeev Kumar Academy of Arts & Performance (SKAAP), also based in Surat, promotes visual arts and performance. Set up in an area of approximately 70,000 square feet, it allows students to learn and develop their performing arts skills, and deserving students are given scholarships. In the near future, this academy will be tying up with international academies for student exchange programmes.

Through the Sanjeev Kumar Foundation, a health camp is also organized every year, involving blood donation, ear and eye check-ups, etc. An ambulance has been placed at the local hospital. The foundation has also entered into tie-ups to provide free spectacles and surgery to the needy as required. Blankets are distributed among the homeless during winter.

6

Why Hari Will Always Remain Timeless

BY AAKANKSHA NAVAL-SHETYE

A true measure of an actor's success is the impact he or she makes on the minds of the viewers and the emotions they stir in the hearts of their audience. Do the generations who come after look up to the actor for inspiration? Do they absorb the finesse that the actor has shown on celluloid? Sanjeev Kumar scores a resounding yes on being one such exemplary actor and inspiration.

I spoke to two fine contemporary actors to understand what Sanjeev Kumar means to them. The first is Pratik Gandhi, the star of *Scam 1992: The Harshad Mehta Story,* who also hails from Sanjeev Kumar's home state of Gujarat. He has an interesting revelation to make before sharing his thoughts on the late actor: 'For the past several months now, we have been looking for a reference point to make a film on Sanjeev Kumar's life or one inspired by him, where I will be essaying his character on screen. So, being approached for this book for me is a sign that I'm on the right path.'

I also reached out to critically acclaimed actor Manav Kaul, who has often expressed his admiration for Sanjeev Kumar and has also been compared with the legendary actor for his realistic approach to acting. Manav and Sanjeev Kumar both have a connection to the late veteran theatre director Satyadev Dubey.

Kaul told me, 'When I came to Mumbai, I started working with the legendary theatre director Satyadev Dubey. A lot of people have worked under him as an actor, including Naseer sahab [Naseeruddin Shah], Rajesh Khanna and even Sanjeev Kumar. I got lucky that I was selected for one of his plays and I started working with him.'

Dubey, born in 1936, was two years senior to Sanjeev Kumar. He enjoyed a five-decade-long prolific career as a theatre actor, director and playwright. Though not many details are available about the plays he and Sanjeev Kumar did together, Sanjeev was the lead actor in *Vishwasghaat,* a movie that had dialogues and screenplay by Satyadev Dubey.

Manav says, 'Sanjeev Kumar and I are gurubhai as we both had a common guru. Dubeyji, being a short-tempered man, would express his chagrin at Sanjeev Kumar's delayed arrival to the rehearsals. He told me, "I always wanted to scream at him [Sanjeev]! Why are you coming late and all of that, but whenever he used to come on stage and start performing, he had such natural talent that I couldn't say anything because of his amazing quality he had; Sanjeev Kumar was masterful at natural dialogue delivery, he would deliver dialogues as if the situation were actually unfolding." This is a quality most actors aspire to learn, with a lot of practice, but Sanjeev Kumar just had it. When he acted, it never felt like he was delivering dialogues. Dubeyji was mesmerized by his craft and his anger would quietly melt away.

'Also, I remember that as actors we would watch a lot of movies … Hollywood films, to study actors and their acting styles. My all-time favourites were Javier Bardem, Al Pacino, Robert De Niro and Leonardo DiCaprio. But when it came to Hindi cinema, we always looked up to Sanjeev Kumar and Yusuf sahab [Dilip Kumar].'

According to Pratik Gandhi, 'Sanjeev Kumar is like flowing water on screen and he could mould himself into any character you wanted, be it a comic-based, intense, dramatic or romantic role. He never let his star-persona dominate the character, and that is a huge (quality), given his stature in the industry. Also, that's his greatness as an actor … to not let the star override the story, and you can see that nuanced, balanced performance in characters where it was easy to go over the top.'

Manav's favourite Sanjeev Kumar film is *Angoor*. 'I've watched it over and over again because of the sheer brilliant and realistic performance of Sanjeev Kumar,' he gushes! 'His style and the film continue to be relevant even today. If I watch it again, I'll laugh and watch it once again.

'Later, when I auditioned for *Tumhari Sulu*, I remember that producer Atul Kasbekar and director Suresh Triveni at the audition called me "the New Age Sanjeev Kumar".'

Pratik, too, has many favourites of Sanjeev Kumar's. 'When I saw *Khilona* for the first time, I was too young to appreciate his work, but when I saw it again, it opened my eyes to the actor's talent. The challenge is in playing a role like that to perfection, as it is easy to go overboard. I did not become a fan overnight, but each time I watched this movie, I came away learning something, imbibing something and taking away so much from the character. He made the character believable and unforgettable. And he did that with amazing grace and ease, like it was the most natural thing to happen and he was not Sanjeev Kumar but that particular character. I also loved *Pati, Patni Aur Woh*, a film I have watched multiple times and still find funny.'

The film critic and the movie buff in me both agree with Manav and Pratik's analyses. Sanjeev Kumar's style was so distinct that unlike many heroes of his time, he never had to rely on props like dialogues or music or camera angles to make him the hero. At a time of larger-than-life heroes, he 'heroed' the common man, and that's what set him apart too. He was in the league of actors over stars, and yet as commercial and mainstream like any other ... but with each of his performances a textbook in acting!

7

A Tribute by Artee and Ashish Patel

Artee and Ashish are children of Gayatri and Ashok Patel.

Ashish Patel, also known as DJ ALX, runs a payment processing company called Genesis Merchant Solutions in Houston, Texas. He has played his own part in keeping the legacy of Haribhai alive by playing remixes of songs picturized on Hari all over the US. He is part of a radio show called GenerAsian Radio in Houston, which showcases artistes from across the music world.

'I've been DJ-ing since 1994 and music has been a passion of mine since I was a child,' says Ashish. That is understandable since parents Gayatri and Ashok Patel had a fondness for music too. Ashish's sacred space is a mix of world sounds, which he infuses with the latest electronic beats.

Ashish refers to Hari as 'Mama'. 'I've played Mama's tracks from San Francisco to Chicago and my home city of Houston, as well as all over Mexico. My way of keeping his memory alive is to add newer beats to classic tracks like "*Thande thande pani se*" and "*O manchali*", so that people remember his songs, and so that this in turn will make them want to watch his movies. I remember Mama singing "*Thande thande pani se*" to us when we were children and this was very special. As I got older, I started to appreciate other songs such as "*O manchali*" and "*Ek ladki bholi bhali si*".'

Ashish believes that his mama was a true talent and legend who had a natural gift; with his unique craft, he could make others experience both happiness and despair at the theatre and movies. 'He could make people relate to his characters and I'm quite certain that I've inherited a taste for music and an inherent sense of rhythm from my Mama,' says Ashish.

Hari's niece Artee Patel won the Miss India Texas pageant in August 2001. She remembers being pampered by her Hari Mama. 'He would always bring us presents every time he travelled out of the country for a shoot. One year he went to Singapore, I had asked for a make-up set from there. He could've easily said that he doesn't know how to choose one. But he made the effort and got me a purple-and-white marble case with eyeshadows, blush and lipsticks inside. He would ask us specifically what we wanted, and he would bring exactly that.'

Artee and Ashish lost their mother when this biography was being written. Artee was grief-stricken: 'My mother has been through so much in her life. She moved to America, lost all her family at a young age, survived cancer and two heart attacks and dealt with a lot of hardships along the way. Despite everything she had been through she was the strongest woman I have ever known.'

Artee also owns a very successful bridal beauty business catering to South Asian brides, teaching group make-up classes and running an online beauty shop. Artee maintains an exhaustive collection of DVDs of her mama's films and talks to her daughter about his work to keep the memories alive. Artee is the only person from Hari's family who has faced the camera after him. She had a guest appearance in the hit TV show *Queen of the South*, where she played a doctor. She has also done commercials and shows.

Uday, Prithvi, Ekta, Ashish and Artee are the children Hari loved with all his heart.

Epilogue

The extent of my fondness for Sanjeev Kumar as an actor is so immense that I have often confessed to Sid, my better half, that he's fortunate that I wasn't born earlier. I was just six years old when Sanjeev Kumar passed away, tragically early. The extent of hubbub at the time (not common for the demise of a Hindi film actor in a south Indian household!) ensured that I became aware of it, while not grasping it fully!

Later, in college, I got exposed to his cinema. I had just begun to believe that there has to be a distinctive chaap to every actor. A style that typifies them. I realize now that the actors who touch our lives are rarely those with distinctive styles—perhaps a rigidly defined style in itself is extremely limiting.

Sanjeev Kumar was limitless because he had no set ways. He imbued truth into the most banal of moments. He made everything believable. He just became the character. The audience never questioned why he was cast—he had complete conviction and his feelings were always palpable. Looking at how effortless his performances seem; I am tempted to believe that he never prepared for any role. The other explanation would be that his effort was way too sublime to be visible. The way he uses his hands, facial expressions and his body movements are all uncanny, and yet they fit perfectly into the situation.

Sometimes, I wonder how he prepared himself for *Koshish*! His projection of abject helplessness in *Khilona* blew my mind; he humanized his characters to perfection. Then there was *Naya Din Nayi Raat* where he played nine different characters. To my mind, Sivaji Ganesan and Haribhai are actors of the same wattage. The difference between them is that Sivaji Ganesan belonged to a milieu where performances required more drama (and I love that too!).

Sanjeev Kumar was a more levelled actor. In the song '*Tere bina zindagi se koi*'—just the way he looks at Suchitra Sen and puts his coat around her would make any woman's heart melt! There is so much history between the couple, so much unsaid from their past. Sanjeev Kumar manages to elicit emotion in his audiences with his aching vulnerability; also, when he lip-syncs, one can see his throat tighten. When you add Gulzar's lyrics to Sanjeev Kumar's song delivery, what you get is a supremely heady cocktail.

His comedy in *Angoor* is every bit as creditable as his gravitas in *Aandhi*. I have watched *Angoor* so many times. Each time the audience wonders, which brother is it? The greatness of his performance is that he makes you guess—that's very difficult to achieve. He doesn't play with different mannerisms to distinguish between the two brothers. This makes the movie all the more confusing and heightens the comedy!

He was always prepared to take risks, and I think this attribute resonates with me. An actor should be living a different life every time they appear on screen. He has influenced me subconsciously. Away from pedestrian and restrictive ideas of what an actor can or cannot do, he was unstoppable in his experimentation and omnipotent in his prowess. I think, though there have been some wonderful actors, there hasn't been another Sanjeev Kumar. It was so brave of him to attempt a film like *Qatl*. Also, there were shades of negativity in so many of his roles. Viewers who have seen *Griha Pravesh*, will readily identify with the middle-class man trapped in the mundane, going through a mid-life crisis. 'I know that feeling,' is how the audience reacts to Sanjeev Kumar. He didn't really set out to have an affair, but it happened. You can feel that the couple [he is paired with Sharmila Tagore] is trapped—you can feel their enervation and their fatigue. As they go from one day to another, hoping that one day things might be better, nothing changes!

I cannot forget the scene in which he tells his wife that he's having an affair. The resignation with which they accept the affair and the simple curiosity with which Sharmila Tagore responds are totally natural. Thereafter, the awkwardness and the embarrassment flow naturally.

Among his many co-stars, I believe that Haribhai and Jayaji had a lovely give-and-take as performers. The song '*Beeti na bitaayi raina*' is one of my all-time favourites. Sanjeev Kumar is brilliant as a fallible protagonist. When something happens to him, one feels that it could happen to anyone. In *Silsila*, he didn't shy away from playing the 'not-so-prominent' role. In fact, everyone knew that because Sanjeev Kumar agreed to play the role, he elevated the role. So many years later, you cannot talk about *Silsila* without talking about Sanjeev Kumar. His conversation in the clinic with Jaya Bachchan—navigating the stickiness of their respective spouses being embroiled with each other—is full of pregnant pauses. Each one is trying to cover something up and yet being honest with the other. The pain and the questions writ all over his face are priceless. The niceness of the man comes through, so much so that when Rekha goes back to him, it's believable. From this performance to that of the stubborn, heartless father in *Trishul* in which the father-son relationship never fructifies is such a paradox! They could be played by two entirely different people.

Sanjeev Kumar was the non-pareil actor he was—despite his heart condition. I wonder whether it could've impeded him in giving us more of his work to cherish. Yes, there must've been unease, but art has been known to be propelled by tragic happenings. We have always supposed that heartbreak is a great fuel for poetry. However, his greatness is beyond that assumption because an actor cannot always draw from personal experience alone. It is in this context that the sheer diversity of roles played by Sanjeev Kumar is a testimony to his craft and not to any personal tragedy. He was believable, no matter which role.

My all-time favourite Haribhai performances are *Griha Pravesh*, *Koshish* and *Sholay*. What thrills me immensely is that this book will help people rediscover his films and enjoy a period of cinema they might've not been introduced to (and choose their own favourites too).

Vidya Balan

Afterword

Here's the story you've read. An exceptionally talented son, Hari, is born to a mother in answer to her prayers. This son loses his father at the age of twelve and moves from a comfortable life to one of struggle, with three younger siblings to take care of. Instead of taking up a safe job, he chooses to become an actor. He begins in theatre and suffers rejections before he gets the elusive break in films. After fourteen years of intense struggle, he revels in fourteen years of success, the last five of which feature more misses than hits. He dies young of a heart attack.

If only stories were that straight.

In early 2019, Hema Upadhyay, a media relations professional, asked me, 'Haven't you wondered why there isn't a book on Sanjeev Kumar?' My mother had once asked me the same too. Sure enough, I started wondering about it and decoded the degrees of separation to reach Uday Jariwala, who eventually became the force behind the book. Like many others, I reached out to actor Darshan Jariwala first, who, with great politeness, told me that he wasn't related. Finally, I got Uday's number from a journalist in Surat, and we started working on the book. First up, the structure—how do I write the biography of a man I had never met? I made a list of people who had worked with him. Every co-star I spoke to was elated. 'I am so thrilled that a book on Haribhai is being written,' said Ranjeeta Kaur, Hari's popular co-star from the 1980s. Hari's family gave me the names of people who were close to him. Then came the innumerable Google searches, where I dabbled with various keywords, hoping to extract the maximum. But most of the articles I picked on the internet portrayed Haribhai as 'the sad man who died lonely'.

I was determined to evaluate this claim. Jyoti Jariwala, the resilient sister-in-law, the only survivor of that generation at the time of finalizing this book, worshipped Hari. I asked her, 'When it comes to a man's bad habits or affairs, the family is usually the last to know. How much could you have known about Bhai's personal life? Whom was he in a relationship with? Where was he spending his late nights? Surely, while looking after his brother's family might've provided Hari with fulfilment, it could not have given him companionship?'

Jyoti nodded sagely, 'I was quiet when it came to Bhai's personal life. But after Nikul's death and before Bhai went for surgery to the US, I mustered up courage and requested Bhai if the kids and I could move out to live in the other house. We wanted him to get married. It was important. I also told him that no one could take care of him like a wife, especially post-surgery. Neither money nor space was a problem. Bhai had already bought another house in Rukhsana building next door in Nikul's name and we could shift there. Bhai refused to listen to me.'

Perrin Villa was a simple home. At the time of Hari's relationship with Hema, Baa had insisted he book a bungalow in Juhu, more suited to the affluent lifestyle of a cinema star. However, this bungalow got trapped in legalese, and Hari never saw it. Later, over the years, Hari also got many proposals for marriage. Many of the women had one condition—that they would marry him only if they did not have to live with his extended family. Jyoti did not want to be the one to come in the way.

And yet, Hari breathed his last, a single man. As millennials would probably agree with me, marriage is no guarantee of happiness. Hari's twin legacy is his enduring art and a grateful family that worships him. That's a life well-lived.

Q&A with Harihar Jethalal Jariwala

1. Which role do you wish you had played?

Kabir Bedi's role in *Anokha Daan*.

2. Who is your competitor?

Sanjeev Kumar.

3. Who inspired you to become an actor?

Raj Kapoor.

4. Who was your first love?

It was more of a great crush! A Muslim woman whom I wooed and romanced when I was just twenty-six years old.

5. What is God to you?

I don't visit any temples. For me, my mother is my God.

6. Who are your closest friends?

Pravin Joshi, Subhash Sanas, Subhash Indori, Satpal, publicist K. Razdan, Tanuja, Sachin Pilgaonkar, Shatrughan Sinha, Moushumi Chatterjee, Gulzar, Basu Bhattacharya.

7. Which actress is like a younger sister to you?

Jaya Bhaduri.

8. Which is your most challenging role?

The speech and hearing-impaired character in Koshish.

9. Is marriage an ambition?

No, marriage cannot be an ambition. Ambition has something to do with work. Marriage is about destiny.

10. Which are your favourite films?

I have a huge collection of video cassettes. My favourites are *Abbott and Costello*, *A Fistful of Dollars*, *The Good, the Bad and the Ugly*, *High Noon* and *For a Few Dollars More*.

11. Who was your favourite comic star?

Charlie Chaplin. I would finish his films and keep rewinding to watch them again.

12. Which was the film you and Gulzar watched together?

Gulzar and I loved to watch *Dumbo* together. It was a film about the separation of a mother from her child, and both of us used to cry while watching it.

13. Whose grave did you go to pay your respects in Toronto?

David Abraham. He was a fine actor, but he died all alone in Toronto. I went to pay him my last respects. He was a part of one of my first films *Ali Baba and 40 Thieves*, in 1966.

14. What is your favourite cuisine?

Chinese.

15. Your lead role in *Manchali* was a re-imagination of which character?

Guru Dutt's role in *Mr. & Mrs. '55*.

16. What was your favourite gift for Shammi Kapoor?

Caviar.

17. What do you love collecting?

Watches, glass artefacts, figurines, perfume bottles.

18. How many National Awards have you won?

Two, for *Dastak* and *Koshish*.

19. Which actor did you publicly say you would marry and why?

I'd marry Daboo because he wouldn't bring his tensions home.

20. What did you want to rename your film *Anubhav* and why?

I wanted to rename it 'Tanubhav' to toast Tanuja's excellent performance in it.

21. Which is your favourite song?

'Que Sera Sera' by Doris Day.

(This Q&A is an imaginative curation borrowed from articles, interviews and family inputs.)

Browsing Books for Hari

Book 1

Makeup Man: From Rocky to Star Trek, the Amazing Creations of Hollywood's Michael Westmore by Michael Westmore and Jake Page, The Lyons Press, 2017.

This book carries a mention of Hari and his gifted make-up artist Sarosh Mody, in the words of Emmy and Academy Award-winning make-up artist Michael Westmore.

> I was first contacted by an East Indian company to create some special make up effects for a very big film, both in size and popularity. It starred one of India's most famous actors Sanjeev Kumar. This was one of India's first attempts to step out of their world of beautiful people. Sanjeev was to wear numerous transitional latex prosthetics as his face was transformed in the Indian version of Dr Jekyll and Mr

Hyde. Each Indian star has his or her own make-up artiste and the name of Sanjeev's artiste was Sarosh Mody. They both arrived in Hollywood and stayed for the next month. Sarosh would show up at my lab every morning and sit and watch me prepare the masks. After a month of sculpting, molding and painting, we were ready to test each phase of the make up. After our application and approval test, I had to manufacture enough faces for Sarosh to take back to India with him, as the mail and Customs couldn't be counted on to deliver.

Book 2

Hero Volume I: The Silent Era to Dilip Kumar, The Bollywood Series, by Ashok Raj, Hay House UK, 2010.

This book offers a comparison between Hari and Guru Dutt.

Sanjeev Kumar's linkages with the Guru Dutt school are far less direct than interpretative. His resemblance to the master as far as appearance and mannerisms were concerned was quite striking. In addition, like Guru Dutt, he projected a kind of sensitivity that would make an actor a class by himself. This resemblance, however, was not imitative but more of a coincidence. In this sense, Sanjeev Kumar represented a continuity of Guru Dutt's screen persona, and he was seen by many as filling the void left by the great master …

His style was unassuming and had a spontaneity and warmth reminiscent of Motilal, Ashok Kumar and Balraj Sahni …

Sanjeev Kumar, like many other credible actors had a massive following among the viewers. There are two main reasons for his immense success. First, he arrived in the post classical period as the antithesis of the prevailing macho, glamorous and stylized hero and thus he was easily recognizable as a down to earth character among the people. He looked far more familiar, the man next door, who did not need an introduction. In this sense, Sanjeev Kumar was the first to challenge the typical hero-centred basis of Hindi cinema and introduce a definite qualitative improvement in characterizations. Second, Sanjeev Kumar represented, in emotionally charged roles, an innate strength of the Indian personality – outwardly vulnerable and yet inwardly strong enough to face the harsh realities of life ...

Book 3

R.D Burman: The Man, The Music by Anirudha Bhattacharya and Balaji Vittal, HarperCollins India, 2011.

Hari was incredibly lucky with the music of his films and with his association and friendship with the Gulzar-R.D. Burman combination. Here are a few excerpts from the book.

What Soumitra Chatterjee was to Satyajit Ray, Max Von Sydow to Ingmar Bergman and Toshiro Mifune to Akira Kurosawa, Sanjeev Kumar was to Gulzar, acting in 6 of the 12 feature films Gulzar directed till 1985. R.D. composed the music in 4 of these films.

The song '*Tere bina zindagi se koi*' was created by Pancham as a puja song '*Jete jete pothe holo deri*'. Gulzar took to the tune and penned the lyrics which fit in snugly.

The kokoro, a wind instrument - one of the more uncommon ones that Pancham used earlier in '*Gulabi aankhen'* in *The Train* - was heard in the Asha-Kishore duet *'Hawa ke saath saath'*.

Gulzar remembers, 'Sanjeev Kumar had a very relaxed disposition towards most things in life. For e.g., he was always the last one to de-board an aircraft, waiting till all the other passengers had done so. This rubbed off on his on-screen persona as well. Sanjiv's maturity as an artiste, the innate calm that he carried in and out of the study despite his troubled personal life is reflected in a number of RD compositions picturized on the actor.'

Book 4

Pran: A biography by Bunny Reuben, HarperCollins India, 2005.

Hari was a superstar and extremely sensitive. Director Tinnu Anand recollects approaching Sanjeev Kumar for a role in *Kalia*, in the book:

> I don't think anyone knows this but I had approached Sanjeev Kumar for the role which I ultimately gave to Pran Saab. I had a very long session narrating my story to Sanjeev and discussing his get up and everything for the role. Then at 4.30 in the morning, he got up and said he was doing my film.
>
> When I went to Sanjeev's place about 1 'o' clock in the afternoon, of the following day, which was about the time Sanjeev used to wake up, I was told by Jamnadas his secretary that Sanjeev Kumar would not be doing my film. This was only because that very morning, a full page advertisement had appeared in *Screen*, which announced that Amitabh had green lighted Kalia. So he felt very hurt, slighted that we had not waited for his announcement before putting in the ad.

... Sadly, I didn't get a chance to work with Sanjeev Kumar again.

Book 5

Gulzar's Angoor: Insights into the Film, by Sathya Saran, HarperCollins India, 2019.

Hari could get away with anything on Gulzar's sets. Deepti Naval, speaks with admiration:

> 'Gulzar is a writer of precision. He had a metre in mind, the rhythm of a sentence in his brain. He knew exactly how a dialogue should be delivered, whether it would end on a high note or a low one. He was strict about it and the only person who could improvise on it was Sanjeev Kumar, who would do so but without changing the inherent structure and rhythm of the line.'

Book 6

Khullam Khulla: Rishi Kapoor Uncensored by Rishi Kapoor and Meena Iyer, HarperCollins India, 2017.

There are some rare anecdotes in this book about Hari trying to lose weight and also about an unreleased film. In the late Rishi Kapoor's words:

> There was a popular slimming centre in Mumbai in the 1970s called Jussawala. Sanjeev Kumar had enrolled there to lose weight for *Love & God* ...
>
> Sanjeev Kumar was a senior actor when I entered the film industry. He was a friendly man and often played cards

with us at Jeetendra's place. He lived close to me in Pali Hill but he was never a close friend like Jeetendra, Guddu or Premji. We used to meet socially. He was a good actor with a wicked sense of humour, he could bitch a lot. Its sad that he passed away so young. But however short his life and career, he managed to do one RK film, *Biwi O Biwi* (1981). He was very friendly with my uncle Shammi and my brother Daboo. He and I also worked on a film together, which is still in the cans. It was called *Maang Sajado Meri* and starred Asha Parekh and Ranjeeta alongside us. A well made social romance, it was written by Manmohan Desai and directed by Pragya Raj. The film was complete and ready for release when a problem erupted between the producer and the financier. The financier decided that it was better for him to scrap the film and not release it, so he could write off the entire cost and gain some tax relief.

Sanjeev Kumar was one of the few who chose to venture off the beaten path.

Book 7

Hema Malini: Beyond the Dream Girl by Ram Kamal Mukherjee, HarperCollins India, 2017.

Hari's talent was always admired by his directors. This is a quote in the book from Ramesh Sippy, the legendary director of *Sholay* and *Seeta Aur Geeta*:

> I have never worked with an actor whose sense of timing was as exact as Sanjeev's for comedy. And he always appeared to be so effortless, so perfect.

Book 8

Smita Patil: A Brief Incandescence by Maithili Rao, HarperCollins India, 2015.

In this book, the author talks about Smita Patil's desire to work with Hari.

> Smita Patil's only excuse to engage in stupidity like working in *Kaanch Ki Deewar,* could be to act with Sanjeev Kumar, who was an actor first, then a star.

Filmography

Gujarati

1. *Ramat Ramade Ram*
Year of Release: 1964
Director: Dinesh Rawal

2. *Kalapi*
Year of Release: 1966
Director: Manhar Raskapur

3. *Mare Javun Pele Paar*
Year of Release: 1968
Director: Chandrakant Sangani

4. *Jigar Ane Ami*
Year of Release: 1970
Director: Chandrakant Sangani

Punjabi

5. *Udeekan*
Year of Release: 1979
Producer: Hari Dutt
Director: Hari Dutt

6. *Faujee Chacha*
Year of Release: 1980
Producer: Dheeraj Kumar
Director: Dharam Kumar

Telugu

7. *Oorvasi*
Year of Release: 1974
Producer: Not identified
Director: K. Bapaiah

Tamil

8. *Bharatha Vilas*
Year of Release: 1973
Producer: A. C. Tirulokchandar, T. Bharathi
Director: A.C. Trilogchander

Sindhi

9. *Ho Jamalo*
Year of Release: 1970
Producer: Rajan Chawla & Hari Motwani

Hindi

10. *Hum Hindustani*
Year of Release: 1960
Producer: Sashadhar Mukherjee
Director: Ram Mukherjee

11. *Aao Pyaar Karen*
Year of Release: 1964
Producer: R. K. Nayyar
Director: Sasadhar Mukherjee

12. *Nishan*
Year of Release: 1965
Producer : Homi Wadia
Director: Aspi Irani

13. *Smuggler*
Year of Release: 1966
Producer: Ratan Mohan
Director: Aspi Irani

14. *Pati Patni*
Year of Release: 1966
Director: S.A. Akbar
Producer: Usman Ali

15. *Husn Aur Ishq,* alias *Alif Laila*
Year of Release: 1966
Producer: Naresh Kumar
Director: Naresh Kumar

16. *Badal*
Year of Release: 1966
Producer: Aspi Irani
Director: Aspi Irani

17. *Naunihal*
Year of Release: 1967
Producer: Saawan Kumar Tak
Director: Raj Marbros

18. *Gunehgar*
Year of Release: 1967
Producer: P. Daswani
Director: R. Thakur

19. *Chhoti Si Mulaqat*
Year of Release: 1967
Producer: Uttam Kumar
Director: Alo Sarkar

20. *Aayega Aanewala*
Year of Release: 1967
Producer: Kewal Misra, K.L. Pandit
Director: Kewal Misra

21. *Sunghursh*
Year of Release: 1968
Producer: Harnam Singh Rawail
Director: Harnam Singh Rawail

22. *Shikar*
Year of Release: 1968
Producer: Atma Ram
Director: Atma Ram

23. *Saathi*
Year of Release: 1968
Producer: T. Govindarajan, S. Krishnamurthy
Director: C.V. Sridhar

24. *Raja Aur Runk*
Year of Release: 1968
Producer: L.V. Prasad
Director: Kolli Pratyagatma

25. *Gauri*
Year of Release: 1968
Producer: Sivaji Films P. Ltd.
Director: A. Bhimsingh

26. *Anokhi Raat*
Year of Release: 1968
Producer: L.B. Lachman, L.B. Thakur
Director: Asit Sen

27. *Aashirwad*
Year of Release: 1968
Producer: Darius Gotla, Hrishikesh Mukherjee, N.C. Sippy
Director: Hrishikesh Mukherjee

28. *Satyakam*
Year of Release: 1969
Producer: Sher Jeng Singh Punchhe, Sher Jung Singh
Director: Hrishikesh Mukherjee

29. *Sachaai*
Year of Release: 1969
Producer: M.C. Ramamurthy
Director: K. Shankar

30. *Jyoti*
Year of Release: 1969
Producer: A. Devdas, Chitra Mitra
Director: Dulal Guha

31. *Jeene Ki Raah*
Year of Release: 1969
Producer: L.V. Prasad
Director: L.V. Prasad

32. *Insaf Ka Mandir*
Year of Release: 1969
Producer: Sherbahadur Singh, Jadgish Singh
Director: B.R. Ishara

33. *Gustakhi Maaf*
Year of Release: 1969
Producer: Gopal Sehgal
Director: Raj Kumar Bedi, Rajkumar Bedi

34. *Dharti Kahe Pukarke*
Year of Release: 1969
Producer: Deenanath Shastri
Director: Dulal Guha

35. *Chanda Aur Bijli*
Year of Release: 1969
Producer: Atma Ram
Director: Atma Ram

36. *Bandhan*
Year of Release: 1969
Producer: G.P. Sippy
Director: Narendra Bedi

37. *Oos Raat Ke Baad*
Year of Release: 1969
Producer: Commercial Cine Corporation.
Director: V.Y.B. Shiras

38. *Priya*
Year of Release: 1970
Producer: Frank Fernand
Director: Govind Saraiya

39. *Maa Ka Aanchal*
Year of Release: 1970
Producer: Jagdev Bhambri
Director: Jagdev Bhambri

40. *Insaan Aur Shaitan*
Year of Release: 1970
Producer: Aspi Irani
Director: Aspi Irani

41. *Gunah Aur Kanoon*
Year of Release: 1970
Producer: Johnny Whisky, K.L. Bhatia
Director: B.R. Ishara

42. *Devi*
Year of Release: 1970
Producer: T.M. Kittu, A.V. Subramaniam
Director: V. Madhusudan Rao

43. *Bachpan*
Year of Release: 1970
Producer: Kolli Pratyagatma
Director: Kolli Pratyagatma

44. *Night in Calcutta*
Year of Release: 1970
Producer: Amrit Mahendra
Director: Amrit Mahendra

45. *Khilona*
Year of Release: 1970
Producer: L.V. Prasad
Director: Chander Vohra

46. *Dastak*
Year of Release: 1970
Producer: Rajinder Singh Bedi
Director: Rajinder Singh Bedi

47. *Paras*
Year of Release: 1971
Producer: M.A. Madhu, N.N. Sippy
Director: C.P. Dixit

48. *Man Mandir*
Year of Release: 1971
Producer: M.T. Boxwala, Sudesh Kumar
Director: Tapi Chanakya

49. *Kangan*
Year of Release: 1971
Producer: M.B. Raj, Jagdish A. Sharma
Director: K.B. Tilak

50. *Ek Paheli*
Year of Release: 1971
Producer: Kuldip Talwar
Director: Naresh Kumar

51. *Purani Pehchan*
Year of Release: 1971
Producer: Kaan, Kan Kimura, Moti
Director: Kewal Misra

52. *Anubhav*
Year of Release: 1971
Producer: Basu Bhattacharya
Director: Basu Bhattacharya

53. *Subha-O-Sham*
Year of Release: 1971
Producer: B. Radhakrishna, Abbas Shabaviz
Director: Tapi Chanakya

54. *Seeta Aur Geeta*
Year of Release: 1972
Producer: G.P. Sippy
Director: Ramesh Sippy

55. *Sabse Bada Sukh*
Year of Release: 1972
Producer: Hrishikesh Mukherjee
Director: Hrishikesh Mukherjee

56. *Rivaaj*
Year of Release: 1972
Producer: K.C. Bokadia
Director: T. Prakash Rao

57. *Koshish*
Year of Release: 1972
Producer: Raj N. Sippy, Romu N. Sippy
Director: Gulzar

58. *Jai Jwala*
Year of Release: 1972
Producer: K.D. Sharma
Director: Manohar Deepak

59. *Parichay*
Year of Release: 1972
Producer: Subhash Kapoor, V.K. Sobti
Director: Gulzar

60. *Suraj Aur Chanda*
Year of Release: 1973
Producer: A.V. Subramaniam
Director: T. Madhava Rao

61. *Manchali*
Year of Release: 1973
Producer: Raja Nawathe
Director: Raja Nawathe

62. *Dur Nahin Manzil*
Year of Release: 1973
Producer: Hari Walia
Director: Hari Walia

63. *Bharatha Vilas*
Year of Release: 1973
Producer: A.C. Trilogchander
Director: A.C. Trilogchander

64. *Anamika*
Year of Release: 1973
Producer: Tahir Hussain
Director: Raghunath Jhalani

65. *Agni Rekha*
Year of Release: 1973
Producer: K.S. Melwani
Director: Mahesh Kaul

66. *Anhonee*
Year of Release: 1973
Producer: Ravi Tandon, G.M. Khwaja, Gullu Kochar, Jagdish C. Sharma
Director: Ravi Tandon

67. *Rocky Mera Naam*
Year of Release: 1973
Producer: Satram Rohera
Director: Satram Rohera

68. *Shaandaar*
Year of Release: 1974
Producer: K.V.V. Arthanari
Director: R. Krishnan, S. Panju

69. *Imaan*
Year of Release: 1974
Producer: Atma Ram
Director: B. Padmanabham

70. *Dawat*
Year of Release: 1974
Producer: Dilip Dutt
Director: B.R. Ishara

71. *Chowkidar*
Year of Release: 1974
Producer: Gopal Ralhan
Director: Shyam Ralhan

72. *Charitraheen*
Year of Release: 1974
Producer: Debesh Ghosh
Director: Shakti Samanta

73. *Archana*
Year of Release: 1974
Producer: Mirchadani
Director: Satpal

74. *Manoranjan*
Year of Release: 1974
Producer: F.C. Mehra
Director: Shammi Kapoor

75. *Aap Ki Kasam*
Year of Release: 1974
Producer: Jagdish Kumar, J. Om Prakash
Director: J. Om Prakash

76. *Naya Din Nai Raat*
Year of Release: 1974
Producer: N.P. Ali, P. Meharoof, N.P.C. Mehmood
Director: A. Bhimsingh

77. *Kunwara Baap*
Year of Release: 1974
Producer: Amarlal P. Chhabria
Director: Mahmood

78. *Uljhan*
Year of Release: 1975
Producer: Sudesh Kumar
Director: Raghunath Jhalani

79. *Dhoti Lota Aur Chowpatty*
Year of Release: 1975
Producer: Mohan Choti
Director: Mohan Choti

80. *Apne Rang Hazaar*
Year of Release: 1975
Producer: Ravi Tandon, Jagdish C. Sharma, Gullu Kochar, G.M. Khwaja
Director: Ravi Tandon

81. *Apne Dushman*
Year of Release: 1975
Producer: Jeetendra Bhandari
Director: Kailash Bhandari

82. *Aandhi*
Year of Release: 1975
Producer: Jagdish Kumar, J. Om Prakash
Director: Gulzar

83. *Aakraman*
Year of Release: 1975
Producer: Jagdish Kumar
Director: J. Om Prakash

84. *Sholay*
Year of Release: 1975
Producer: G.P. Sippy, Sascha Sippy, Shaan Uttamsingh
Director: Ramesh Sippy

85. *Faraar*
Year of Release: 1975
Producer: Alankar Chitra
Director: Shankar Mukherjee

86. *Mausam*
Year of Release: 1975
Producer: P. Mallikharjuna Rao
Director: Gulzar

87. *Do Ladkiyan*
Year of Release: 1976
Producer: Gope Dadlani
Director: Kolli Pratyagatma

88. *Arjun Pandit*
Year of Release: 1976
Producer: L.B. Lachman
Director: Hrishikesh Mukherjee

89. *Zindagi*
Year of Release: 1976
Producer: Romu N. Sippy, V.K. Sood
Director: Ravi Tandon

90. *Vishwasghaat*
Year of Release: 1977
Producer: Johny Bakshi
Director: Mahesh Bhatt

91. *Paapi*
Year of Release: 1977
Producer: O.P. Ralhan
Director: O.P. Ralhan

92. *Dil Aur Patthar*
Year of Release: 1977
Producer: Krishan Sethi
Director: Kanak Mishra

93. *Apnapan*
Year of Release: 1977
Producer: J. Om Prakash
Director: J. Om Prakash

94. *Angaaray*
Year of Release: 1975
Producer: S.P. Malhotra
Director: Govind Saraiya

95. *Alaap*
Year of Release: 1977
Producer: Hrishikesh Mukherjee, N.C. Sippy
Director: Hrishikesh Mukherjee

96. *Immaan Dharam*
Year of Release: 1977
Producer: Premji
Director: Desh Mukherjee

97. *Yehi Hai Zindagi*
Year of Release: 1977
Producer: B. Nagi Reddy
Director: K.S. Sethumadhavan

98. *Shatranj Ke Khilari*
Year of Release: 1977
Producer: Suresh Jindal
Director: Satyajit Ray

99. *Dhoop Chhaon*
Year of Release: 1977
Producer: S.N. Jain
Director: Prahlad Sharma

100. *Mukti*
Year of Release: 1977
Producer: Raj Tilak
Director: Raj Tilak

101. *Tumhare Liye*
Year of Release: 1978
Producer: Raj Tilak
Director: Basu Chatterjee

102. *Swarg Narak*
Year of Release: 1978
Producer: Ram Chabbra, B. Nagi Reddy
Director: Dasari Narayana Rao

103. *Sawan Ke Geet*
Year of Release: 1978
Producer: R. Bhattacharya
Director: R. Bhattacharya

104. *Muqaddar*
Year of Release: 1978
Producer: Ravi Anand
Director: Ravi Tandon

105. *Trishul*
Year of Release: 1978
Producer: Gulshan Rai
Director: Yash Chopra

106. *Pati Patni Aur Woh*
Year of Release: 1978
Producer: B.R. Chopra
Director: B.R. Chopra

107. *Trishna*
Year of Release: 1978
Producer: G.P. Sippy, Ramesh Sippy
Director: Anil Ganguly

108. *Devata*
Year of Release: 1978
Producer: N.N. Sippy
Director: S. Ramanathan

109. *Maan Apmaan*
Year of Release: 1979
Producer: N.V. Deshpande
Director: N.V. Deshpande

110. *Ghar Ki Laaj*
Year of Release: 1979
Producer: Satram Rohera
Director: B.R. Ishara

111. *Bombay by Nite*
Year of Release: 1979
Producer: Upendra Jha
Director: A. Shamsheer

112. *Hamare Tumhare*
Year of Release: 1979
Producer: F.C. Mehra, Parvesh C. Mehra
Director: Umesh Mehra

113. *Inspector Eagle*
Year of Release: 1979
Producer: Vishwamitter Adil, Laxminarayan Khanna, Bhagwan D. Pabreja
Director: Vishwamitter Adil

114. *Jaani Dushman*
Year of Release: 1979
Producer: Rajkumar Kohli
Director: Rajkumar Kohli

115. *Griha Pravesh*
Year of Release: 1979
Producer: Basu Bhattacharya
Director: Basu Bhattacharya

116. *Kaala Patthar*
Year of Release: 1979
Producer: Yash Chopra
Director: Yash Chopra

117. *Nauker*
Year of Release: 1979
Producer: Govindram Ahuja, Ismail Memon
Director: Ismail Memon, Jyoti Swaroop

118. *Takkar*
Year of Release: 1980
Producer: Aadi Sheshagiri Rao Ghattamaneni
Director: K. Bapaiah

119. *Swayamvar*
Year of Release: 1980
Producer: B. Nagi Reddy
Director: P. Sambasiva Rao

120. *Patthar Se Takkar*
Year of Release: 1980
Producer: Gulab Mehta
Director: Gulab Mehta

121. *Abdullah*
Year of Release: 1980
Producer: Sanjay Khan, Asghar Ali, Zarine Khan
Director: Sanjay Khan

122. *Jyoti Bane Jwala*
Year of Release: 1980
Producer: Prasan Kapoor
Director: Dasari Narayana Rao

123. *Be-Reham*
Year of Release: 1980
Producer: K.D. Shorey
Director: Raghunath Jhalani

124. *Hum Paanch*
Year of Release: 1980
Producer: Boney Kapoor, Surinder Kapoor
Director: Bapu

125. *Waqt Ki Deewar*
Year of Release: 1981
Producer: T.C. Dewan
Director: Ravi Tandon

126. *Chehre Pe Chehra*
Year of Release: 1981
Producer: Raj Tilak
Director: Raj Tilak

127. *Ladies Tailor*
Year of Release: 1981
Producer: Khalid Akhtar
Director: Khalid Akhtar

128. *Itni Si Baat*
Year of Release: 1981
Producer: K. Raghavan, K. Umakanth
Director: Madhu M.

129. *Biwi O Biwi*
Year of Release: 1981
Producer: Raj Kapoor
Director: Rahul Rawail

130. *Silsila*
Year of Release: 1981
Producer: Yash Chopra
Director: Yash Chopra

131. *Sindoor Bane Jwala*
Year of Release: 1982
Producer: A. Shree Ram Reddy
Director: K. Bapaiah

132. *Namkeen*
Year of Release: 1982
Producer: Jayant Malkan, Kutti Krishnan
Director: Gulzar

133. *Log Kya Kahenge*
Year of Release: 1982
Producer: B.R. Ishara
Director: B.R. Ishara

134. *Khud-Daar*
Year of Release: 1982
Producer: Anwar Ali, F.K. Rattonsey
Director: Ravi Tandon

135. *Angoor*
Year of Release: 1982
Producer: Jai Singh
Director: Gulzar

136. *Haathkadi*
Year of Release: 1982
Producer: Pahlaj Nihalani
Director: Surendra Mohan

137. *Shriman Shrimati*
Year of Release: 1982
Producer: B. Nagi Reddy
Director: Vijay Reddy

138. *Suraag*
Year of Release: 1982
Producer: Jag Mundhra
Director: Jag Mundhra, Ambrish Sangal

139. *Sawaal*
Year of Release: 1982
Producer: Yash Chopra
Director: Ramesh Talwar

140. *Ayaash*
Year of Release: 1982
Producer: Shakti Samanta
Director: Shakti Samanta

141. *Vidhaata*
Year of Release: 1982
Producer: Gulshan Rai
Director: Subhash Ghai

142. *Hero*
Year of Release: 1983
Producer: Subhash Ghai
Director: Subhash Ghai

143. *Pakhandi*
Year of Release: 1984
Producer: Robert D'Souza
Director: Samir Ganguly

144. *Meraa Dost Meraa Dushman*
Year of Release: 1984
Producer: Johny Bakshi
Director: Raj Khosla

145. *Bad Aur Badnaam*
Year of Release: 1984
Producer: K.D. Shorey
Director: Feroz Chinoy

146. *Lakhon Ki Baat*
Year of Release: 1984
Producer: Basu Chatterjee
Director: Basu Chatterjee

147. *Yaadgaar*
Year of Release: 1984
Producer: R.C. Prakash
Director: Dasari Narayana Rao

148. *Ram Tere Kitne Nam*
Year of Release: 1985
Producer: Harish Shah
Director: P. Madhavan

149. *Zabardast*
Year of Release: 1985
Producer: Mushir Alam, Mohammad Riaz
Director: Nasir Hussain

150. *Rusvai*
Year of Release: 1985
Producer: Surjit Aujla
Director: Rajat Rakshit

151. *Haathon Ki Lakeeren*
Year of Release: 1986
Producer: Chetan Anand
Director: Chetan Anand

152. *Chhota Aadmi*
Year of Release: 1986
Producer: Mahesh Naresh
Director: Krishnakant

153. *Bijli*
Year of Release: 1986
Producer: Shridhar Prasad
Director: Anant Marathe

154. *Badkaar*
Year of Release: 1986
Producer: H. Kohli
Director: Shiv Kumar

155. *Baat Ban Jaye*
Year of Release: 1986
Producer: Nitin Manmohan, Anil Hanspal
Director: Bharat Rangachary

156. *Qatl*
Year of Release: 1986
Producer: R.K. Nayyar
Director: R.K. Nayyar

157. *Kaanch Ki Deewar*
Year of Release: 1986
Producer: Kamal Chowdhary, M.N. Yasin
Director: M.N. Yasin

158. *Love and God*
Year of Release: 1986
Producer: Akhtar
Director: K. Asif

159. *Raahee*
Year of Release: 1987
Producer: Lakhan Sinha
Director: Raman Kumar

160. *Hiraasat*
Year of Release: 1987
Producer: Sunil Sharma
Director: Surendra Mohan

161. *Namumkin*
Year of Release: 1988
Producer: Bidhu S. Jha
Director: Hrishikesh Mukherjee

162. *Do Waqt Ki Roti*
Year of Release: 1988
Producer: M.P. Agrawal
Director: Satpal

163. *Oonch Neech Beech*
Year of Release: 1989
Producer: Jagdish Varma
Director: Wasi Khan, Prayag Raj

164. *Professor Ki Padosan*
Year of Release: 1994
Producer: Kant Kumar
Director: Shantilal Soni, Ravi Tandon

Index

Acknowledgements

When Narendra Modi inaugurated the Sanjeev Kumar Auditorium in Surat on 14 February 2014 as the then chief minister of the state, he expressed his appreciation for how carefully the actor's trophies and records had been preserved by Uday Jariwala and handed over to the auditorium authorities.

Modi's remark had an important context because Hari Jariwala never married and has left behind no child to preserve his belongings or to carry on his name. Yet, close friends of Hari's vouch for his strong relationship with his extended family, which was palpable to all. It went far beyond a mere feeling of duty towards his siblings. Hari was a loving man. His vast affection for the children of his sister Gayatri and brother Nikul (Hari's other brother, Kishore, had no children) and their wholehearted reciprocation of it is the reason this book could be written, nearly four decades after his death.

Uday recalls how Modi spoke about Hari's films *Koshish, Khilona* and *Angoor* in particular and with nostalgia. As part of the inauguration ceremony of the auditorium, two National Award trophies earned by the legendary actor were handed over by Uday to Modi, who in turn handed them over to Niranjan Zanzmera, then mayor of Surat, to place them in the auditorium. After the event, as Modi was leaving, he said to the mayor, 'Send me all the details [of the inauguration]', and tweeted those later.

By inaugurating the auditorium, Modi had discharged his duties, both as a fan as well as an administrator, towards perhaps the best-known Indian film star from his home state. This gesture stands testimony to Harihar Jariwala's contribution to cinema as well as to the adulation of his fans, who have ensured that he has a road, a stamp, a school and an auditorium to his name.

Uday and his mother Jyoti Nikul Jariwala have preserved Hari's diary, several articles on him, fan mail, letters, invitation cards and clippings about him from the year 1971 onwards. Some of those clippings are now torn or have faded with time; luckily, several articles carry the name of their writer and publication clearly. Every single contribution has been credited in the book. *Hari-philes* (a term we will use for Hari's innumerable fans) from across the world reached out with memorabilia and anecdotes—those that could be verified became part of this book.

I express my deepest gratitude for the untiring work of the journalists of the 1970s and '80s who interviewed Hari Jariwala and gave us a way to know him in his own words. My thanks to all the friends, colleagues and scribes who gave us their time and memories for this book.

About the Authors

Uday Jariwala is the heir to the legacy of Sanjeev Kumar. He runs the Sanjeev Kumar Foundation, an NGO that works towards the promotion of theatre, art and education. He is a businessman and lives in Mumbai with his wife Neelam and their two children, Aryan and Saachi.

Reeta Ramamurthy Gupta is a prolific biographer, reviewer for CNBC TV18, and a bibliophile. She is credited with the acclaimed Red Dot Experiment, a ten-year-long and six-nation study on how culture impacts communication. This is Reeta's third book.